WALK WITH ME

God Seen, God Heard, God Revealed: A 365-Day Devotional

Dr. Albert E. Russell

3GIMM Publishing

WALK WITH ME
God Seen, God Heard, God Revealed: A 365-Day Devotional

DEDICATION

This book is dedicated to my children Donovan and Genesis. Thank you for inspiring me to get up and shoot for the stars every, single day.

WALK WITH ME: God Seen, God Heard, God Revealed

ACKNOWLEDGEMENTS

Writing a book like this takes a lot of time and effort. It took me roughly three years to complete this work. In those three years were multiple events that slowed down my productivity. But thanks to the grace of God, I was able to bring the devotional to completion. I would like to thank Les'Lee Gilberry for your undying support. You're a constant source of joy and love in my life and I appreciate you very much. Thank you to Dr. LaKeacha Jett for your edits and advice. It was a tremendous help. Thank you to Dr. Valerie Wright for helping me through the first round of edits and pushing me to finish this work. I want to thank my children who are a constant source of inspiration. Thank you to Grace for always being supportive of my family and my life outside of church. Thank you to my many friends on social media who send constant encouragement and support. There are too many of you to name but know that I appreciate you. Thank you to my family, especially my mom, who always supports everything that I do. Thanks to Evangelist Gail Woods who is another fervent supporter and a constant giver of love and encouragement. Thank you to all of my students and colleagues at Tuskegee University. Special thanks to Ms. Ayannah Page and Ms. Makaela Williams for the constant and daily encouragement and inspiration.

WALK WITH ME: God Seen, God Heard, God Revealed

WALK WITH ME

JANUARY 1ST

"RESERVED SEATING"

Ephesians 2:6 "And God raised us up with Christ and seated us with Him in the heavenly realms in Christ Jesus..."

Money can buy lots of things. It can buy friends. It can get us access into the most exclusive places. Money can even buy happiness. However, there is one thing could never be purchased by money. No amount of money in the world can purchase a seat in heaven. These seats were purchased with the blood of Christ. He gave up his life so that we could have access to them. It is Jesus who brings us into the Holy of Holies; into the very presence of the Father. Scripture says God raised us up with Christ and God seated us with Him in the heavenly realms in Christ Jesus. When Christ was raised (resurrected) and seated, believers too were raised and seated. Every believer has been raised from death to life. Every believer has a reserved seat in the heavenly realms. Being seated is indicative of our works being completed. This is good news for us! Christ's work has been imputed unto us. We are not saved by works but by His grace! Here is the beauty of the Gospel, once we accept Christ's purchase of this seat, it is there for us until the Lord calls us home. **Today, let us reflect upon the fact that although the seat is free, it cost Him His life.**

The New
Place

Keep yourself cover

Thank you for the process,
Yes Lord?

Nevertheless - Inspire or
Luke 5-5

Something come out of your
devotion.

JANUARY 2ND

"A LIFE SENTENCE"

John 10:10 "The thief comes only to steal and kill and destroy; I came that they may have life, and have it abundantly."

For the most severe crimes, a life sentence may be given by an earthly court system. This means that the perpetrator is resigned to spend the rest of their life behind bars. In John's gospel, Jesus describes Satan as a thief who comes to do three things: steal, kill and destroy. Keep in mind that this is taught in the context of a pasture full of sheep following their shepherd, knowing his voice and not running after another. So, the thief would have to deceive the sheep in order to get them out of the pasture and into his clutches. This would be a death sentence. Satan hands out death sentences daily. Thanks be to God for the Good Shepherd Jesus Christ. Not only is He the antithesis of Satan, He is greater than the thief. Jesus gives a great gift: Jesus sentences us to life! When the prison system says LIFE, it's tragic but when Jesus gives us a life sentence, we should rejoice! Although the Thief has pronounced a death sentence upon us, God said you shall live and do so abundantly! **Today, thank God for life and reflect on the eternal life sentence that has been handed down from the Supreme Judge of the universe, meted out by the Good Shepherd on all who would believe!**

Judge 20-18

JudaH - PraisE

Victory is All ready mines !

Depend on God,

JANUARY 3RD

"HYPOCRISY OR CORRECTION"

*Matthew 7:1,2 "Do not judge, or you will be judged.
For with the same judgment you pronounce, you will be
judged; and with the measure you use, it will be
measured to you."*

Jesus gives us a stern rebuke in Matthew's gospel.
He says do not judge or you will be judged. The
word judge here is literally where we get our word
hypocrite from. What Jesus is saying is do not
judge hypocritically. Do not call your brother out
for a speck when you have a beam. Do not be
guilty of the same sin for which you judge others.
However, in modern times many use this scripture
to avoid correction. Many believe that if immoral
behavior is identified and rebuked, that is
judgment. Jesus says that we ought to make
righteous judgments (Matt 7:24). The Bible says
that the spiritual person makes assessment of all
things (1 Cor 2:15). Spiritual being the operative
word. We mustn't mistake correction for judgment.
People who correct us if they see us in a fault are
not judging us. If they don't correct us, but rather
walk away shaking their heads in condemnation,
making assumptions or determining that we aren't
worth correcting, that's judgment. **Today, let us
learn the difference and not be so quick to get
angry when correction is applied.**

Nevertheless
the Lord is steching us

Let redeemer of the Lord
say so.

Power is in the tongue.

Refill me with the Holy Ghost

Stay with us

Worship him and get Tap into
another level of God

When we worship we tell
God, I Trust you for who
you are.

JANUARY 4TH

"WORTHY OF CELEBRATION"

Hebrews 1:2,3 "…spoken to us in His Son, whom He appointed heir of all things, through whom also He made the world. And He is the radiance of His glory and the exact representation of His nature, and upholds all things by the word of His power…"

The resume of Jesus is amazing. His credentials supersede those of any human being. I often wonder why mere men receive more honor than the King of Kings. It's because we live in a culture of hero worship. We especially celebrate cultural icons when they pass away. The irony is that their posthumous impact, no matter how extensive, can never reach that of Jesus. It is Jesus who is the appointed heir of all things. That is, the Father has decided to leave all things to Him. It is Jesus who is the logos (Word) of God that caused everything to come into existence. It is Jesus who reflects God the Father more accurately than any cultural icon. Jesus is the inspiration for more hits than any musician; He's changed more lives than any philanthropist and those who are gone are still gone, Christ Jesus rose again! The eternality of Jesus means that He has no grand finale. **Today, celebrate Jesus, the living God, the one who was dead but behold, He now lives forevermore.**

37 Miracles of JESUS

I Yield, Nevertheless
I yield to you God, only God

4-25-21 Pastor Jason Clarke
God, He not asking you to lose
your life or kill yourself, but to
sacific forgive them
son - mother
God God   foreshaken
I thirsth
Finish, Hands, Spirit
HE DIED
This why Jesus Die
God is the
JESUS is the Greatest John 15:13
see you like son, That you like a
mother
Eph1

"I WAS BLIND BUT NOW I SEE"

2 Corinthians 4:4 "…in whose case the god of this world has blinded the minds of the unbelieving so that they might not see the light of the gospel of the glory of Christ, who is the image of God."

I once watched a documentary on teen-aged prostitution. One thing was abundantly clear, the key to pimping was mental slavery! The first to engage in mental slavery of human beings was Satan himself. He engaged in mind control/mental slavery from the very beginning. Anytime humans can be coerced into doing something that we know is bad for us, there is something amiss. Scripture refers to Satan as the god of this world and reminds us that he blinds the mind. He literally uses a smokescreen to cloud our judgment but more importantly to keep us from seeing the light of freedom in Christ. Traffickers and pimps use drugs, threats of death etc. to achieve this end with human subjects. Not surprisingly, so does Satan. He has no shortage of tricks to keep us in a state of mental blindness. Thanks be to God that Jesus is the way out of slavery. It is for freedom that we have been set free. The light of the gospel is a beacon of hope! **Today, remember that Jesus WILL break the shackles of slavery because Jesus came to set the captives free!**

I give your name Slory.

Now word, Acts 1 - 8
Don't stop until you have
a Book of Acts experince

Holy Ghost help you to
operate in the earth,

Fill me again
fill us again
with your Holy Ghost powe
Pls 136

JANUARY 6TH

"WHO ARE YOU?"

Gen 32:25 "When the man saw that he could not overpower him, he touched the socket of Jacob's hip so that his hip was wrenched as he wrestled with the man."

We know the story of Jacob well. Genesis 32 recounts his experience at Phenu-El. From his experience, a thought emerges. No one knows what we have been through but God; no one knows our true identities but God. What we have endured prepared us to live up to our true identities, not the names that someone else may have given us. The oil cannot come out of the olive unless the olive is first crushed. We have all had a "hip socket" experience. Those moments make our struggle against God so one sided, in His favor, not ours, that we have no recourse except to surrender to Him. The beauty of God is that we are able to ask for a blessing in return for our surrender! Scripture bears this out. Jacob said emphatically that he would not let go until the Lord blessed him. Indeed, the Lord blessed him, changed his name and altered history and Jacob's story (his-story) in the process. **Today, look at your circumstances, count your blessings and ask yourself, what is this situation going to bring forth from me and for me that will glorify God?**

Bishop Derrick Lee 4-25-21

3 Sunday Straight
Orange
I am the Lord
NEW 7
Completion 8
84
NEW Furniture,
Thank you.

business great

ALL IS WELL
wear purple a couple time
this week,
Hissop oil rub my leg legs

Bishop Lee Tell
Anna
I Love
Anna

JANUARY 7TH

"THE SOVEREIGN GOD"

Isaiah 44:6 "This is what the Lord says—Israel's King and Redeemer, the Lord Almighty: I am the first and I am the last; apart from me there is no God."

My daughter said once asked my late wife what the definition of a brat was. Danielle answered her and said "...someone who always wants to have their way..." to which my daughter replied, "Well God is a brat because we have to do everything he says!" This was an amazing revelation and gives a glimpse into the minds of many. While Genesis has since changed her stance, many still maintain that God is a hypercritical, self-indulgent bully. What is lost on many is the sovereignty of God. God has a right to do whatever He pleases because He is GOD! He is King and Redeemer and the only one who is able to fill all things and all roles perfectly. He is The Almighty i.e. El Shaddai, the One in whom there is no lack of power. He is the first because He precedes time. He is the last because when time is no more, He will still remain. The last part of this verse is critical, "apart from me, there is no God". Think about this: many claim to be a god but none of them can claim to be THE God. **Today, reflect on the sovereignty and magnitude of God.**

When you love God you should
not mind being contrated.

Everything should give God glory
God went all the glory,
I give you glory.

Pray we get our fire back
Pray we get our compassion back
Deal with the mess in the
Temple.

I went be more like Jesus
Every day

JANUARY 8TH

"STAY IN YOUR LANE"

1 Corinthians 12:4 "There are different kinds of gifts, but the same Spirit distributes them."

I thoroughly enjoy being a teacher. I believe that this is what God put me here and gifted me to do. There is something about working within the gift that God has given us that is supremely satisfying! Our culture teaches us to usurp what others have and to make so-called "boss moves" but in all honesty, there is only so much that we can do. A better alternative is to stay in our God-given lanes and work within the confines of what God gives us. Some of us have multiple gifts and can do multiple things. Some of us do not. The lack of multiple gifts does not diminish our roles in God's kingdom. We are all running the same race, we are all competing against ourselves and not the person in the opposite lane; and we all have to use God's gifts to glorify Him. Staying in our lane requires humility. It requires us to be willing to encourage and not to envy. Staying in our lane means being content with what God does in and through us and knowing that He gets just as much glory from small accomplishments as He does from major ones. **Today, whatever your gift is, thank God for it and use it to help someone!**

Bishop M. Densmore, Q & A
4-26-21

Mandate of God, got to have people in your life to push you in your

* I been talking and teaching of the empowerment of the Holy Ghost, we need the Holy Ghost to fill the will of God.

* I am a servant,

** what God call you to he cover you to do the work he call you to do.
                                              anoint
You can't kill what God ~~anitin~~ it.

Be careful where you sit,

Whatever you need, Become the WORD

① Spend time with God,

② Submitt yourself to God   He will put you
                           under a prophetic

③

When your spouse walk out on you
Stay ~~Prayer~~ Prayerfull

Roman 10:9, 10   the beginning   set you in the
                                              door
Acts1:8 & Acts 2:38   Holy Ghost is   the
                                              souler
Gal 5:22   to maintn
                                     his power

JANUARY 9TH

"TAKE THE LOW SEAT"

Galatians 6:3 "If anyone thinks he is something when he is nothing, he deceives himself"

People are, by nature, self-indulgent and self-centered. We have all taken part in this circus atmosphere of wanting to be noticed and wanting to be the center of attention. Saying that we are nothing in today's culture seems so condescending. Many would be offended and put off by such a statement. However, it is true. Consider the magnitude of the universe, the multitude of galaxies that exist, the size of the stars, the size of the planet and now consider that we are nothing more than specks of dust in the universe. Remember that all glory belongs to God and He will not share it with anyone. We don't need or deserve the accolades, the praises or the adulation. Whatever we do, we do it by the power of God, not in our own strength! As long as our eyes are fixed upward on Christ, we are not able to look down on anyone. **Today, be reminded that the world doesn't revolve around us. Let us stay humble and resist the temptation to be prideful. May Jesus keep us all near the cross!**

Bishop M. Densmore   Q & A

ConIX 4-26-21

repent when you been hurt by
Christian people or people, get heal
from that, cause you can't help people
when you hurt, how do you know
       prophetic gift?
You begin to hear the spirit and share it
with man of God.
honor your a shepard,
being rejected

          Virtual Pastor, Bishop, M. Densmore
Reset
     B 20 sowing Seeds

JANUARY 10TH

"UNDER CONSTRUCTION"

Phil 1:6 "For I am confident of this very thing, that He who began a good work in you will perfect it until the day of Christ Jesus."

There are two words that should never leave the lips of a Christian: "I've arrived." If we are to grow to the measure of the stature of the fullness of Christ, and if Christ fills all things, then He is immeasurable which means that we NEVER stop growing as Christians. Paul writes this very thing. His confidence is based on past experience. He knows that the work of completion comes directly from the Lord and His Spirit transforming us. He also points to a future time: He will perfect it until the day of Jesus Christ. So, the time limit on transformation is Christ's return. None of us know the day nor the hour of His return. Those of us who are still alive at that moment will be transformed in the twinkling of an eye. Those who are asleep will awaken to God's glory. We don't ever arrive because there is no endpoint for Christian growth/maturity. We all remain "continuous improvement" projects. **Today, reflect on the things that God has changed in your life. Reflect on your growth as a Christian. Know that God is not finished with you yet.**

JANUARY 11TH

"MORE LIKE THEE, LESS LIKE ME"

2 Corinthians 3:18 "But we all, with unveiled face, beholding as in a mirror the glory of the Lord, are being transformed into the same image from glory to glory, just as from the Lord, the Spirit."

God is a God of transformation. He is able to do anything. There are many self-help books on the market but the Bible offers secrets to transformation at no monetary cost to the reader. Paul makes this plain here. We are being transformed and conformed to the image of Christ who is the glory of God. Paul writes this passage to reflect the progressive work of God, through the Holy Spirit, in our lives. The transformation occurs as we behold the image of Christ. The more we look to Jesus, the more we begin to look like Jesus. As Christians we ought to reckon ourselves as slabs of marble, life through the Holy Spirit as the chisel and God as the sculptor. He is using the chisel of life, in the hands of the Holy Spirit, to conform us into the image of His Son; causing ALL things to work together to produce a holy masterpiece. **Today, reflect on the fact that although the chiseling may hurt, God's glory is worth it and we are being perfected through each experience in this life.**

JANUARY 12TH

"WATCHING YOUR BACK"

Ephesians 6:12 "For our struggle is not against flesh and blood, but against the rulers, against the powers, against the world forces of this darkness, against the spiritual forces of wickedness in the heavenly places."

When we mention anything related to the spiritual realm, many seek to dismiss us as weird or even crazy. Newsflash: you are not paranoid, crazy, insane or mentally unstable. There is indeed an unseen realm that coexists with the visible realm. There is a ruler of that unseen realm who is referred to as "the god of this world" or the "prince of the power of the air". Indeed, there are forces that want to take us out. Scripture bears this out. There are even levels to that unseen realm. There are rulers, powers and forces who work together to oppose God and His people. Knowing this can be frightening, but we also know that they must all bow to Christ Jesus! GREATER is He who is in us than he who is in the world. If you notice, the armor of God does not include protection for the back of the soldier. That's because God has that part secured and no enemy will ever pull a sneak attack on His children. **Today, stay on the battlefield, hold up the bloodstained banner of the One who loves you...the man, Christ Jesus! At His name, every knee, spiritual or physical, will bow.**

"LIFE'S TWO GREAT CERTAINTIES"

John 16:33 "These things I have spoken to you, so that in Me you may have peace. In the world you have tribulation, but take courage; I have overcome the world."

Jesus, in the 16th chapter of John's gospel, Jesus is preparing His disciples for His departure. He is getting ready to go to Calvary and He is revealing himself clearly to the disciples. He is no longer speaking in parables. He gives two great certainties to His disciples that they can hear, understand and believe. First, He says, "in Me you may have peace". It is written as an axiomatic statement. It is a certainty. The beginning of the second statement is the second certainty: "In the world you have tribulation". This is the truth. The world is basically a raging storm because of the destructive nature of sin. When we walk with Christ, we are called out of the world system, but we still live in the world itself. Therefore, tribulation is certain because of the conflict between Christ and the world system. The closer we get to God, the more static we can expect to catch. If it seems as if you are catching static for no apparent reason, you are probably getting ready to go to a new level in God! **Today, know this, that while tribulation may be certain, so is the overcoming power of Jesus Christ.**

JANUARY 14TH

"NO THANK YOU"

Galatians 2:20 "I have been crucified with Christ, and I no longer live, but Christ lives in me. The life I live in the body, I live by faith in the Son of God, who loved me and gave Himself up for me."

It's interesting how new age and new thought philosophy has infiltrated the Christian church. We hear people say "look in the mirror" or "look inside yourself" or "have faith in yourself" and declare this or decree that. Question: why would I look to the exact person who had my life jacked up before I met Jesus? Self was the reason my condition was what it was! This is just Christian common sense. The man in the mirror did not/cannot save us. The Man, Christ Jesus, did. New Age thinking tells us that all the 'power' we need is already within us. True, if they mean the power to sin and screw up everything that we touch! We must dethrone self and enthrone Jesus if ANY real power is to be experienced in our lives. Nothing good resides in the flesh. **Today, let us look to Jesus who hides our lives in Himself, who justifies us and who reminds us to DIE to self so that we might live through Him and He through us. Let us say "no thank you" to egotism and trust in the living God.**

JANUARY 15TH

"THE TRUTH OF THE MATTER"

John 14:6 "Jesus said to him, "I am the way, and the truth, and the life; no one comes to the Father but through Me."

Here is a little-known secret: there is no such thing as "your truth". We hear this often. Live your truth. Speak your truth. Celebrities have popularized this way of thinking. Think about it, if everyone has their version of the truth, how do we know what's real? There is, however, such a thing as the truth i.e. absolute truth. We've been dragged into relativism by folks who are looking to justify their sin by creating their truth while seeking to suppress the absolute Truth of Jesus Christ for their lie. Your relative truth and His absolute truth cannot both be the truth. This is a logical fallacy known as the principle of non-contradiction. It will either be one or the other. They can coexist but cannot both be true. Jesus Christ is the absolute truth and His words are absolutely true without any equivocation. The Word of God is absolute truth that every believer must stand on. **Today, let us exchange our truth for His truth, our words for His words and our sin for His righteousness.**

JANUARY 16TH

"HE DOESN'T REALLY KNOW"

Luke 22:31,32a "Simon, Simon, behold, Satan has demanded permission to sift you like wheat; But I have prayed for you..."

Sometimes we give the devil too much credit. He is not omniscient. He is not omnipresent. His advantage lies in the legions of demons and principalities he with whom colludes to oppose us. Here is a piece of good news for every believer: Satan doesn't know our future. There is a reason that he only knew about Job after God informed him of Job. There is a reason that the Holy Spirit speaks to the Father in a language that only they understand. What Satan can see is our potential. As we get closer to God, and our gifts start to manifest, Satan identifies them as dangerous to him and to his mission. That's when he attacks, in an effort to keep us away from our God-ordained destiny. Scripture says that he demanded permission to sift all of the disciples as wheat. Sifting was allowed because Jesus understood that what would remain after the sifting would be the purified wheat. In the case of the disciples, those trials and that shaking would further conform them to the image of Christ. **Today, let us press toward the mark, regardless of the obstacles!**

JANUARY 17TH

"WHY ARE YOU HERE?"

1 Kings 19:9 "There he went into a cave and spent the night. And the word of the Lord came to him: "What are you doing here, Elijah?"

Elijah was running for his life. He had just come off a spiritual victory over the prophets of Baal. He had outrun a chariot ahead of the rain shower that God told him was imminent. After these demonstrations of God's power, Elijah began reflecting of the viciousness of Jezebel and he became afraid. Herein lies the blessing, Elijah, seeking solitude, praying for God to take his life and remove him from trouble, got asked a pointed question: "What are you doing here?" God is simply asking, "Why are you running?" You've already seen my power and my glory, what can Jezebel do to you? It was in this midnight that Elijah heard from God. God is closest to us in the midnight hour. When we are alone and in solitude, that's when God can whisper into our spirit and show us all of the things that make us love Him more each day. Today, let us not fear man nor any enemy in our pursuit of God's destiny for us. **Trust Him, believe Him and love him all the more.**

WALK WITH ME: God Seen, God Heard, God Revealed

"LISTEN UP"

John 10:27-28 "My sheep listen to My voice; I know them, and they follow Me. 28I give them eternal life, and they will never perish. No one can snatch them out of My hand..."

The Bible tells us that if we are followers of the Good Shepherd, we know his voice. I love the agrarian imagery that Jesus uses here. Shepherds confine their sheep to areas that are manageable. Shepherds were armed with staffs that were used to fend off enemies. Some of those enemies were human and others were predatory animals like wolves. When the shepherd calls out to the sheep, they know his voice and are usually within a distance that they are able to hear the shepherd clearly. Sometimes, the sheep wander off and are unable to hear the voice of the shepherd. We do this often as Christians. We drift away from the pasture, sometimes in search of something greener and other times because we are disillusioned with our lives. Jesus is the Good Shepherd. Today, let us be reminded that if the voice of the Shepherd is inaudible, the Wolf is, without a doubt, not very far away. **Grace tells us that if we are ever out of pasture, Jesus the Good Shepherd is calling and waiting for us to come back in.**

JANUARY 19TH

"SINGULAR FOCUS"

James 1:8 "...being a double-minded man, unstable in all his ways."

Social media has given us license to live multiple lives. Many of the images we see are not real. Since there is no way to go behind the screen or peek behind curtain, we have no way of knowing who the real person is behind the profile picture. Often times, as a consequence of the protection that social media provides for us, we are able to say and post whatever we feel without accountability. Many vacillate between "scripture" on Sunday and "foul language, photographs, thoughts & actions on Monday-Saturday." I liken this to a pendulum. The closer the weekend gets, the rowdier the posts become. When this is our way, we are being double minded and thus unstable in all of our ways. Double minded literally means having two minds or two psyches. This leads to instability not just in one area but in all areas. A weak foundation with cracks in it has problems in multiple areas because cracks usually spread throughout. This is reminiscent of what Jesus meant when he said "No one who puts their hand to the plow and continues looking back is fit for the kingdom of God." **Today, with one mind and one heart, let us wholeheartedly follow Christ. Pray today for a renewed mind and a singular focus on what matters.**

JANUARY 20TH

"TEMPORAL OR ETERNAL?"

Nehemiah 8:10 "…Do not grieve, for the joy of the LORD is your strength."

Joy is defined as "the emotion evoked by well-being, success, or good fortune or by the prospect of possessing what one desires". Under normal conditions we deal with joy as a feeling or an emotion; however, we may also consider a different function of joy. Not only can joy be an emotion, joy can also be a place. In Matthew 25 the scripture says for the two servants to "enter into the joy of your Master." In today's scripture, the Jewish people are coming back from Babylonian exile. They have completed the wall along with Nehemiah and now they are also reconciling themselves back to God. The word joy in Hebrew is the word chedvah (khed·vä') which simply means gladness but it only exists in the Bible once in this particular context. The passage can be translated as "The joy that belongs to God is my stronghold." Why is this important? Joy is a place where we reside. It is not just a place but it is a stronghold that cannot be penetrated by the attacks of the enemy. This joy is where God desires for us to reside. Happiness is but a vapor but joy has a strong, lingering aroma. Joy is eternal and is not predicated on my mood or my circumstances. **Today, be resolved to live in the stronghold of God's joy.**

JANUARY 21ST

"CARNIVOROUS CHRISTIANS"

Hebrews 5:12 "For though by this time you ought to be teachers, you have need again for someone to teach you the elementary principles of the oracles of God, and you have come to need milk and not solid food."

Immature Christians seek after different things to make them feel like they've been to church. Whether it's a certain preaching style, a certain program or a certain song, when the focus is not Christ, the person will not mature past where they are. Mature Christians need a word. We must get past presentation to get to the power of Christ. The Hebrew writer recognized this as he chided his readers for their immaturity. Apparently, they had been a part of the Way for some time but they were not growing. They were so stagnant that the writer says they needed to be taught the rudiments again. They had regressed to the point that they could not handle solid food, which he later says is for the mature. This passage is instructive for us. We have to be willing to grow so that we are not tossed to and fro by every wind of doctrine. We must grow in order to become disciple makers. If not, we are in danger of being like the fruitless vine, cut off and thrown into the fire. **Today, let us crave the pure milk of the Word and the power that only comes from being connected to the vine.**

_____

_____

_____

_____

_____

_____

_____

_____

_____

_____

_____

_____

_____

_____

_____

_____

_____

_____

_____

_____

_____

JANUARY 22ND

"GOD OF A SECOND CHANCE"

Joel 2:25 "Then I will make up to you for the years That the swarming locust has eaten, The creeping locust, the stripping locust and the gnawing locust, My great army which I sent among you."

God's grace is so amazing. Every day we are beneficiaries of His grace and mercy. Every morning, His mercies are new. Every evening, He calls out to us. In the cool of the day, He walks with us. In the darkness of night, He comforts us. When we are out of line, He chastises us. Judah was being chastised and Joel was the prophet who delivered God's message to them. The chastisement of God is necessary and it is indicative of His love for us as His children. Even with chastisement, God is a God of restoration. He tells Judah here that everything that you've lost, I will make up to you. The years that were lost will be restored. God's grace ensures that every believer has access to the three R's. Restoration: God promises to restore what was lost, ask Job. Renewal: we are renewed by the washing and regeneration of the Word. Redemption: we are redeemed by the blood of Christ. Many of us have lost years, at times due to our own indiscretions. **Today, trust that recovery can and will happen by His own doing.**

JANUARY 23RD

"MORE THAN ONE WAY TO GLORIFY HIM"

Colossians 3:23 "Whatever you do, do your work heartily, as for the Lord rather than for men..."

Many times, we think that we can only glorify God by going to church or by giving to the poor or doing some selfless deed. While those things do bring God glory, there are other ways to glorify Him as well. Have you ever been to work and noticed coworkers milking the clock or just doing enough to get by? Maybe some of us are guilty of this ourselves. Have you ever half-stepped or put in minimal effort on a project? Laziness, slothfulness, a poor work ethic or a decidedly nonchalant attitude towards our jobs is not a godly attitude. Paul says here that whatever we do we should work heartily. Sometimes our attitude towards work is based on who we work for. Paul quashes that as well by telling us to work as if we are working for the Lord and not men. This is not the only scripture that encourages hard work. Proverbs 26:15 states that the sluggard thrusts his hand into the bowl but is too lazy to bring it back to his mouth. God gives us energy and strength. He gives us the ability to create wealth. He gifts us with intelligence and creativity. **Today, let us praise and glorify God through giving 100% effort on our jobs and in our careers.**

JANUARY 24TH

"DOERS OF THE WORD"

James 1:22 "But prove yourselves doers of the word, and not merely hearers who delude themselves."

The Bible is the inspired Word of God. It is not a cherry tree from which scriptures can be cherry picked. We cannot pick and choose scriptures to fit our ideas. Instead, our ideas should be shaped by and rooted in the scriptures. Rather than sifting through verses in the Bible, getting rid of the ones that make us uncomfortable and trying to reinterpret what has always been common sense, why don't we find out what God's plan is and see how those uncomfortable verses help in establishing it and following it. We are warned no to add or subtract from the Word of God, but rather we are to take the whole counsel of God. Doers of the word simply do what the word says, even when it is uncomfortable or unpopular. Doers of the word prove to be doers by their actions. We prove to be doers of the word by exercising discipline in areas where the word tells us to have restraint. We prove to be doers of the word by heeding God's command to love one another. Doers do, hearers look into the mirror but forget what they see. **Today, let us be doers of God's word regardless of the consequences.**

_____

_____

_____

_____

_____

_____

_____

_____

_____

_____

_____

_____

_____

_____

_____

_____

_____

_____

_____

_____

_____

JANUARY 25TH

"SPIRITUAL ENGINEERING"

Romans 8:28 "And we know that God causes all things to work together for good to those who love God, to those who are called according to His purpose."

Have you ever been in a situation where you doubted only to see that situation turn for the good? Have you ever been in a situation that did not turn but rather, ended badly and later you realized that there was still some good in that situation for you? Romans 8:28 ensures that we realize that no matter the outcome, God will eventually get glory and we will benefit, somehow, from the outcome. This is not some blanket statement that everything will be good all the time. Paul is addressing those who are suffering in the present time here. Seeing things come together that we know are orchestrated by God lets us know that God is for us; and if God is for us, He is more than the whole world against us. D.A. Carson says that we shouldn't interpret this text in selfish terms, but rather we should understand that although bad things are befalling God's people, we can be certain that even in the midst of such misery that God is at work for those who love Him! There is a synergistic effect between all experiences that have an end that God ordained. **Today, remember that God engineers every *thing*.**

WALK WITH ME: God Seen, God Heard, God Revealed

JANUARY 26TH

"WHY ARE YOU HOLDING ON?"

1 Peter 5:7 "Cast all your anxiety on Him, because He cares for you."

Problems and anxieties are like Velcro. They seem to stick to us and we seem reluctant to let them go. Yes, this is easier said than done. The reason we hold on to our issues is because sometimes we believe that we can straighten them out ourselves. We feel some semblance of control when the problems are in our hands. It's not that God CAN'T fix our problems. The issue is whether or not we are willing to GIVE our problems to God to be fixed. Peter, here, instructs us but a plain reading of the text doesn't reveal that the word cast is written in the past tense. It can be translated as having already cast your anxieties upon him. Casting gives the idea of hurling forcefully. Imagine taking every issue that besets us and hurling them at the feet of Jesus! Jesus tells us to come to him if we are heavy laden and if we need rest. The reason is simple: He cares for us. There is concern for us! Here is the God of the universe, hung every star in the sky, created all things and yet He cares for us. **Today, put what you're facing up against the Almighty God and God wins every time.**

JANUARY 27TH

"WHAT'S DONE IS DONE"

Philippians 3:13,14 "Brethren, I do not regard myself as having laid hold of it yet; but one thing I do: forgetting what lies behind and reaching forward to what lies ahead, I press on toward the goal for the prize of the upward call of God in Christ Jesus."

The past can hold us captive. Sometimes, good memories cause us to reminisce often. We tend to rest on those accomplishments without realizing that there is more work to do. In the same way, bad experiences can be just as captivating. We harp on mistakes, we beat ourselves up and we play the woulda-coulda-shoulda game rather than letting what is done be done. Our pasts are like books. They are there for reference and for a testimony, but like a book, the words on the paper are not the present reality. Therefore, we may reference the past but we cannot stay there. When we do, the past becomes a ball and chain. We learn from the past but we can't let it hold us back. Paul rightly instructs us here. Forgetting is active, conscious and continual. The things that are behind, good or bad, are forgotten on the way to what lies ahead. We must press which requires exerting some spiritual energy! **Today, let us remember that the only thing that matters is the upward calling of Christ Jesus!**

JANUARY 28TH

"BY ANY MEANS NECESSARY"

Haggai 2:7 "I will shake all the nations; and they will come with the wealth of all nations, and I will fill this house with glory,' says the LORD of hosts."

As a young Christian, I used to think that every no was the final answer. After walking with God for some time, I realized that a no often diverts us into the direction of God's yes and not the yes that we may have desired. A closed door, if closed with enough force, can shake several other doors open. Haggai prophesied about 15 years after the return from Babylonian exile. The temple was in ruins in Jerusalem. As you can imagine, the nation was poor and there were very few resources for rebuilding anything. God reassured the nation through Haggai that His no, which led the people into captivity, was only a detour to His yes but, the yes would have to be on His terms. He says in response to the dearth of resources that He would shake the nations and they would provide the resources. The resources belong to Him, and therefore, He can distribute them however He sees fit. **Today, be encouraged and let us pray for God's YES and that we would trust Him totally for everything.**

"DISCIPLINE YOURSELF"

1 Corinthians 9:27 "No, I beat my body and make it my slave so that after I have preached to others, I myself will not be disqualified for the prize."

In the ninth chapter of Paul's first letter to the Corinthians, he is giving some life lessons. He's talking to the Corinthians about the principles of holy living. I love the imagery used by the Apostle Paul. He compares Christians to boxers and runners. The imagery is related to Greek athletes preparing for a contest. He associates physical strain, discipline, strength and fighting with being a Christian. Hebrews 10:36 says that we need endurance to receive what is promised to us! Our stamina is directly related to how long we train. Our training takes place when we spend time in the word of God. The less we train, the weaker we are when it's time to fight. Our fiercest opponent knows our every move and knows everything about us; our favorite punch, what makes us angry and how to throw us off our game. It's not Satan, it's SELF. We must discipline ourselves as we fight against our flesh; beat our bodies into submission and not let them win. Discipline is saying no when EVERYTHING else around us is saying yes. **Today, let us run in such a way so as to win the crown. Godliness is profitable for this life and the next.**

"ALL DAY, ALL NIGHT"

Hebrews 7:25 "Therefore He is able also to save forever those who draw near to God through Him, since He always lives to make intercession for them."

Jesus is a priest forever in the order of Melchizedek. Priests have a specific function: to minister on behalf of those whom they represent. There is a reason that Jesus replaced the Aaronic and Levitical priesthoods. He did so because His life is indestructible and His ministry does not stop at the temple! Therefore...he is able to save fully those who draw near to God through Him. This is an amazing testimony to the unfailing ability of Jesus. He ministers day and night on behalf of those who have drawn near to God through Him. He never gets tired, He never sleeps, He never slumbers and He never quits...He intercedes all day and all night for all eternity. This is necessary because the enemy, who we face, is just as relentless, but for a different purpose. Now for the good news, what you are dealing with right now has been dealt with already...in heaven because Jesus has already made intercession on your behalf. **Today, know that not only does Jesus never sleep; He has never lost a case.**

"STAY PUT"

2 Chronicles 5:14 "...so that the priests could not stand to minister because of the cloud, for the glory of the LORD filled the house of God."

We often spend inordinate amounts of time wondering how much longer we'll be in service. Some churches put clocks within the view of the preacher to ensure that he/she knows not to preach too long. We get preoccupied with devices and games and sometimes miss out on what God is saying and doing. We look for entertainment and for pomp and circumstance when in church. There will be times when fire falls from heaven and God's glory shows up during the service. We shouldn't be in a rush. Don't rush out the door thinking "those folks are crazy". These are the times when we should stay there and let the Holy Ghost work on us! God's glory surpasses tradition, time or agendas. Forget about all of the other superfluities and stay in the presence of the Lord. He showed up in this scripture because everyone in service to Him was on the same page. The priests, musicians and ministers all glorified God together. When this happened, the glory of the Lord fell and no one could minister because His glory was so thick in the temple. **Today, make yourself a promise to stay in the presence of the Lord and get what He has for you.**

FEBRUARY 1ST

"THE REASON FOR THE BLESSING"

John 15:6,7 "If you remain in Me and My words remain in you, ask whatever you wish, and it will be done for you. This is to My Father's glory, that you bear much fruit, proving yourselves to be My disciples."

We often wonder why God is so good to us. When we are connected to the vine, we cannot help but to absorb some of the nutrients. We will grow and be nurtured as long as we stay connected. Jesus makes a conditional statement here. He says if we remain (abide) in Him and if His words remain (abide) in us, we can ask whatever we desire and it will be done for us. This sounds like a blank check but it's not. The second part of the statement is the key to understanding this passage. God does not bless us simply to increase our possessions, He blesses us because we are to bear fruit and glorify His name. It brings glory to God when we bear fruit. The fruit that we bear is spiritual food that can be used to bless others. The fruit is our actions towards others. The fruit is to be used to add to the kingdom! **Today, let us abide in Christ so that we will have everything that we need and so that we might bring glory to God the Father!**

FEBRUARY 2ND

"RESOLVED"

Isaiah 50:7 "For the Lord GOD helps Me, Therefore, I am not disgraced; Therefore, I have set My face like flint, And I know that I will not be ashamed."

It's the second month of a new year. It's around the time when those resolutions start going out the window. It's around the time when we look down at our bellies and see that we've overdone it, yet again. Those resolutions are oftentimes half-hearted. We are already knowing that we will fall off the wagon. Walking with God is a daily proposition and not merely a resolution made on December 31st. Our model is Jesus. Scripture says that we can be resolved when we know two things: 1) The Lord God is our help and 2) The Lord God will not allow us to be disgraced. The scripture referenced above is actually an OT reference to Christ. He had stubborn, immovable faith as He walked the earth working while waiting for His appointment with those Roman soldiers at Calvary. He sets a great example for us. We need stubborn faith in tough times! That kind of faith where we set our face toward the LORD, dig our heels in and wait to see what the end is going to be! **Today, be resolved to stay encouraged this day and every day!**

FEBRUARY 3RD

"THE ROD OF CORRECTION"

Hebrews 12:7 "Endure hardship as discipline; God is treating you as his children. For what children are not disciplined by their father?"

There are two interpretations of struggle that most of us offer up. Either we have done some immoral act and are being punished for it or God is using our struggle to bring something out of us that will bless someone else. The fact that trials drive us to our knees is not a bad thing. It is the intended outcome of God's training! It is the proper posture as we approach the throne of grace. It is the correct mindset of humility as we approach an omnipotent God. Trials ensure our dependence on Him and not ourselves for sustenance. While on our knees, let us not waste time griping, which we are all guilty of, but rather use that time to move ever closer to our comforter, Christ Jesus, through prayer and supplication. The scripture admonishes us to bear up under hardship as discipline; a term which comes from a root word that brings children to mind. **Today, let us remember that we are children who are in need of correction in order to grow properly.**

"A LIFETIME OF FOLLOWING"

Mark 8:35 "Then Jesus called the crowd to Him along with His disciples, and He told them, "If anyone wants to come after Me, he must deny himself and take up his cross and follow Me."

There are generally two types of "Christians". There are fringe followers who get close enough to be blessed but not close enough to get splattered by the blood from Calvary. Then, there are those who sell out and risk everything to follow Jesus. Notice in the scripture above, Jesus summoned both to Himself. He called His disciples and the crowd and he made a very exacting statement. He said, IF anyone. He says this to His disciples to suppress their pride. He says it to the crowd to determine who is serious about getting closer to Him. He then gives the criteria in the form of three commands: 1) deny yourself 2) understand the ultimate end of this journey and 3) follow Me. Denial of self means His will supersedes my will; the cross tells me that death is a distinct possibility as a result of my journey; and following means emulation of the ways of my Teacher. **Today, let us remember that following Jesus is a lifetime proposition that we choose, knowing the outcome from the beginning.**

"THANK YOU JESUS!"

Job 9:33 "There is no umpire between us, who may lay his hand upon us both."

Job's situation was unique. He was a righteous man who was allowed, through the permissible will of God, to be tested by Satan. It looked like an unwarranted attack. Job began to search for answers. He did not understand and thus, asked for an umpire. His thinking is prophetic. The word umpire gives the idea of a mediator or a go-between, between Job and God. The imagery of a cosmic courtroom comes to mind. Satan is the prosecutor, and, therefore, the mediator i.e. defense attorney, would have to be Jesus. We have an advocate, Jesus Christ the righteous. Job's status as pre-priesthood and pre-law is even more significant, showing how God's redemptive acts preceded even scripture itself. There is one mediator between God and man, the man Christ Jesus. He is able to lay His hand on sinful man, not be tainted by our sinfulness and be our bridge to a thrice holy God, keep us from falling and present us as blameless. We all have a case pending in the eternal courtroom of God. **Today, let us thank Jesus Christ, the Supreme Advocate, who has dismissed our case and cleansed us of all unrighteousness.**

"LIGHTS, CAMERA, ACTION"

2 Peter 3:8 "But do not let this one fact escape your notice, beloved, that with the Lord one day is like a thousand years, and a thousand years like one day."

Many times, we rush God. We look at others prospering while doing evil and we wonder when Christ will part the clouds and set everything right! Peter, addressing that sentiment here, gives the reasoning. He says that God is giving sinners time to repent. Within this is another thought. A rough calculation based on this scripture puts our entire lives into perspective. If 1000 years is but a day to God, then our lives are about the span of a short movie. One hour and forty minutes for a life of seventy years, to be exact. Rather than focusing on what others are doing, let us make life beautiful, make others beautiful; love with fervor, love in deed and not just with words and love God with all our hearts. If God produces, directs and edits the film that we call our life, the ending will always show the main character in a favorable light. **Today, let us remember the preciousness of time and spend it wisely.**

FEBRUARY 7TH

"HONEY OR VINEGAR?"

Jeremiah 31:3 "The LORD appeared to him from afar, saying, "I have loved you with an everlasting love; Therefore, I have drawn you with lovingkindness."

We are called to evangelize as we go. We are called to share the gospel with those who are unsaved, unchurched, un-whatever and to do it with love. How did the good news of Jesus Christ become unloving, critical, mean spirited and judgmental? Because there are times when we deliver the good news using our own eyes to see people's faults rather than using the eyes God gives us to see people's needs. Christ Jesus paid the price for all of our sins...past, present and future. Not a license to sin but definitely a reason to celebrate! We should tell folks how they can be sin debt free, how much God loves us all and how Jesus exchanges our uncleanness for His cleanness. We must show people Christ with love then instruct them in righteousness. More flies are caught with honey than vinegar. If the Father drew us in with lovingkindness, how can we do anything less? **Today, let the love of Christ permeate every evangelistic effort.**

FEBRUARY 8TH

"GOD DIDN'T SAY THAT"

1 Kings 13:18 "The old prophet answered, "I too am a prophet, as you are. And an angel said to me by the word of the Lord: 'Bring him back with you to your house so that he may eat bread and drink water." (But he was lying to him.)"

This passage of scripture is a cautionary tale for every believer. When God gives us an assignment, we must carry it out as He commanded. This young prophet, Jodan, was sent to prophesy against King Jeroboam for his wickedness. The LORD gave the prophet specific instructions to return home by a different route and not spend the night. The king's entreaties did not work to get Jodan to stay so Satan found another way in, an old false prophet. This man was bedridden but when he saw the chance to one-up God's prophet, he saddled his donkey and went to find Jodan. Jodan's immaturity and spiritual fatigue made him vulnerable. The old prophet took advantage of this and got him to disobey God. Jodan ended up being eaten by a lion as a result of his disobedience. We must be careful who we allow to speak over and into our lives. Any word from MAN that is contrary to what God already told us is subject to question. **Today, let us pray for discernment so that we are not led astray**.

"RESETTING"

Luke 8:49 "While He was still speaking, someone came from the house of the synagogue official, saying, "Your daughter has died; do not trouble the Teacher anymore."

Jairus was a man who had to deal with multiple setbacks. His daughter was dying and he had to humble himself and bow at the feet of Jesus. He had to deal with a woman's blood issue holding him up. The text never says that he got frustrated or upset. Jesus never left his side. Once the distractions were over, they were on their way to his home; and Jesus was about to do a miracle for Jairus' daughter. It was looking good. I can imagine Jairus smiling as he walked and talked with Jesus. Enter a person from his home telling him that his daughter was not just sick anymore…she was dead and that he should leave Jesus be. Jairus had two choices. Jesus helped him to decide. He told Jairus not to fear but to believe. In life there are setbacks and there are hurdles. We will all face them. Listen to Jesus, do not fear, only believe. A setback only gives you an opportunity to develop a strategy for getting over a hurdle. **Today, let us have the mind of Jairus and trust Jesus in spite of the setbacks and hurdles that seek to postpone His work.**

"SOUND ASLEEP"

Psalm 121:2, 3 "He will not allow your foot to slip; He who keeps you will not slumber. Behold, He who keeps Israel will neither slumber nor sleep."

Life is one mountain after another. There is new trouble with each passing day. When we reach the top of one mountain, we look and we see more mountains off in the distance. Not the pie-in-the-sky existence that many of us crave, but definitely a reality. This psalm reminds us that mountains are a part of life and when we see them, we often wonder, "How am I going to climb this?" The writer reminds us that as we look to the mountains and we wonder where our help is going to come from, we can be certain that the Lord is an ever-present help in times of trouble. As we climb, we realize that it can get slippery. This imagery is prevalent in the Old Testament because of the goats and deer observed by shepherds in this culture that climbed mountains to escape predators. Again, the writer reminds us that God will not allow our feet to slip. Finally, he reminds us that this same God who guides our feet never sleeps. How comforting is that to know? Problems and worries often rob us of sleep. We develop insomnia wondering "what if?" **Today, let us make our minds up to sleep well knowing that God is always awake and working for us.**

FEBRUARY 11TH

"GOD IS LOOKING"

2 Chronicles 16:9 "For the eyes of the LORD range throughout the earth to strengthen those whose hearts are fully committed to him."

Many shy away from believing in God or submitting to Christ because in that submission is a tacit admission of dependence. Christians depend on God, period. There's no equivocation regarding this fact. His Word says whoever hopes in the Lord will never be put to shame. Dependence is a requirement to follow God because it is He who supplies our every need. Some see this as weak. There is strength in dependence, however. Dependence means that I am in a position to hold God to His Word and expect that He will keep it. It also means that I depend on God to the exclusion of anything (one) else. In context, today's scripture is an admonition to King Asa for his dependence on foreign allies. The point is very clear, God is looking for the opportunity to strengthen us if we are committed to depend totally on Him! He will provide everything that we need and do so tangibly. The danger for us is that we cannot always see, feel or hear God but human beings are always in our midst that we can see, feel and hear. This makes it easy to trust in humans, especially in times of distress. It is true that sometimes God sends some people as allies for us. **Today, let us remember that even these allies are not meant to replace Him.**

FEBRUARY 12TH

"WE KINDA EARNED IT"

2 Timothy 3:6 "For among them are those who enter into households and captivate weak women weighed down with sins, led on by various impulses."

Christianity has been maligned for centuries. There is good reason for it. Many of those who claim to be leaders are actually corrupt wolves in sheep's clothing. They use God's name as a cover for all manners of foolishness and still have the nerve to claim moral superiority over those who are "unsaved" or different from them. It is not the sin but rather the self-righteousness that is the issue. They have a form of godliness but deny its power. Their intentions are bad and they know upfront that they are not honoring God in what they do. As long as charlatans continue to represent the kingdom of God, the name of God will continue to be stomped upon by the enemies of the cross. We should not ever hide false intentions behind the name of God. The mere thought of God causes many to relax and let their guards down, making them vulnerable. When the true intention is revealed, often by God Himself, the outcome can be disastrous. One thing is certain, if God's name is used for personal advancement and ill-gotten wealth, God IS NOT PLEASED and HE will not let evil stand! **Today, let us be vigilant and discerning to recognize the wolves when they show up.**

"BEING PERFECTED"

Romans 8:29a "For those God foreknew, He also predestined to be conformed to the image of His Son..."

America longs for perfection. We look for perfection in our leaders. We look for perfection in our children. We want the perfect body. We want everything to be just perfect. One thing to remember is that perfection didn't start out that way. Perfection is an unattainable goal that will elude us every time we seek it. A wedding that seems perfect did not just happen, there were many people who worked hard behind the scenes to ensure that it went off without a hitch. The perfect photograph may have required 100 takes. In other words, what we see as a perfectly finished product actually took some work to get there. We think as Christians that perfection is a requirement. Nothing could be further from the truth. We cannot ever be perfect. We can, however, be perfected, which is a long, arduous process. The scripture says that we have been predestined to be conformed to the image of Christ. Conformed is a descriptive word, not a verb. God's plan is to cause us to look, act and think like Jesus. **Today, let us long to be like Jesus and allow God to cause that to happen daily.**

_____

_____

_____

_____

_____

_____

_____

_____

_____

_____

_____

_____

_____

_____

_____

_____

_____

_____

_____

_____

_____

_____

_____

"NOTHING GOOD RESIDES HERE"

Romans 7:18 "For I know that nothing good dwells in me, that is, in my flesh; for the willing is present in me, but the doing of the good is not"

There was a song by a popular gospel artist that insinuated that God somehow sees the best in us and that is why God chooses us. At the time of the song and at the height of its popularity, it was amazing to see churches take hold of such a humanistic theology and promote it so readily. Man's best is no more than filthy rags to God. On our best day, we could never please Him because we are nothing more than sinful creatures apart from Him. The question is, did God see the best in us or, did God see the Blood of Jesus covering us? There is nothing within the human being that warrants God's favor or grace. It is given at His own discretion. It is only the blood of Jesus that gives us peace with God. It is because of that blood that God lavishes His righteousness, blessings and love upon us! Paul here tells us plainly that nothing good dwells in our flesh. **Today, let us recognize our depravity, thank Jesus for His unconditional love and thank the Father for His undying mercy!!!!**

FEBRUARY 15TH

"WHO IS THE DRIVER?"

1 Corinthians 10:13 "No temptation has overtaken you but such as is common to man; and God is faithful, who will not allow you to be tempted beyond what you are able, but with the temptation will provide the way of escape also, so that you will be able to endure it"

There is vigorous debate now from the Vatican that the Lord's Prayer should be edited so that it cannot be inferred that it is God who leads us into temptation. While James reminds us that God does not tempt anyone, every temptation that comes our way must indeed pass by God before it ever gets to us. In His permissive will, God allows us to be tested. Paul reminds us that these things are common to man. He reminds us that although God sees the temptation before we do, He is faithful to limit what we are exposed to and will even give us a way out of it. Often, when we are led by lust, we miss the escape route. Lust focuses on the physical and the material. Anything rooted in lust, marriages included, will crumble because both the physical and the material will pass away. The vehicle of LUST will drive us to do many things that we wouldn't have if we had not accepted the ride in the first place. **Today, when the escape route avails itself, take it.**

FEBRUARY 16TH

"THIS LOVE"

John 13:35 "By this all men will know that you are My disciples, if you have love for one another."

Did you know that we are witnesses to the reality of Jesus Christ? As a Christian and as a disciple, we are the reflection of Jesus to the world around us. This is a conditional statement given by Jesus to His disciples. If we have love for one another, then all men will know that we are His disciples. It is by this; this is a demonstrative pronoun that points to something tangible. This is what the world will see. This is our love for one another. This is the tangible, beautiful, awesome expression of love that comes through God's people. If we learn that we need one another, and that others depend on us...then the world will be a much better place. We are meant to be one in Christ and to love one another despite our flaws. We have to get it right within the church so that the world can see what Jesus looks like, talks like and how He treats people. **Today, make it a point to show love to your fellow disciples and in doing so, show the world what true discipleship looks like.**

"HIGH HORSE, LONG FALL"

1 Peter 5:6 "Therefore humble yourselves under the mighty hand of God, that He may exalt you at the proper time…"

Proverbs 16:18 says that pride precedes destruction and haughtiness precedes a great fall. Peter provides great insight to us here in his epistle. He warns us that God opposes the proud but He gives grace to the humble. He is speaking of the dynamics between the older men and the younger men within the body of Christ. The younger ought to submit to the elders and yet all ought to clothe themselves in humility. That is, the elder should not lord authority over the younger but rather he should exercise grace. It's amazing to know what can be accomplished with others when we operate in humility and not pride. He then refers to God's mighty hand which is in stark contrast to our feeble hands. It is not our pride that will exalt us. Pride only puffs up. It is God who looks down, sees the humble and then exalts them in the time that he deems proper. **Today, let us remember our position within the kingdom, show respect to those who are elder to us and be mindful of the power of God's mighty hand.**

"WHAT'S HOLDING YOU BACK?"

Acts 3:2 "…whom they used to set down every day at the gate of the temple which is called Beautiful, in order to beg alms of those who were entering the temple"

Do you have a "Beautiful Gate" in your life? A "Beautiful Gate" is something that: 1) you cannot get past 2) the people that you deal with cannot/will not take you past and/or 3) you "feel" is not right but you have grown comfortable with. The man referenced in scripture had friends who did a noble deed for him by taking him to the gate on a daily basis. However, these friends had limitations and could only take him so far. By the same token, he had gotten accustomed to being carried and begging to subsist. Once he got to the gate, there was nothing the beggar could do. The friends never thought to take him any further or take him closer to the temple to solve his real issue. Lack of money was only a symptom but it was not the root issue. Fortunately for us, no matter the gate, Jesus is portable and can come to us and get to the root of our issues. Peter and John met this man where he was and raised him up. They asked no questions or offered no judgments. **Today, know that Jesus desires to raise us up from our seemingly "beautiful" experiences!**

"WAR WITH GOD"

Romans 5:10 "For if while we were enemies we were reconciled to God through the death of His Son, much more, having been reconciled, we shall be saved by His life."

God's grace is an amazing thing. It is at once unfathomable and bold. Unfathomable in that we cannot understand why God does what He does. Bold because He does it right in our faces and to our amazement. Prior to our salvation, we were at war with God. We were hopeless enemies of the cross. Here, the scripture reminds us of the unfathomable nature of God's grace. While we were actively God's enemies, the death of Jesus reconciled us to God! God's justification is contrasted with our status as His enemies. Who can understand that? Now for the boldness, because of the life of Jesus, that eternal, indestructible life, we shall be saved. Saved, in this sense, means a future salvation from the power, penalty and presence of sin. Justification ensures future salvation! The life of Christ means that He will return to set all things right! Every promise God ever made was pointing to a singular moment in history: the resurrection of Christ Jesus! Because of him, we are no longer at war with God. **Today, let us thank Him for His mercy and for peace.**

"HE MAKES IT ALRIGHT"

Luke 7:38 "...and standing behind Him at His feet, weeping, she began to wet His feet with her tears, and kept wiping them with the hair of her head, and kissing His feet and anointing them with the perfume."

The woman in the scripture referenced above was in a bad place. She was trapped in a lifestyle that she did not know how to escape. She heard that Jesus was eating at the house of Simon the Pharisee and she crashed the party. As she wept in repentance, she wept enough to wet his feet. She then proceeded to wipe them with her hair. She recognized that the escape from her struggle was reclining here at this table. We all struggle with different things. Besetting things. Just know this, God is searching for one with a repentant heart and He is waiting to put you back together again. He is waiting to make it alright. Jesus did not condemn this woman, although Simon did. Jesus touched her, although Simon wouldn't. Jesus forgave her, although Simon wouldn't. Jesus told Simon, the one who is forgiven much loves much. We all have heavy debts. **Today, let us remember that the blood of Jesus has already been spilled for our sins; turning from them is up to us.**

"POPPYCOCK"

Colossians 2:4 "I say this so that no one will delude you with persuasive arguments."

The church at Colossae dealt with many heresies in its day. Not only were the heresies dangerous, they were also coming from very skilled rhetoricians who were able to make a very good case for their doctrine. However, those nuanced points are the types of poison pills that Satan plants to disrupt the church. Jude refers to them as hidden reefs. Unfortunately, there is nothing new under the sun. Today, there are also famous, influential and powerful rhetoricians who deal in nuance and subtleties. They delude the masses with their smooth talk. Some are inside the church. Some are outside the church. The bottom line remains the same: it's all poppycock. We must be careful to test everything in light of scripture, to pray for discernment, to not allow our sin to force us to seek safety in a false doctrine and to not be afraid to have a Berean type discipline in vetting every doctrinal argument. Elders have a saying "everything that 'sound' good ain't always good." If a doctrine is based on limited scriptural evidence, fallacious interpretation of scripture or no scripture at all, it's probably faulty and should be avoided. **Today, be vigilant.**

"ALL HAVE SINNED"

Romans 3:23 "for all have sinned and fall short of the glory of God..."

In God's kingdom, there is no room for judgment of others. Hypocrisy has no place because none of us are any better than the other. There are no gradations on sin. No levels to sin. It is all filth to God. Our righteousness is as filthy rags before God. God understood and understands this. This is why a surrogate in the person of Jesus Christ came to be the supplier of righteousness for all of us. None of us will ever attain perfection. None of us will ever approach God's holiness. There is none that is righteous, no, not one. But this is Christ's role as the one who imputes His righteousness unto us! For this, we ought to thank God. He sent Christ Jesus to be our righteousness and the propitiation for our sins. **Today, let us remember what Jesus has done for us in forgiving our sins.**

"RIPE FIELDS"

Luke 10:2 "And He was saying to them, "The harvest is plentiful, but the laborers are few"

The gospel ministry i.e. telling others the good news about the death, burial and resurrection of Christ takes place in the trenches as well as the church. Often times, the workers are sitting in the building instead of flooding the streets. We cannot allow ourselves to get so comfortable in the church that we forget that the world is dying around us. Within this comfort zone, we tend to let the four walls of the building limit our impact. We can go in twos just as the disciples did. We can pray for opportunities to witness daily. We can pray for openings to introduce the Gospel to someone who may not know it. We can pray for more workers, just as Jesus said we could. A ripe harvest can be a daunting task. There may be thorns surrounding the crops. It may be hot or dusty. Maybe it's a winter crop. Whatever the case, the Lord will supply. We will either plant or water but what we don't want to do is destroy. **Today, let us ask God to prepare our hearts for ministry and for witnessing to those who are lost. The harvest is plentiful but the workers are few.**

"JARS OF CLAY"

2 Corinthians 4:7 "But we have this treasure in jars of clay to show that this all-surpassing power is from God and not from us."

We are all just jars of clay. Fragile, cracked, chipped, burnished and sometimes overworked. God uses these fragile vessels for a reason. It is an awesome demonstration of His power that He is able to work through such fragile objects. It is indicative of His delicacy in dealing with us. If you've ever worked with something fragile, you know that it must be handled with care. It also shows His wisdom. Our trials and tests are like a furnace that burnishes us and in doing so, builds strength so that we are not so easily shattered. Another reality of being a jar of clay is that every jar of clay has a crack in it somewhere. Practically, a broken vessel has no use. Spiritually, a broken vessel's contents leak out as a blessing to others. Before we get too prideful, remember that if our crack is invisible to the naked eye, let's say, under the bottom of our vessel, we are still in no position to judge those whose cracks are easier to see. **Today, let us endeavor to build each other up knowing that we are but broken vessels.**

"HE WANTS THE BEST FOR US"

Ephesians 2:11 "For we are His workmanship, created in Christ Jesus for good works, which God prepared beforehand so that we would walk in them."

When we have children, we often have dreams for them before they have dreams for themselves. We want them to be doctors or lawyers or ball players or something that will make us proud. These are our little bundles of joy and we want nothing but the best for them. Jesus once said if we, as humans, know how to give good gifts, how much more does our heavenly Father know how to give good gifts? We are the workmanship of God, His doing and therefore, like a parent, surely, He wants the best for us! That is why He pre-planned the way that we should walk. The scripture reminds us that we were created in Christ Jesus for good works and that those good works were already prepared for us to walk in them. Walking indicates a way of life that God has already prepared for us. Not a perfect way of life, but as good as possible under the circumstances. God never stops trying to make us the best that we can be. Therefore, we should never stop trying to be the best we can be. **Today, let us walk in the good works that God has already prepared for us.**

FEBRUARY 26TH

"DO YOU CARE THAT I AM PERISHING?"

Mark 4:38 "Jesus Himself was in the stern, asleep on the cushion; and they woke Him and said to Him, "Teacher, do You not care that we are perishing?"

One day, my late wife and I were boating on Lake Martin in Dadeville, Alabama. We were headed to a location known as Chimney Rock. People frequented this site to climb the rock and jump off into the lake. Being novice boaters, we made a wrong turn and got lost. Boating is infinitely easier with a navigation device. Then, the app that I was using on my phone, malfunctioned. After we righted the boat, we could finally see our destination. We thought we were home free until it started raining. We had two choices, turn back or keep pushing. We pushed through the rain to an area where there was no rain. We were able to enjoy the destination despite the rough trip. God has a lesson in everything. In life when we get lost, we must turn around rather than continuing in error. When the things we depend on malfunction, we must remember that God never does. When the rain comes, this doesn't necessarily mean turn back. Storms are temporary and God will eventually guide us to a place of safety. **Today, thank God for every lesson and everything learned therein.**

"EVER INCREASING DISORDER"

Colossians 1:17 "He is before all things, and in Him all things hold together."

According to the Second Law of Thermodynamics, in a natural thermodynamic process, the sum of the entropies of the interacting thermodynamic systems increases. In thinking about entropy, it should be understood that disorder is the natural tendency of the universe. Everything is tending towards disorder. Even our bodies. Some things are moving towards disorder slower than others. Even the universe is continually expanding. How does this square with evolutionists and atheists who don't believe that a creator brought order from chaos? Are we to believe that randomness and natural selection somehow bucked the entropic trend toward steadily increasing disorder and caused ordered, highly complicated and intricately designed species to come into existence? It's far easier to see God's hand in creation than it is to put my faith in a theory that is the equivalent of the universe finding a winning biological lottery ticket billions of times. **Today, know that there is indeed a God whose hand guides all things from complex to mundane.**

FEBRUARY 28TH

"KEEPING PACE"

Ecclesiastes 9:11 "I again saw under the sun that the race is not to the swift and the battle is not to the warriors, and neither is bread to the wise nor wealth to the discerning nor favor to men of ability; for time and chance overtake them all."

In life, we face two certainties. While they do not always occur concomitantly, they do so often. These two things we cannot outrun. They are age and death. Age slows us down while death catches up to us. Solomon in all his wisdom, did not disagree with this assessment. Swift people run races because in their swiftness, they are built to run. Warriors fight battles because in their fierceness, they are built to fight. Wise men rarely go hungry because in their wisdom, they know how to get bread. Discerning men can become wealthy because in their discernment, they are able to make good decisions. Men of ability are often shown favor because of their ability. But, in all of this, none of these are superior to the other because none of them can outrun time. The hourglass elapses for each of us although we do not all have the same number of days. Chance cannot be predicted and thusly, neither the fortunes of these who we assume that things will be handed to. **Today, let us resolve to do as Solomon said, fear God and keep His commandments.**

"I CAN'T SEE IT YET!"

Hebrews 11:1 "Now faith is confidence in what we hope for and assurance about what we do not see."

The only way to see the unseen is by faith. The future and God's promises can be distorted because of storms that we find ourselves standing in. That's when we must shift our focus from the physical to faithful. What is unseen is eternal. Think about God's master plan for our lives and the fact the plan was in place before we were even formed in our mothers' wombs. IF God says that it won't rain forever then we can't allow the storm to stop us from believing that! The rain from the storm is watering the seeds of hope and faith! The Hebrew writer says that faith has two components. One is being confident that our hope (expectation) is well founded and well placed. The second component is being sure that although we do not see what we hope for just yet, we are certain that it is coming. Joy always comes in the morning, rainbows after every storm, peace during and after every test. **Today, hold on to your mustard seed and watch God turn it into a tree!**

"DO SOMETHING DIFFERENT"

James 2:15, 16 "Suppose a brother or a sister is without clothes and daily food. If one of you says to them, "Go in peace; keep warm and well fed," but does nothing about their physical needs, what good is it?"

We live in an era where the poor and the disenfranchised are scorned and looked at as enemies. Truthfully, except for the super-rich in this nation, every last one of us is probably one or two paychecks from being on the streets. We like to brag about how hard we work and castigate those who we deem as lazy or fruitless. We complain about "socialist" programs and "handouts" as if no one has ever helped us. We offer up platitudes to those who are hurting rather than real relief. The Bible has a different take, one that every Christian should be mindful of. To paraphrase James, words don't matter, especially if we have the means to assist. John says in his first epistle that to have the world's goods, see someone in need and overlook them does not demonstrate the love of God (1 John 3:17). **Today, come down off the high horse and do something different! Let us think about someone other than ourselves.**

MARCH 3RD

"WHY AM I HERE?"

1 Timothy 1:16 "Yet for this reason I found mercy, so that in me as the foremost, Jesus Christ might demonstrate His perfect patience as an example for those who would believe in Him for eternal life."

The apostle Paul gives a synopsis of his life here in his letter to Timothy. He tells the truth that he was a violent aggressor, a blasphemer and the chief sinner. There is nothing wrong with honesty when it comes to testifying about the transformative power of God in our lives. Too many seek to sanitize their stories and in so doing, rob the testimony of its power. Paul indicates here that despite all of his flaws, God used Him to show someone else His patience so that they would see Paul's example and potentially come to Christ. The kindness of God leads us to repentance! Some of us are wondering what our purpose is or why God has strategically positioned us in our current predicament. I've pondered this numerous times. We must embrace God's will and live out His purpose for us. **Today, if God has you in a "place", stay there. Someone is watching to see how you handle it so they can learn how to handle it. God is sovereign over everything.**

MARCH 4TH

"STICK TO THE BUSINESS AT HAND"

2 Tim 2:4 "No soldier in active service entangles himself in the affairs of everyday life, so that he may please the one who enlisted him as a soldier."

Life is much like a spider's web. There are so many things that come at us, to distract us. These distractions can be detrimental to our spiritual lives as Paul so eloquently states here. The military reference is very appropriate. The military is mission minded and structured. Nothing distracts from the mission. Weather doesn't, people don't, conditions don't...nothing does. Have you ever seen an army movie where soldiers were wading through some murky swamp without even a thought as to what might be lurking under the water? That's the kind of focus Paul is discussing but he did so in the context of human interactions. He was directing Timothy to steer clear of distractions because they are entangling and will eventually keep him from carrying out his mission. **Today, let us remember that our primary objective in this battle is to please our commanding officer.**

"TWINS"

Psalm 23:5 "Surely goodness and lovingkindness will follow me all the days of my life, And I will dwell in the house of the LORD forever."

When we love the Lord, when we devote ourselves to Him and see Him for who he really is...we can count on two things to always follow us...goodness and mercy! God's goodness is so necessary for our survival. The world is a cold place and sin has turned it on its head. Mercy comes from a Hebrew word that can mean kindness but also fidelity or covenant loyalty. In other words, God's fidelity to His word follows us. How awesome is it for us to know that God keeps His promises to us. Does this not make the valley a little less scary? Yes, it's dark and overwhelming but the goodness and the fidelity of God are behind us through the entire process. David emphasized the certainty of this happening by using the word "surely". **Today, let us glorify God for His certainty, His goodness and His mercy.**

"OLD DOG, NEW TRICKS"

Ecclesiastes 1:9 "That which has been is that which will be, and that which has been done is that which will be done. So there is nothing new under the sun."

A deer hunter can hunt with corn every time they go into the woods because deer crave corn and cannot resist it. Why would they do anything different if what they use is working? Prostitutes use the same lines to lure in male customers because those lines have always worked. Advertisers use the same advertising methods, just with better analytics, because people repeatedly fall for the same thing. There is a reason why there is NOTHING new under the sun. It is simple. Why would Satan develop new tricks when the old ones still work just as well? There is an old saying that goes: the game hasn't changed, just the players. Satan knows exactly what every human weakness is and how to exploit it. He has been studying/tempting human beings for millennia. The beautiful thing is, Jesus also knows our weaknesses. He experienced them, but He was without sin. He is our High Priest because of these experiences. **Today, let us follow His model and turn from sin and turn to God.**

MARCH 7TH

"THE GREAT GOD"

Genesis 18:14 "Is anything too hard for the Lord?"

The prophet Isaiah tells us plainly that God's arm is not too short to save. He tells us that God can do anything. God asks Moses in Numbers 11:23 "...is My power limited?" The angel told Mary, after announcing to her that she would carry the Messiah in her womb, with God, nothing shall be impossible. The record is clear. God cannot fail. Here in this text, Abraham and Sarai got news that they would have a child. They were both a bit incredulous because they were both very old and beyond child bearing, child yielding years...or so they thought. When Sarah laughed, the Lord called her on it. I'm sure that God gets this response often from humans. He gives a promise. We find it incredible that it could ever happen and yet, He follows through and it does happen. The Bible tells us that Abraham's faith was credited to him as righteousness. Facing challenges becomes easier when we know the ONE that stands between us and the challenge. It also helps to know that the challenge never surprises God and is often allowed by Him! It is our faith in this great God that helps us to navigate the strange and complex turns that life takes. **Today, remember and believe, there is nothing too hard for God.**

_____

_____

_____

_____

_____

_____

_____

_____

_____

_____

_____

_____

_____

_____

_____

_____

_____

_____

_____

_____

_____

_____

"WHAT WE DON'T DESERVE"

Ezekiel 20:44 "Then you will know that I am the LORD when I have dealt with you for My name's sake, not according to your evil ways or according to your corrupt deeds, O house of Israel," declares the Lord GOD."

Much of our theology is based on the false premise that happiness is somehow owed to us. Surely, no one wants to live miserable, paltry lives but we will not always be happy. When we really think about the whole "favor isn't fair" attitude and theology, it is based on us having something that someone else does not have or cannot get. It is true, favor is not "fair" but neither is it deserved. If God blessed us based on what we deserved, we'd all be broke, poor, homeless and empty because we are all undone before Him. Thank God that He is merciful and loving and that he sees Christ and not us as he lavishes His grace upon us. What God does, He does for His own sake and because of His own promises. **Today, let us thank Jesus for covering us up so that only He shows up on God's radar.**

MARCH 9TH

"ENCOURAGE EACH OTHER DAILY"

Hebrews 10:25 "Let us not neglect meeting together, as some have made a habit, but let us encourage one another, and all the more as you see the Day approaching."

Social media, the current social and political climate have made it acceptable to eviscerate one another without a second thought. Christians have seemingly succumbed to the world's way of thinking and acting. We hurl obscenities at one another, insult each other's intelligence, brag and boast about political candidates and at the end of the day, we don't see the obvious contradiction of our actions and our beliefs. Here's a piece of advice, before we hit the pillow...instead of talking about each other, poking fun at one another, scandalizing each other, backbiting or just flat out being ornery towards one another, let's try the alternative and pray for one another and build one another up! Thank God for the privilege of prayer and the gift of edification. The writer here uses the coming of Christ as an hourglass and tells us to encourage one another all the more as we see the Day approaching. Christ is indeed coming back. What will He find us doing? **Today, remember that we all need encouragement and we all need prayer!**

MARCH 10TH

"SURGICAL PRECISION"

Hebrews 4:12 "For the word of God is living and active and sharper than any two-edged sword..."

One of the most common misconceptions about church is that the preacher is somehow preaching at the congregation. Truthfully, if we carefully survey the Bible, we see that God dealt with his spokesperson before that spokesperson ever dealt with anyone else. When those who are charged with delivering God's word somehow believe that it is for those other folks but does not affect them, there will be a serious disconnect between minister and the ones to whom they minister. The gospel should not only minister to the people but also to the preacher. We all need the gospel because all have sinned and have fallen short of the glory of God! God's word will remind us of that as it cuts us with surgical precision. The words here are telling. The word is continually living, it is energetic, it is sharp, it is able to pierce and separate things that are very tightly compressed like joints and marrow and it judges our thoughts and intentions. Whatever we think has to line up with God's word and if it doesn't, the word judges our thoughts and intentions as inaccurate and in need of revision. **Today, take heed to the word. There is life in the word.**

MARCH 11TH

"AVOIDING THE TRAPPER'S SNARE"

Psalm 91:3 "For he will deliver you from the snare of the fowler, and from the deadly pestilence."

Harping on the past will not change anything. Fretting about the future won't change anything either. Instead, we should divert our energy towards living in the present, thanking God for new mercies rather than swimming in streams of past pain or dreading future storms. God has already gone before us so whatever is coming; He has already seen it and will prepare us for it. God has already delivered us from what is behind us; what's behind us is already completed. So, let us look at today with thanksgiving and praise and adoration that we are able to see another sunrise. Let us look to our heavenly Father who gives good and perfect gifts. Let us live for Him today in full assurance of His power. **Today, let us be grateful, let us empty our hands of problems and leave them at the base of Calvary, let us remember that pain is temporary and let us embrace the calling of this day.**

"BE TRANSFORMED"

2 Corinthians 5:17 "Therefore if anyone is in Christ, he is a new creature; the old things passed away; behold, new things have come."

Transformation can be a slow process. Salvation, however, is instantaneous. Who we are is an aggregate of all of our life experiences; they mold us and shape us. Those things have whatever effect we allow them to have. Negative experiences can affect us negatively, only if we allow them to. The same can be said for positive experiences. At our core, we are someone. Who we are matters but sometimes, the "who" has been bestowed upon us by others. We must be careful not to let others define us or give us our identity. Thanks be to God through Jesus Christ our Lord that He can change who we are and what we are! He is able to go to the core of a person and transform us, remake us. By the same token, whatever label the world has "affixed" to us, Jesus can liberate us from it. This is not limited to any select or specific group; the word says if anyone is in Christ they are a new creation. Jesus specializes in causing new things to emerge, even from places that were old and decrepit. **Today, if you are reading this, let him set you free!**

"THIS IS NOT WHAT I PRAYED FOR"

Romans 8:26 "In the same way the Spirit also helps our weakness; for we do not know how to pray as we should, but the Spirit Himself intercedes for us with groanings too deep for words..."

When we pray, the Bible instructs us to pray, believing that we already have what we ask for if we ask according to God's will. How in the world am I supposed to know what God's will is? His will coincides with His word. When we pray with specificity, we expect specific results. That is warranted because we know that God knows how to give good gifts. What we often don't know is that our prayers on a specific topic or for a specific thing can be and often are misguided. God has a mechanism in place to take care of this. We pray and the Bible says the Holy Spirit takes our prayers before the Lord and intercedes on our behalf. He prays for us but He does so in a language that is indecipherable by anyone else except for the Father (and the Son). This can cause some consternation on our part because what we want and what God wants for us are two different things. Therefore, when the prayers get answered, we get what we need but it doesn't look like what we asked for! **Today, let us learn gratitude knowing that God always knows best.**

MARCH 14TH

"HE HAS ALREADY MADE A WAY"

Deuteronomy 31:8 "The LORD is the one who goes ahead of you; He will be with you. He will not fail you or forsake you. Do not fear or be dismayed."

God knows our ways, our thoughts and our hearts and yet, He still loves us. Today was known in His mind before we ever saw it. All of our days were written long ago, so there is absolutely nothing that happens today of which God is not acutely aware. We can walk in confidence knowing that God has gone before us, cutting down unseen enemies and plowing the road for us to tread. Moses writes here that it is the LORD, YHWH (Yahweh) who goes before us. This may seem simple but the name YHWH carries so much weight that there is no one who is able to stand in His way. The name indicates that The LORD is the supreme and sovereign of the universe. Not one other god or power or principality can resist Him or overtake Him. **Today, let us reflect on that fact and know with certainty that God cannot fail, He will never leave and He is always going before us to prepare the way for us to glorify Him.**

MARCH 15TH

"LET GO AND LET GOD"

Philippians 4:6 "Be anxious for nothing, but in everything, by prayer and supplication and with thanksgiving, present your requests to the Lord."

Patience and dependence go hand in hand. To be patient is to be dependent on God alone and to be dependent on God alone is to be patient. He does not work on our timetable and we cannot do anything apart from the vine. It is not a symbiotic relationship. Our relationship with Him is totally one sided. He supplies, we consume. We cannot give Him anything nor does He need anything from us. A word of advice to all who worry about what we cannot control: relax, take a deep breath and stop fretting. God is in control. The origin of anxiety is our desire to control the outcome of a situation. Anxiety means "I want to do it myself." Not being anxious for anything but rather, in everything we hand it over to God. He can do more with our messes than we can ever do with His perfection. We have to let God do it. We have the prescription for anxiety here in the passage given. By prayer and supplication and with thanks, we should present our requests to God. Paul could've easily said prayer but here he uses two words. Prayer indicates the direction i.e. to a higher power and supplication indicates the urgency. **Today, give it to God.**

"DETHRONING SELF"

Isaiah 6:5 "Then I said, "Woe is me, for I am ruined! Because I am a man of unclean lips, And I live among a people of unclean lips; For my eyes have seen the King, the LORD of hosts."

Idols are often thought of as little trinkets that ancient people carried around with them to curry favor with the deity of their choosing. While this may be true, there are other idols as well. We often idolize people. We lift athletes, actors and actresses, leaders, political figures and all types of famous human beings onto pedestals that they do not deserve. We can even idolize ourselves. We can, knowingly or unknowingly, usurp God's position. When God renders a decision that we do not like and we decide to rebel, we are no longer worshipping God, we are idolizing ourselves. Isaiah may have had a high opinion of himself but it wasn't that way after he experienced the holiness of God. His response to seeing God's majesty up-close and personal was one that we would all be wise to emulate. He understood his brokenness in the face of God's completion, his filthiness in the face of God's holiness and His utter terror at the realization that he was unfit to stand before the LORD of hosts. **Today, let us be resolved to dethrone ourselves and magnify God!**

MARCH 17TH

"BOUGHT SENSE"

Joshua 5:6 "For the sons of Israel walked forty years in the wilderness, until all the nation, that is, the men of war who came out of Egypt, perished because they did not listen to the voice of the LORD..."

There is an old saying that wisdom gained from mistakes is called bought sense. In other words, the mistake and what it extracted from us cost us something; and therefore, we know to avoid that particular situation if it comes up again. We can all testify to having some wisdom that we paid a price for. Like the Israelites, much of our bought sense comes because we refused to go where God sent us. Instead, we decided to go our own way, only to find out that we are not nearly as smart as God! The journey to Canaan should have taken eleven days. Instead, it took forty years. I always wondered why the Israelites were always in the same predicament. In a revelation that was an answer to my own situation, God reminded me that we will constantly face the same situations until we prove faithful to withstand them. God keeps us in places until we learn total dependence on Him and His desired response. **Today, let us not circle the same mountain but rather learn the lesson and move forward in obedience to the place where God is directing us.**

"BY HIS OWN DOING"

2 Corinthians 8:9 "For you know the grace of our Lord Jesus Christ, for though he was rich, He became poor for our sakes so that through His poverty, we might become rich."

We cannot say it enough: God's grace is an amazing thing. It gives us what we do not deserve. It removes burdens that we are meant to carry. The grace of God was never more evident than when it was actualized in the person of Jesus Christ. This scripture is a testament to grace. When Paul says that Jesus Christ, our Lord, was rich, he does not mean while He lived on earth. He was a poor, nomadic carpenter who depended on the hospitality of others when He was in ministry. But, prior to coming to earth, Jesus, the second person of the Godhead, God the Son, was rich. Think of the adornments of heaven: golden streets, priceless gems, glorious riches; no earthly billionaire's trappings could ever compare to this. He owns the cattle on a thousand hills and if that doesn't say enough, He can create anything by simply speaking it into existence. Now, knowing this, consider the fact that He became poor. This is a cause/effect clause. He made a decision to enter into poverty with the outcome being that we might become enriched. Not monetarily but spiritually. **Today, thank God for Jesus!**

"USE ME, GOD?"

Ezekiel 24:18 "So I spoke to the people in the morning, and in the evening my wife died. The next morning, I did as I had been commanded."

Low hanging fruit in ministry make it easy to accept pats on the back. The easiest part of pastoring is preaching. Most pastors would take a preaching assignment on two minutes notice. The hardest part of pastoring is having a knife stuck in your own gut but still having to offer comfort to the wounded. Ezekiel lost his wife and was told, by God nonetheless, not to even mourn or take his sandals off! I offer no sugarcoating or platitudes when I tell you that life sucks sometimes. We are not exempt from trouble. It is quite understandable that people chase temporary solutions to numb the pain that life inflicts. We must know, however, that temporary numbing, like pain meds, wears off and the pain remains and often intensifies. Jesus is a much better alternative. He doesn't necessarily numb the pain; He just gives us the courage and strength to withstand it. God told Ezekiel that He was about to take his wife. He prepared him and I am certain, in that loss, God offered some comfort or at least, some strength to press forward. **Today, know that we must continue with God's plans even in the midst of our own pain.**

_____

_____

_____

_____

_____

_____

_____

_____

_____

_____

_____

_____

_____

_____

_____

_____

_____

_____

_____

_____

_____

MARCH 20TH

"SIMPLIFY YOUR LIFE"

Jonah 1:17 "And the LORD appointed a great fish to swallow Jonah, and Jonah was in the stomach of the fish three days and three nights."

We know the story of Jonah very well. Jonah was a prophet but he did not really enjoy his job. I guess, when we think about it, none of the prophets really enjoyed what they did. That's a far cry from the fancy-schmancy, lifestyles of the rich-and-famous preachers of today. Jonah had a simple mission but we must acknowledge that it was a very daunting one. The Ninevites were not nice people and they did not worship God. This is the furnace that Jonah was thrown into. This is why he tried to abort his mission. This is why he was willing to go a different way; because he did not like his assignment and he probably felt like God gave him a raw deal. So, he hitched a boat ride to Tarshish, put the lives of the sailors and passengers in danger and ended up spending three days in the belly of a great fish. Although there is some significance being in the fish's belly and the length of time that he was there, he did not have to go through any of that. His life could have been a whole lot simpler had he just trusted God and obeyed his command. **Today, let us simplify our lives through obedience.**

"A LIVING WITNESS"

Zephaniah 3:20 "…I will give you honor and praise among all the peoples of the earth when I restore your fortunes before your very eyes."

Judah endured much pain and suffering as the result of their disobedience. Judah and Benjamin, the southern kingdom, could be described as the opposite of the ten tribes in the north. The split in the kingdom resulted from the disobedience of Solomon's sons. They were wicked and God allowed an exiled, former enemy of King Solomon to come back and rip the kingdom apart. Judah could not avoid the influences of the world and eventually succumbed to worse idolatrous practices than Israel did. Because of this, Judah was taken into exile by Babylon. As heart wrenching as it sounds, that chastisement had a cleansing effect. It also had a deeper purpose; God would show His redemptive and restorative power to them through their pain. The prophet Zephaniah prophesied against Judah but as with many prophetic books, he did not only prophesy doom but also redemption. Here, God tells His people that He will gather them and restore them and that they would see it with their own eyes. **Today, give God thanks if you have been a witness to His restoration!**

MARCH 22ND

"A BITTER TASTE"

Revelation 3:16 "So because you are lukewarm, and neither hot nor cold, I will spit you out of My mouth."

Having a casual relationship with God is almost like saying "I'm kinda pregnant." You either are pregnant or you're not pregnant but there is not really a middle ground. In America, we've perfected the casual relationship with God. We've perfected the excessive works to compensate for the lack of love. We've perfected the art of political Christianity where we align our faith with our favorite political candidate(s) or party and believe that we are somehow pleasing God by voting a certain way. None of this will compensate for actually having a real relationship with God where His word is our guiding principle and His pleasure is our only goal. The Laodicean church had the casual relationship perfected. John's references to the temperature of the church are important. Laodicea was located in a region where the water, transported by aqueduct, would be polluted with limestone deposits unless it was either hot or very cold. Lukewarm water, in this area, could literally kill a person. This is why Jesus threatens to spit them out. **Today, let us pray for the Holy Spirit to keep us hot for the Lord, always!**

MARCH 23RD

"LAVISHING LOVE"

1 John 3:1 "See how great a love the Father has bestowed on us, that we would be called children of God; and such we are..."

There is no greater love in the entire universe than the love that God has for us. This eternal, invincible, unchangeable, immovable love was on display at Calvary. Because of what happened at Calvary, Jesus made our adoption as sons and daughters certain. What happened at Calvary made it certain that the Holy Spirit would come into the world, mark every believer and seal us until the day of redemption. God has lavished His grace upon us in the person of Jesus Christ! He died and He rose! What happened after Calvary guarantees that we will rise again after the corruptible has put on the incorruptible. John asks us to "see" how great this love is. Look around you. See the sun at the proper distance from the earth. See the birds who are a reminder to us that we don't have to worry about anything. See the seasons change at their proper time. Look down and see the inflation and deflation of the abdomen and know that the oxygen taken in and CO_2 exhaled all come from God. See how great a love He has given to us! **Today, remember that there is no greater love that could be lavished upon us than to be called His children.**

"THE WIND IN THE SAILS"

1 Corinthians 3:7 "So then neither the one who plants nor the one who waters is anything, but God who causes the growth."

Joan S. Gray, noted Presbyterian theologian, used an analogy in her book Spiritual Leadership for Church Leaders. She compared the church to either a rowboat or a sailboat. An egocentric church is destined to only be as strong as its leader. As we know very well, leaders are human and fallible. A man-centered church is nothing more than a rowboat powered by human effort. Rowing hard, rowing against the wind and sometimes, going nowhere. The extent to which the leadership pushes will be as far as the church can go. Contrast this with a church that depends on God alone and operates on faith. A theocentric church is a sailboat whose sails are filled with the mighty, rushing wind that the Spirit provides. Paul knew this well. The people of Corinth were eager to be egocentric; looking to Paul and Apollos to be their leaders and be the ones on whom they hung their collective hats. This was a mistake and Paul corrected it swiftly. It is God who gives the increase and He is able to do it regardless of who the leader of the congregation is. **Today, let us remember that any growth will be facilitated by God.**

"TONE IT DOWN"

Matthew 23:5 "Everything they do is done for people to see..."

In America and in the Christian church in particular, we have a choice as to how we live out our Christianity. Some choose to live outwardly as Christians but inwardly as they please. Others know that it is the heart that matters and not the outward display. The way that this is played out in the church today is no different than how the Pharisees operated in Jesus' day. The Pharisees lived loud, long and large. They prayed loud prayers to ensure that they were heard by everyone. They wore long robes to ensure that they were seen by everyone and they bound large phylacteries to their heads to show their devotion to the Word. To update this, loud prayers, nice suits and big bibles do not equal having a relationship with God! If God is truly working on the inside the fruit will be evident without us having to trumpet it. **Today, let us pray for clean hands and a pure heart and to serve God sincerely!**

MARCH 26TH

"INNER STRENGTH"

1 John 4:4 "You are from God, little children, and have overcome them; because greater is He who is in you than he who is in the world."

There is an old hymn, Hold to God's Unchanging Hand, that says "time is filled with swift transition, naught of earth unmoved can stand, build your hopes on things eternal, hold to God's unchanging hand…" The fact that God's hand never changes is great consolation in an ever-changing world. Although the world doesn't stand still for anyone, we must understand that we have a treasure in jars of clay that keeps us from being crushed, even when hard pressed. There are two inevitable outcomes in life, trouble and the end of trouble. With the instability of the world, we mustn't be surprised by the trials we face; they are promised to us all. Because of the immutability of God, we mustn't be surprised by our ability to handle tribulation either. The One who lives within us gives us strength. He is greater than he who is in the world and is the root of all instability! **Today, let the joy of the Lord, the joy that lives inside of every believer, be our strength! Joy comes from knowing that as we endure hardship, we have an eternal and unfailing God to see us through!**

MARCH 27TH

"REJOICE IN THE MIDDLE OF IT"

Colossians 1:24 "...I do my share on behalf of His body, which is the church, in filling up what is lacking in Christ's afflictions."

Paul says something here that is very interesting. He says that he is filling up what is lacking in Christ's afflictions on behalf of the church. How is this possible? Christ did everything once and for all. There was nothing lacking. If there were anything lacking, He would not have been resurrected. The resurrection is proof that the Father was satisfied with what the Son had done at Calvary [see Romans 3:25, 26]. Christ's afflictions were many. Calvary was brutal, the road to Calvary was an overwhelming display of hatred and punishment and here we have Paul, to interpret his phrase, picking up Calvary's leftovers and doing so gladly. He was willing to take the 40th lash, the fourth nail, the second crown of thorns. Not that there was anything left but he was willing to suffer for the name of Christ. If you've been serving the Lord and you find yourself in a bind, know that regardless of your predicament, God's opinion of you has not changed...HE STILL LOVES YOU! **Today, let us remember that we share in the afflictions of Christ and He is in every trial with us.**

"WHO ARE YOU, ANYWAY?"

Genesis 32:28 "He said, "Your name shall no longer be Jacob, but Israel; for you have striven with God and with men and have prevailed."

Jacob was an interesting character as far as biblical characters go. He stole Esau's birthright, ran from him for years, tricked his father-in-law out of the choice livestock using some clever breeding techniques, snuck away from the same man with his daughters only to be caught and accosted, finally and dreadfully faced his brother who ended up forgiving him and oh, by the way, he wrestled with God. This "man" that Jacob wrestled with all night, until daybreak, had to severely injure Jacob in order for Jacob to give up. So, not only was Jacob conniving, He was tenacious as well. After the wrestling match was over, Jacob was given a new name, Israel. Jacob means "heel grabber or supplanter" which was his nature. Israel means "God strives". This may be interpreted as meaning that Jacob would no longer have to resort to his nature but that God would now fight for him. God causes change in our lives not because he "can't" use us the way that we are but because He doesn't want to. God is constantly putting us in position to glorify Him. **Today, remember that in His sovereignty, He conforms us to His plans not the other way around.**

"NOT POSSIBLE"

Acts 1:7 "He said to them, "It is not for you to know times or epochs which the Father has fixed by His own authority..."

Many have undertaken, each time to their own chagrin, attempts to predict when Jesus will return or, for non-Christians, when the "world will end." Each time someone tries to predict this event, they fail. Yet, men keep trying! Matthew 24:36 details Jesus' words to His disciples and even Jesus said that no man, including His human self, knew the day or the hour of the end. What makes anyone else so special that they'd know? There was a recent time where so-called Christian prognosticators made their predictions of the end based on the Mayan calendar. There was a noticeable uptick in documentaries dedicated to covering this topic. How can a so-called prophet depend on any source other than the Holy Spirit (God) as a means of prophesying? Any so-called prophet that resorts to divination, psychic powers or other demonic force is no prophet at all. Anyone who defies biblical advice and still tries to predict the end is not a prophet. The end times began as soon as Christ ascended back to heaven. **Today, let us live every day as if He was returning.**

"OUT OF STEP"

Isaiah 48:3 "I declared the former things long ago and they went forth from My mouth, and I proclaimed them..."

Once, I was walking through the airport and I saw a baby walking hand-in-hand with her dad. He was a huge man and she looked to be no more than 2-years old. Every step he took she had to take four to keep up because her legs were so short. It was cute but it showed me something profound. God spoke in that moment and reminded me and is reminding us that it's impossible for us to keep up with Him because He is so far ahead of us and ever going before us. He knows the end from the beginning. His steps are much longer than ours. His ways and thoughts are higher than ours. This is why He must carry us. God is saying, "Stop trying to keep step with Me and let Me carry you instead." God reminds us daily that His ways are unfathomable. **Today, we would be wise to allow Him to quarterback the game while we play our respective positions.**

MARCH 31ST

"MORTGAGING THE FUTURE"

Psalm 106:37 "They even sacrificed their sons and their daughters to the demons..."

Deceased singer Whitney Houston had a song in which she sang that the children are our future. This is so true. Oftentimes, we overlook this fact as we allow our children to wander aimlessly while we sit by and wag our fingers at them. Or, we give them too much leeway and allow them to get swept up in this world's current. We open doors to them that God intended to be kept shut. We expose them at an early age to things that we were not exposed to until we were adults. We give in to their desires rather than setting boundaries. This Psalm speaks of parents who actually sacrificed their children in fire. This was common practice for those who worshipped Molech. They'd make the children walk through fire as a sacrifice to this false god. **Today, let us pray for our children! No longer shall they be cut down like weeds but let them grow up to be oak trees for God! Pray against the spirits of death and apathy that have enshrouded and blinded many of our youth. No longer will parents be enablers or cosigners to foolishness! You are the sovereign God, Amen.**

APRIL 1ST

"EASY STREET"

Matthew 8:20 "Jesus *said to him, "The foxes have holes and the birds of the 1air have 2nests, but the Son of Man has nowhere to lay His head."

It is fitting that on April Fool's day that we debunk a myth. Many churches preach that there is a trouble-free, easy and financially lucrative life that awaits those who put their faith in Jesus. We can have whatever we speak into existence. I like to call this place, Easy Street. On this first day of April, know that the Easy Street is only a myth; a bad April Fool's day joke. Jesus says here in the text to the scribe who wanted to follow Him that He had nowhere to stay! We can also infer that He did not necessarily know where His next meal was coming from and following Him would indeed be a struggle. But notice, Jesus calls Himself the Son of Man to a scribe who would recognize this Messianic title. So, Jesus is warning of the danger in following Him and beckoning the scribe to come with Him at the same time! Knowing that He is the Son of Man means the hole of the fox and the materials for the birds' nests were provided by the Father and therefore you too can expect that the Father will provide for us on this journey! **Today, let us realize that there is no Easy Street when following Jesus, but there is one that awaits, if we stay on the narrow path.**

"HE NEVER CHANGES"

Hebrews 13:8 "Jesus Christ is the same yesterday and today and forever."

There is something to be said for the cohesiveness of the Bible. Whether it is the accuracy of the prophecies, the recurrent connections between the Old and New Testaments or the use of Old Testament scriptures by New Testament authors, there is great connectivity and integrity in the biblical text. For those who question the integrity of the scriptures, it must be considered how Isaiah could write about the crucifixion of Jesus 750 years before it happened. It's not like there was a note passed down for 750 years for the actors in the New Testament to carry out. No, God spoke through Isaiah and revealed His eternal plan to him. The thread that binds the two testaments is the idea of God's redeeming purpose for mankind. He redeemed Israel from her enemies in the Old Testament. He redeemed the Gentiles by sending Christ as a light to Jacob and the nations as well. **Today, let us thank God for His immutability!**

"DON'T TOUCH MY CROSS"

Matthew 27:32 "As they were coming out, they found a man of Cyrene named Simon, whom they pressed into service to bear His cross."

Simon the Cyrene was pressed into service. He was a man from the continent of Africa who was standing on the side of the road leading up the hill to Calvary. He saw Jesus in his weakest hour. He was not aware that he'd be presses into service. The odd thing is, he never protested. He stepped up and assisted Jesus with the cross. You can imagine that Jesus, after hours of torturous beating was extremely weak and could not make the ascent up the hill in His condition. Now, consider that Jesus asks us to deny ourselves, take up our own crosses and follow Him. He said this having witnessed crucifixions and knowing the agony involved in carrying your own cross. He said it also knowing the outcome of the crucifixion is death. Our crosses get heavy and there are times when we need a break to rest. We must ask ourselves who is on the side of the road in our lives; do we have a Simon the Cyrene? The truth is, not many will help you pick up your cross to follow Jesus, but there are plenty that will help you lay it down to follow them. **Today, if you have a Simon who is there for you at a moment's notice, be thankful.**

_____

_____

_____

_____

_____

_____

_____

_____

_____

_____

_____

_____

_____

_____

_____

_____

_____

_____

_____

_____

_____

_____

APRIL 4TH

"THE FORGETFUL CHRISTIAN"

James 1:24 "…for once he has looked at himself and gone away, he has immediately forgotten what kind of person he was."

The Word of God is a like a mirror. When we look into it, we can see our flaws. When we look into it, we can see what we need to change. Just like a mirror in the restroom, when we look into it, we can see immediately where correction is needed. James says that one who looks into the mirror and forgets what he/she looks like is the same as one who hears the word but does not do the word. The word is not minced, especially when spoken by Christ. The Bible says that we are laid bare before God. No pretenses, no masks and no fronts. The Word is only as effective if we hear it and apply it. We must be willing to let it crush us, cleanse us and then restore us. The Word comes to life when we realize that what we are reading is for us before it is for anyone else. **Today, thank God for His word and for its transformative power in our lives!**

APRIL 5TH

"THROUGH THE FIRE"

Zechariah 13:9 "This third I will put into the fire..."

Psalm 91:15 says that the Lord will be WITH us in trouble. He did not say He would take us around or over trouble but into/through it! We might ask, "Why doesn't God, in His omniscience, just avoid the trouble and spare me?" The reason is simple, trouble holds gifts like faith, perseverance, hope and trust that it must yield to us as God carries us through. We can't get those gifts without going through the experience of the trouble! Then we are truly able to say "what was meant for bad, God has used it for my good." Truly, the LORD is good! The prophet Zechariah prophesied to Jerusalem that two-thirds of the people would perish but one-third would be taken through the fire and in doing so would be tested and purified. The fires that we face move us closer to sanctification. That is a lifelong process and we will face many furnaces along the way. If God takes us through the fire, that means that God is also in the fire with us. **Today, let us remember that trouble, does not last forever and, although prickly and hard to wrestle sometimes, does indeed bear gifts that will transform us from glory to glory.**

WALK WITH ME: God Seen, God Heard, God Revealed

APRIL 6TH

"A MIGHTY GOOD LEADER"

1 Corinthians 11:1 "Be imitators of me, just as I also am of Christ."

Leadership is an interesting concept. Many believe that to be a leader you must be tough and have a take-no-prisoners attitude. Others are anti-micromanagers and decided to allow people to work and contribute in their own way and by their own merits. Christian leadership is not based on worldly ideals but rather, how Christ led. We can implement all of the paradigms and business models that we want but if we don't exemplify the character of Christ, we are failing our constituents. It's not just about being the boss but rather being a servant-leader that people can look to for guidance and as a model. We must ask, am I worthy of being imitated? Leadership is a lifestyle and, many times, a calling. We should lead not with the index finger but with the feet and not ask anyone to do anything that we are unwilling to do. Jesus led with his feet. He showed people how to do it rather than telling them what to do. **Today, let us take up the mantle that Christ left behind and lead as He led.**

"WHAT ARE YOU GOING TO DO ABOUT IT?"

Hebrews 10:36 "For you have need of endurance, so that when you have done the will of God, you may receive what was promised."

We are instructed to not get weary in well doing. The problem is we do indeed get weary. We are humans with a limited capacity for suffering and for pain. We do no enjoy being in painful situations. We like comfort. Liking comfort means that sometimes, when easy situations arise, we succumb to them. Temptation to sin is no different. When we see temptation and we indulge it to the point of actually sinning by doing what the temptation presents, we have a problem. We must repent and turn from that thing immediately. The Christian life is about persistence and resistance. Our resistance must be persistent. We must be persistent in our struggle of resisting sin. We must also be consistent in removing ourselves from situations that cause us to sin. This sounds like a man-centered message. It's not. The Holy Spirit, living in and through us, makes any resistance to sin possible. The Hebrew writer says we need endurance so that we can hold out until our change comes. **Today, let us listen for His voice and obey it, especially if there is an avoidable situation before us.**

APRIL 8TH

"P.O.W. M.I.A."

Matthew 11: 2, 3 "Meanwhile, John heard in prison about the works of Christ, and he sent two of his disciples to ask Him, "Are You the One who was to come, or should we look for someone else?"

There are times, like John the Baptist, when we get trapped behind enemy lines. John was essentially a prisoner of war (POW) in the spiritual chess match that has been going on since before the beginning of time. John was in prison because of his fidelity and faithfulness to the gospel message. So, when Jesus is working miracles, healing the sick and raising the dead, while John was in prison, I imagine that John was a bit perturbed. He was stuck in prison after he had worked all his life in preparation for the coming of the Messiah. Maybe he expected that things would be different. Here is a great point to ponder: how do you handle being a POW? How do we handle times when it seems as if God has forgotten about us? We have to remember His Word and know that we are never missing in action (MIA). He knows everything about where we are and what we are going through. He has not changed His mind about us. Jesus spoke glowingly about John meaning that Jesus had not forsaken him. **Today, remember that the situations that we face don't change God's opinion of us and He still loves us.**

APRIL 9TH

"LET ME IN"

Acts 2:2 "And suddenly there came from heaven a noise like a violent rushing wind, and it filled the whole house where they were sitting."

Pentecost was a special, historical event. God orchestrated the appointed time and place and made sure that what occurred would never be forgotten. He went for maximum effect doing several things. First, He sent a great noise and that noise, which sounded like the wind, filled the house were the disciples were. Then, he enabled them, through His Spirit, to speak in other languages. There were roughly fifteen different regions represented and the disciples were able to get through to each of them. Then, He used Peter to preach and three thousand people were saved. None of this would have happened had the disciples been resistant to the Holy Spirit. It was the noise from heaven that signaled that the Holy Spirit was coming but it was the Holy Spirit who filled the disciples and gave them abilities that they would not have had without Him. The Bible says that the noise filled the whole house but it was the Spirit who filled the believers there. **Today, let Him in and do not be resistant to His filling. Without the Holy Spirit, there is no power for the believer.**

APRIL 10TH

"IS ANYONE HOME?"

Revelation 3:20 "Behold, I stand at the door and knock; if anyone hears My voice and opens the door, I will come in to him and will dine with him, and he with Me."

One thing that Jesus will not do is force Himself on anyone. Some believe that somehow His irresistible grace compels us to believe. But whenever Jesus spoke to unbelievers He always gave them a choice to believe. He would speak in parables and make the rhetorical statement, "if anyone has ears to hear, let them hear." When Jesus speaks here in the book of Revelation however, He is actually talking to believers. He is talking to a church that had lost its way and people who had lost sight of what was important. This is why Jesus is standing on the outside of this church looking to get in. This is a great testament to His grace. Yes, He passed judgment on the church but He also gave the church a chance to repent. He says IF anyone answers, He will come in and eat with them. He will come in and get intimate with them. An image used to illustrate this scripture often shows Jesus standing outside a door with no knob. Jesus will never kick the doors to our hearts in, He desires to be invited in. **Today, let us open our hearts to Jesus and then we will truly see transformation in our lives!**

APRIL 11TH

"REAL TO ME"

John 5:39 ""You search the Scriptures because you think that in them you have eternal life; it is these that testify about Me..."

An existential approach to scripture means that we approach the text believing that it can actually have a transformative effect on our lives. We think that the words on the pages are able to guide us to the better self that we desire. What we don't study for, is mere information. We don't approach the Word of God simply to be informed by it. Information is much less important than transformation. Jesus here is talking to the religious leaders, who studied the scriptures diligently. They studied, but without application. They sought eternal life through the information that they ingested. However, Jesus says here that the Scriptures testified about Him. He said this because of their patent rejection of His messianic claims. They had the law and the prophets, they all pointed to Jesus. So, while the religious leaders were well informed, they were not transformed. People who are merely informed use the Scriptures to support their positions but are unwilling to move from those positions when new, contrary information is presented. **Today, let us not be libraries of knowledge that have not undergone a spiritual renovation.**

_____

_____

_____

_____

_____

_____

_____

_____

_____

_____

_____

_____

_____

_____

_____

_____

_____

_____

_____

_____

APRIL 12TH

"THE MESSIAH'S MARINA"

Hebrews 6:19 "This hope we have as an anchor of the soul, a hope both sure and steadfast..."

America has tricked us into putting out hopes into temporal, fleeting things. We base our worth on the size of our houses or our bank accounts. We put our hope in political leaders and hitch our wagons to the aspirations of a political party. Jesus even said that it is easier for a camel to go through the eye of a needle than it is for a rich person to enter into heaven. He meant it to say that rich people tend to trust in their riches far more than they trust in God. Rather than pursuing the American dream, we should pursue the eternal hope that is in Christ Jesus. Dreams are not always realized but hope in Christ does not disappoint! Hope carries with it an expectation that the thing hoped for will be delivered. We cannot trust in princes or chariots. We cannot trust in institutions. All of these things change. Hope in Christ is likened to an anchor for the soul. That hope is the hope of a resurrection after this life. This anchor holds us steady in the Messiah's marina, no matter how hard the wind blows. **Today, remember that the one who endures until death will receive the crown of life.**

APRIL 13TH

"THE BEST LAID PLANS"

James 4:14 "Yet you do not know what your life will be like tomorrow. You are just a vapor that appears for a little while and then vanishes away."

When people die suddenly, it confirms the obvious: each of us has an appointment with death. We are born into a state of decay. We are dying from the moment we begin living. No matter what our plans are, God has his own plan and we all have a limited number of days upon this planet. Often, we plan our lives as if we know exactly how life will shake out. I'm a living witness that this is not the case. This is what James cautions us against. It's not that we are not trusting God, either. The context of this scripture indicates that some make plans and do not even bother to consult with God. He reminds us that our lives are but a mere breath, a mist, snag in the fabric of time. If we know that this is an appointment we cannot break, we should make sure that we are dressed to meet death. BLOOD OF THE LAMB red is a good color to wear. **Today, let us all be cognizant of the fragility of life and live with the humble expectation that it is God who's the author and we are merely the pens.**

APRIL 14TH

"UNPLUGGED"

John 15:5 "I am the vine, you are the branches; he who abides in Me and I in him, he bears much fruit, for apart from Me you can do nothing."

Once, I was in the airport and I was looking for a seat in the terminal. I looked for one thing, a seat next to a power outlet. Why? To recharge my batteries, of course. I refused to sit in a place with no power. Without power, the things that I need to function don't function. What's the point? We should never align ourselves with dead stuff but we should always want to be seated close to a power source! For the believer, Christ is our power source! He is SEATED above all rule, authority, dominion and power and if we are in Christ, we are seated in heavenly places with Him. Stay plugged in to the power and your batteries will never die! Remember, apart from Christ, we can do nothing! The cross makes us think of a simple question: "At which table am I seated?" If not seated with The Power, Christ, then we're seated at a dead table with no power or life or ability to give life. **Today, let us plug in and also be in prayer that someone in a dead situation today will turn and get connected with the Author of Life, Jesus Christ and live!**

APRIL 15TH

"WHEN THE DEVIL SHOWS UP"

2 Kings 18:13 "Now in the fourteenth year of King Hezekiah, Sennacherib king of Assyria came up against all the fortified cities of Judah and seized them."

Hezekiah had his hands full as king of Judah. Not only was Judah a part of a two-tribe southern kingdom, it was constantly on the watch for enemies. Sennacherib, the king of Assyria, was particularly unnerving. He was irreverent, arrogant, mean-spirited and relentless. You can imagine that when he showed up, Hezekiah was probably a little nervous. Sennacherib even spoke to the people, through his envoys, and told them that God was no match for him! He told them to give up and surrender to him. There was no need to fight, no need to resist and no need to call on God! But, Hezekiah, although nervous, did just the opposite. He went to the prophet Isaiah and took this matter to the Lord in prayer. Of course, God stood up for His people and Sennacherib was eventually defeated. **Today, remember, the devil will keep telling us to give up. We must keep telling him that he's not fighting us; he's fighting our God, and there is no quit in Him.**

_____

_____

_____

_____

_____

_____

_____

_____

_____

_____

_____

_____

_____

_____

_____

_____

_____

_____

_____

_____

"STAND STILL"

Exodus 14:13 "But Moses said to the people, "Do not fear! Stand by and see the salvation of the LORD which He will accomplish for you today; for the Egyptians whom you have seen today, you will never see them again forever."

The Bible says that we do not wrestle against flesh and blood but against powers and principalities and world forces of darkness in high places (see Ephesians 6). This is very true. The question is, why do we try in the flesh to battle those things which exist in a metaphysical, spiritual realm? We must turn those battles over to God. In this text, the Hebrew people indeed faced a physical enemy but that enemy was energized by forces that were not physical but rather spiritual. Our battles may be in the physical realm but what we must understand are their metaphysical origins. So, every time the enemy tries to con us into quitting we must remind him that he is not fighting against flesh and blood but against the Almighty God who stands for us. **Today, reflect on Yahweh Nissi who fights for us in our times of struggle!**

"CUT DOWN"

Numbers 21:6 "The LORD sent fiery serpents among the people and they bit the people, so that many people of Israel died."

Have you ever cleaned your closet out to make room for new things? Now and again, we have to declutter. In order to receive something new, we may have to depart with something old. The same is true in God's economy. When the Israelites were leaving Egypt to go into Canaan, God was doing something new. Some did not understand it and did not accept it. The Israelite demographics reflected all age groups. Some of the older ones were more recalcitrant and they grumbled…a lot. God knew the effect this would have on the younger generation. Grumbling is contagious; and therefore, in this passage of scripture, God used snakes to cut down the grumblers and thereby lessen their influence on the future generations. There is some hope in this story. Just as the grumblers were cut down, the remnant went to Moses to ask him to pray to God for relief. Moses prayed and God had him to raise a bronze serpent, upon which the people looked and were saved. **Today, let us lift up Jesus so that some grumbler may look upon Him and avoid the viper's venom.**

WALK WITH ME: God Seen, God Heard, God Revealed

APRIL 18TH

"IMMUTABLE"

Isaiah 51:6 "Lift up your eyes to the sky, Then look to the earth beneath; For the sky will vanish like smoke, And the earth will wear out like a garment And its inhabitants will die in like manner; But My salvation will be forever, And My righteousness will not wane."

Today, some Christians have exchanged their righteousness for power. Some have exchanged their righteousness for friendship. Some have exchanged their righteousness for fame. When so-called religious people excuse the sins of an unrepentant president for the sake of winning Supreme Court seats or anti-abortion legislation, something is wrong. When churches line up behind the LGBT movement, never addressing the sin of homosexuality, for the sake of being inclusive, something is wrong. When we pack colosseums and cathedrals with a watered down message of the gospel, something is wrong. In a society that seeks to normalize sin, the only way to tell what is NOT normal is to compare everything to the Word of God. If it doesn't line up with God's Word, then it's not normal. **Today, let us reflect on the absolute truth of the Word of God in spite of societal distractions.**

_____

_____

_____

_____

_____

_____

_____

_____

_____

_____

_____

_____

_____

_____

_____

_____

_____

_____

_____

_____

APRIL 19TH

"SUCH IS LIFE"

Luke 12:22,23 "Then Jesus said to His disciples,
"Therefore I tell you, do not worry about your life, what
you will eat, or about your body, what you will wear.
For life is more than food, and the body more than
clothes."

There are times when we get hung up on the minutiae. Life is such a complex thing. There are innumerable variables that we must deal with on a daily basis. We worry about the smallest things. Jesus here in this text tells us that life is more than food and the body is more than clothes. There are such deep intricacies to life that we do not really have time to focus on each and every dust particle floating in the air. Instead, our focus should be on God's ability to guide us through the intricacies, the pain, the heartaches and the disappointments, the anxiety and the uncertainty. When we hear Jesus telling his disciples that God will take care of their every need, He is telling them the truth. When we have needs, we must be cognizant that God has a plan for those needs to be met. He cares for us, even when it seems as if he is simply a metaphysical myth with no empathy for the human condition. Such is life is a phrase that means that we accept things for the way that they are. **Today, let us reflect on this: while life is indeed what it is, we have a God who is working out all of life's issues for our good.**

APRIL 20TH

"WHO HELPS THE HELPER?"

Exodus 17:12 "But Moses' hands were heavy. Then they took a stone and put it under him, and he sat on it; and Aaron and Hur supported his hands, one on one side and one on the other. Thus his hands were steady until the sun set."

One day, I was driving and I saw something very interesting. There was an Auto Zone repair van broken down on the side of the road. I wondered "Who was going to come and assist them?" They are supposed to help folks yet they were on the side of the road themselves. It made me think of those in ministry or those who care for others. We help folks all the time but sometimes we break down, get flat tires, broken belts and our radiators sometimes run hot...we're fallible too. Who can we call since everyone believes that we have it all together? If Moses got tired, if Jesus grew weary of his disciples' constant lack of faith, why do we think that we will somehow always be at optimum efficiency? We must resist the temptation to give that illusion! We need people on our team who we can count on to pray for us as we pray for others! We should never be afraid to remind folks that we are human, just like everyone else. **Today, let us reflect on the fact that we are indeed flesh and are susceptible to failure and in need of assistance just like everyone else.**

"THE TURBINE OF THE MIND"

Ephesians 4:23 "...and that you be renewed in the spirit of your mind"

The fourth chapter of Ephesians is a manifesto for Christian ethics and behavior. Paul draws some stark contrasts between unsaved Gentiles and those who have been saved. In all of his writings, the mind is a major focus. In Greek thought, the mind, distinct from the heart, is the origin of our thoughts. Those thoughts turn into actions. It is the seat of our reasoning and intellect. So, it stands to reason that our minds are as important in the process of becoming more like Christ as our bodies. It is the mind that drives the body. All sin originates in the mind before it ever materializes in our members. Paul tells us here that we are to be renewed in the spirit of our mind. We can interpret that as saying that we change what gives our mind its energy. We change the fuel which will eventually change the ever-turning turbine that drives the mind. The Holy Spirit can and will handle this renewal. **Today, let us focus on what is being put into our minds and how we can better screen out things that will cause us to stumble.**

APRIL 22ND

"TEMPLES OF THE LIVING GOD"

John 15:13 "Greater love has no one than this, that one lay down his life for his friends."

John's gospel gives an intimate account of a particular encounter between Jesus and His disciples where Jesus is conferring a change of status upon them. He says that they are now His friends and no longer as slaves who do not know what the master of the house is doing. It is an amazing thing to be considered a friend of God. The fact that Jesus calls them friend and then tells them exactly how far this friendship would go is heavy, considering His revelations to them in the subsequent chapters. He says the ultimate expression of love is being willing to die for your friends. That is and there is no greater love than this. With the way the words love and friend are so cavalierly spoken, we need to take inventory of our collective vocabularies. Loving and being a friend are deep, abiding concepts that we would do well to fully understand. So, if Jesus is our friend, do we love Him enough to die for Him? Figuratively dying for him means that He can be reflected through me in my words, thoughts and actions. Literally dying for Him means that I did not value my own life over His cause. **Today, reflect on His love for us as compared to our love for Him.**

APRIL 23RD

"TREASURE STORED UP ON EARTH"

Haggai 1:9 "...Why?" declares the LORD of hosts, "Because of My house which lies desolate, while each of you runs to his own house."

We are enamored with material items. We love shiny new stuff. We often chase this "stuff" much to the chagrin of God and what He desires for us. We are to love the Lord our God with all of our heart, soul, mind and strength but many times we love things more. Haggai was a prophet during the temple reconstruction under the reign of King Darius of Persia who had given permission for the Israelites to resume building. During the hiatus, the people had forgotten about the temple and focused on decorating their own homes. They were more concerned with storing up treasures on earth to the detriment of God's desires. We may not have a physical temple that we are neglecting but when we neglect our spiritual lives, our prayer time, our time spent in the Word for the pursuit of worldly desires and the enlargement of our own personal empires, our metaphysical temples are in ruins. The good news is, just like God gave them what they needed to restore the temple, He has already given us what we need in the person and work of Jesus Christ. **Today, let us reflect on the fact that He is the temple restorer.**

"AND?"

Mark 10:28 "Peter began to say to Him, "Behold, we have left everything and followed You."

Peter's admission is a stunning one. It comes on the heels of the rich young ruler whom Jesus instructed to go sell all of his possessions, give to the poor and follow Him. The Bible says that the man went away sad because he owned much property. I too found myself struggling with this very concept. After burying my wife, I struggled intermittently with the idea that I had given up much to follow Him, and I still took major losses. It was and is a frustrating predicament. But, what bought me back to my senses was one word. The word "and" in a question form is equivalent to "so what?" It's not that God is dismissive of our predicaments but more that we are not cognizant of the sacrifice(s) that He has made on our behalf. Think of the fact that the God of the universe condescended in order to save a wretched, pitiful, blind and naked humanity and our sacrifices don't seem so great, after all. Think about the fact that the God of the universe gave Himself over (in human form) to die on a Roman torture instrument and our sacrifices don't seem so great. In light of His great sacrifices, ours do not seem so grand. **Today, reflect on what He has done to better put in perspective what we have to do.**

_____

_____

_____

_____

_____

_____

_____

_____

_____

_____

_____

_____

_____

_____

_____

_____

_____

_____

_____

_____

APRIL 25TH

"HE KNEW ALL THE TIME..."

John 16:33 "These things I have spoken to you, so that in Me you may have   peace. In the world you have tribulation, but take courage; I have overcome the world."

Have you ever been on an adventure with someone who knew that it was about to be a wild ride but didn't inform you? Like, my son. We have to trick him into getting onto roller coasters because he doesn't like them. We have to minimize the danger in order to get him to comply but the whole time, we are knowing that this roller coaster is pretty scary! That's not very nice. The Christian life is not like this. Not only are we told to expect trials and fiery darts, we are told that it is not strange but rather commonplace. This information is given to us up front by the leader of the whole of Christianity, Jesus Christ. He told the men who wanted to follow him in Matthew 8, "foxes have holes, birds have nests but the Son of Man has nowhere to lay His head." He beckons the men in John 1 to "come and see" where he was staying. Here is a hard truth: When Christ compels us to follow him, He does so while being fully aware of the tribulation that lies ahead. Here is the good news: We need to be fully aware that while there may be tribulation, He has overcome the WORLD and also whatever the tribulation in the world might be! **Today, reflect on the good news!**

APRIL 26TH

"RECLAMATION PROJECTS"

Titus 3:5 "He saved us, not on the basis of deeds which we have done in righteousness, but according to His mercy, by the washing of regeneration and renewing by the Holy Spirit..."

If we had to be saved on the merits of our past deeds or even our current deeds, many of us would be in a lot of trouble. I think about my own past and look back in wonder as to why I wasn't already dead or locked away in someone's prison. But the mercy of God and the grace of God operate independently of our personal worthiness. In truth, none of us are worthy or righteous enough to be saved without the blood of Jesus. No matter how many good works we've done, it is not enough to claim righteousness. On the flip side of that, no matter how many bad works we've done, it is not enough to be thrown away. Regardless of whether we were "good" or "not-so-good," we are all reclamation projects to God. We all needed redemption and regeneration. I thank God for the regenerative POWER of the Holy Ghost. When I look back over my life and I see how much God has changed me, I am truly thankful and awestruck because I was a train wreck and now He has salvaged the pieces and made it into something. **Today, reflect on the fact that there is NOTHING too hard for God!**

_____

_____

_____

_____

_____

_____

_____

_____

_____

_____

_____

_____

_____

_____

_____

_____

_____

_____

_____

_____

_____

APRIL 27TH

"ACTIVE FAITH"

James 2:26 "For just as the body without the spirit is dead, so also faith without works is dead."

We often debate works versus faith. We say "Well, if I have faith, I don't need works" or "If I do enough works that ought to be enough." Here is a candid assessment, we need both. A living, active faith is going to produce fruit in the form of works. The works are a natural outworking of an inward faith in an amazing God. James here says that a body without the spirit is dead. He is talking about the spirit or the pneuma that the ancients believed to be the animating force for human beings. A body with no spirit/breath is lifeless. That is the same as the Christian life without works. We do not live a solitary, singular, siloed existence where we just hole up and wait for Jesus to return. Instead, we live vibrant and active lives where we actively seek out opportunities to reflect the love of Jesus to others. So, while good works cannot save us, they can be indicative of one who is saved. Faith means being both hearers and doers of the word. It means taking Micah 6:8 to heart and living it out for the world to see. **Today, let your works reflect the God living inside of you to the world around you!**

"THE DEFINITION OF INSANITY"

Rom 12:2 "And do not be conformed to this world, but be transformed by the renewing of your mind, so that you may prove what the will of God is, that which is good and acceptable and perfect."

If we want anything in our lives to change we must first have a change of mindset! You can change location, color, setting, temperature, but if the mindset is the same, the outcome will be the same also. The definition of insanity as posited by Albert Einstein is repeating the same actions but expecting different results. We live lives of conformity to the world's standards and yet we expect God's results. That doesn't compute. Paul warns us not to be pressed into the world's mold but rather to be transformed by having our minds renewed. This breaks the cycle of insanity. Why should we continue in a pattern to fit into a "system" that doesn't really care anyway? We should desire to be who God intended, not what the world insists on. The church and the word being rightly divided assist with transformation and are not simply there for the exchange of information. If "transformation" is not as fast as you would like, that is a good sign that you are actually being transformed. **Today, let us desire to be changed and conformed into the image of Christ, a desire that God will ALWAYS grant.**

_____

_____

_____

_____

_____

_____

_____

_____

_____

_____

_____

_____

_____

_____

_____

_____

_____

_____

_____

_____

_____

APRIL 29TH

"STOP COMPARING"

Isaiah 64:6 "For all of us have become like one who is unclean, and all our righteous deeds are like a filthy garment; And all of us wither like a leaf, And our iniquities, like the wind, take us away."

Holiness should be the aspiration/desire of everyone who follows Christ. Peter says that we are called out, a royal priesthood. There are standards of Christian behavior that come along with being a part of this priesthood. In American/Western Christianity, we have problem. There are those who think they are "holier" than others. They compare their holiness to the holiness of their neighbor and somehow feel as if they have arrived. This is not holiness, this is self-righteousness. True holiness removes the concept of competition with others and focuses on self in relation to God! True holiness does not allow us to judge another brother or sister for their deeds without first making sure that our deeds are up to par. We don't pluck out logs from the eyes of others without first getting our own eyes together. Holiness is not a competition but rather a lifestyle. Holiness is not just a noun it is also an "action" word. The pursuit of holiness is not the pursuit of perfection, but the pursuit of becoming more like Christ and less like yourself. **Today, let us focus on our own walk and pray for others who are walking as well.**

"ABOUT THIS LIFE"

Mark 8:35 "For whoever wants to save his life will lose it, but whoever loses his life for My sake and for the gospel will save it."

In western Christianity, we are rarely faced with the prospect of death for our beliefs. Yes, violence has happened in churches across America but not necessarily as tribulation against those Christians who were there. Some of it was carried out by scorned lovers or racist white supremacists but in America we face nothing like our brothers and sisters face in other countries. However, if we believe Scripture to be true, we can rest assured that the same intolerance that Christians face in other nations will, eventually, occur here in America. There is a popular quote that says "For God I live and for God I will die." One day, those words will be tested. It happened to Jesus. It happened to 10 of the 12 disciples and there is a distinct possibility that it can and will happen to us. The beauty of losing our lives for Christ means that we gain it to eternal life. All of us must come to the point where we say "My life is in your hands, God, do with it as you please." This must be said with confidence, faith and sincerity. **Today, meditate on what you would do if your life was required of you for your belief in the Gospel.**

"WELL EDUCATED"

Philippians 3:4b "If anyone else thinks he has grounds for confidence in the flesh, I have more…"

The apostle Paul was probably the most educated of all of the apostles who contributed to the canon of Scripture. If God based His calling on our credentials, this man would be, hands down, the most qualified and most decorated apostle in the ancient world. He lays his credentials out in the third chapter of Philippians. His lineage, his educational pursuits, his lofty status in the community were all notable and very impressive. However, God did not have to strip him of these things, but rather, he willingly relinquished them in pursuit of Jesus Christ and the high calling that Jesus placed on his life on the Damascus road. Contrast that with our current culture where titles and degrees mean everything. So much so, that degree mills exist for the sole purpose of issuing out hollow doctorates and, by extension, false credibility to those recipients. God is no respecter of person, degree, reputation or pedigree. The same way God raised up Paul, he raised up Peter the fisherman. Jesus was a carpenter, not a Pharisee. **Today, let us remember that the only degree that matters is the degree to which we put our faith in the living God who cannot fail.**

"WHEN ALL HEAVEN BREAKS LOOSE"

Revelation 21:4 "He will wipe away every tear from their eyes, and there will be no more death or mourning or crying or pain, for the former things have passed away."

There is an old euphemism that is used when things get really bad. I've heard it all my life, especially as a child. It goes something like, "everything was OK, but then, all hell broke loose." Think of the prospects of that. Think about hell, what you know about it, and imagine that being unleashed on the planet or, in your life. It is a chilling thought. Hell is a place reserved for Satan and his demons but will also be filled with people who have rejected God. The opposite, but not equal, of hell is heaven. This is where believers will finally be rewarded and spend eternity with the Lord. Heaven is the place where there will not be any problems, only praise and worship of the Almighty God. There is an old song that says "what a day of rejoicing that will be!" Life can get complicated very quickly. **Today, be encouraged and know that when all else fails, rest assured that all hell cannot break out in heaven. God will be on His throne, we will be His people and He will be our God. The other shore is our true home.**

"QUALIFIED TO TRAIN"

Proverbs 22:6 "Train up a child in the way he should go, even when he is old he will not depart from it."

Training can and should be rigorous. We train for marathons. We train for competitions. We train to play sports. Training is understood to have a purpose. We don't train for without reason, we train because we will eventually implement that training. The Bible says that physical training is of some worth but godliness has worth in this life and the life to come. There are two presuppositions that the writer of this proverb makes. First, when they write "train up a child," it is understood that the one doing the training knows what they are doing. Whatever we "train" them up in, that is what they will "not depart from". We must sow good seeds into their lives. The second presupposition is that the training will last a lifetime. Many of us have witnessed children who got all the training in the world and yet, rebelled. We have to understand that although we train properly, the trainee bears some responsibility of implementing the training. When we don't see the fruit, we can get impatient. **Today, remember that every one of us, trainers and trainees are works in progress. Trust God to handle the implementation, trust God to give the trainer instructions to give to the trainee.**

MAY 4TH

"GET IN WHERE YOU FIT IN"

Luke 14:10 "But when you are invited, go and recline at the last place, so that when the one who has invited you comes, he may say to you, 'Friend, move up higher...'"

American culture can be very cutthroat. We're taught to be up-front and loud because the 'squeaky' wheel is the one that gets the oil. What we are not always taught is to be humble. I've witnessed some rude behavior in my life, much of it coming from so-called church people. Jesus teaches us a valuable lesson in this parable. This is not about weakness but rather, respect and honor. He says to His hearers that we ought to take the lowest seat. We often think the reverse of this because of how our culture values assertiveness. Know this, we will never have a seat that we haven't earned, no matter how many overnight success stories exist. He uses the parable to illustrate how readily we overestimate our importance. The world does not revolve around us and we are not nearly as important as we think we are. It is God who elevates. Therefore, we don't have to elevate ourselves. Peter says that we are to humble ourselves under God's mighty hand and He will exalt us in due time. **Today, let us not think of ourselves more highly than we ought but rather, let us recognize that God is sovereign and we are not.**

"HIS WAY OR NO WAY"

Proverbs 14:12 "There is a way that appears right to a man, but in the end it leads to death."

The writer of Proverbs shares enough wisdom that we could read through the book multiple times and get something new every time we read it. Every one of us will go through this life and have numerous decisions to make. We make decisions from the time we are born until the time that we die. The problem is, every decision that we make may not be a God-centered one. We sometimes make decisions based on emotion, lust, greed, ignorance or even stubbornness. However, the decisions that we make today don't just stay in today. They follow us through the rest of our days. What may appear as right to us could indeed be a costly decision. A man has a way that "seems" right but in the end, it leads to destruction. This is why Jeremiah was warned that the heart is desperately wicked and unknowable. We are told to follow our hearts, but what about a heart that is not lined up with God's will? That heart will lead us to places that are not meant for us. **Today, let us remember that God has a plan for us! His plans are made to be followed, not flouted.**

WALK WITH ME: God Seen, God Heard, God Revealed

_____

_____

_____

_____

_____

_____

_____

_____

_____

_____

_____

_____

_____

_____

_____

_____

_____

_____

_____

_____

_____

_____

MAY 6TH

"WE CAN'T TELL GOD WHO TO SAVE"

Isaiah 55:8 "For My thoughts are not your thoughts, nor are your ways My ways," declares the LORD."

The church crowd can be a very haughty one. We sometimes think that we can pick and choose who comes in. We also have the audacity to sometimes believe that we can pick and choose who is going to heaven. Here is a trustworthy saying that deserves full acceptance, God…Loves…Everyone. He loves the Muslim, the Buddhist, the drug addict, the prostitute…every created being, God loves. How do I know? Scripture bears this out. John said that God so loved the world. In a later epistle, he says that Jesus Christ died for the sins of the…whole world. Whether or not they accept the payment for their sins is a different story, but that does not diminish God's love for all. This passage in Isaiah is preceded by a call to the wicked to turn from their ways and for the unrighteous to turn from their thoughts. God says my ways are better than the wicked one's and my thoughts are purer than the unrighteous one's. But also, He is saying this: if you turn, I will have compassion. God's compassion is unfathomable. Man has compassion on whom he chooses, God has compassion on all who come to Him. **Today, let us remember that whomever God chooses, we should rejoice!**

_____

_____

_____

_____

_____

_____

_____

_____

_____

_____

_____

_____

_____

_____

_____

_____

_____

_____

_____

_____

_____

"REALLY GOD?"

Job 21:22 "Can anyone teach God knowledge, in that He judges those on high?"

We have all had those moments in life where we just look up and ask, "Really, God?" If you haven't had one of them, I commend you. Life is full of befuddling circumstances and crazy happenings. When these things occur, our minds are in overdrive trying to process them. The more we learn to trust God, the more we develop a comfort level with His decision-making process. Surely, it involves more wisdom than ours. His wisdom is infinite and He cannot learn because He already knows everything. When God makes a decision that we don't understand, remember three things: 1) That He is sovereign and can do whatever He pleases 2) He is not obligated to reveal the reason to us and 3) He sees and knows the purpose behind the decision when we only see the immediate outcome. We just have to trust Him. **Today, remember that in our finite humanity, there will be things that happen that we will never understand. We only see in a mirror dimly.**

"KEPT"

Jonah 1:17 "And the LORD appointed a great fish to swallow Jonah, and Jonah was in the stomach of the fish three days and three nights."

There is no place safer than in the arms of God. That is a common saying but it is also a true saying. God is indeed a keeper. He is the One who never sleeps nor slumbers. Daniel slept on the lions as pillows. David's life was never ended by Saul, although several attempts were made. The life of Jesus was not touched until the Father appointed the time. When I think of Jonah, I think about the fact that God not only keeps but God can even preserve. Preservation under all circumstances is a testament to the fact that God will get glory, no matter what. Preservation in situations where we have been disobedient is a testament to the mercy of God. From a scientific perspective, not only should Jonah not have survived, he should have been consumed. But again, God is a keeper. Think about it this way, if God was able to keep Jonah in the belly of a great fish with no acid damage, no enzymatic degradation, no decomposition and Jonah came out better than He went in, He can and will do the same for us, regardless of how bad the situation looks. **Today, believe that God has all things worked out for our good, especially when it doesn't look good.**

"CHARISMA"

Acts 8:9 "Now for some time a man named Simon had practiced sorcery in the city and amazed all the people of Samaria. He boasted that he was someone great..."

Simon was what we would call a counterfeit. Simon boasted of himself and acclaimed himself. We see this, a lot, in today's church. There are scores of counterfeit preachers who take advantage of parishioners for money, sex and numerous other things. The one thing that many of these men and women have is charisma. The Greek word charis is used when speaking of the gifts of the Spirit but that is not what I am talking about here. This charisma comes from somewhere else. But charisma has never saved anyone. I'd much rather be a boring preacher that preached the truth than an exciting and charismatic liar, which is exactly what Simon was. The people attributed his power to God but it was not from God. Yes, God affirmed the apostles with signs and wonders but the apostles also lived exemplary lives of faith. It was not just about doing magic tricks. This is what the people were attracted to. When the apostles showed up, the Holy Spirit exposed Simon. **Today, be sensitive to the Holy Spirit and pray for discernment. Know the truth and the counterfeit will always be able to be spotted.**

"A WAY OF ESCAPE"

1 Corinthians 10:13 "...but with the temptation will provide the way of escape also, so that you will be able to endure it."

I recall a time when I first gave up eating meat. Every craving that I had was for something associated with meat. I'd crave burgers, chicken, and one of my favorites, hot dogs; especially ones with chili, kraut and relish. These temptations eventually went away when I found a suitable substitute and eventually began eating fish as a pescatarian. In a practical sense, Satan operates the same way. Our wants and desires, especially those contrary to scripture, seem to be amplified as we seek to die to those things. Sometimes, the very things we crave are the ones that could eventually destroy us. The drinking or drugs seem glamorous until we die of an overdose or drive drunk into a telephone pole. We are always going to be faced with temptation because we face an enemy who does not sleep. He accuses the brethren day and night. But God, who knows our weaknesses and our faults, always provides a way of escape. He gives us the strength to say no and resist the devil. **Today, let us turn from temptation and use that way of escape that God provides. It is always there.**

"PLAYTIME IS OVER"

Job 1:8 "Then the Lord said to Satan, "Have you considered my servant Job? There is no one on earth like him; he is blameless and upright, a man who fears God and shuns evil."

We are not wrestling against flesh and blood. This passage of scripture bears that out. We are wrestling against powers and principalities and spiritual wickedness in high places. Satan is not in some underground cave plotting against us. He is in the earth and the heavens working his schemes. Unfortunately, for humanity, we are trapped in a cosmic death match between God and Satan. He is constantly on the attack and God is constantly on our side. As much as our culture tries to tell us that compromise is ok, it's not. There is no middle. We have to choose a side. Joshua tells the Israelites to choose this day who you will serve! Elijah asks, how long will you limp between two opinions? Jesus said, plainly, he who does not gather with me, scatters. What am I saying? **Today, let us make up in our minds that playtime is over.**

"THE UNSTOPPABLE PLAN OF GOD"

Ephesians 3:9 "and to bring to light what is the administration of the mystery which for ages has been hidden in God who created all things..."

Nothing has ever stopped God. Once God puts a plan in motion, it does not matter who does what, God's plan will always prevail. Here, Paul, speaking of the plan to include the Gentiles in the salvific work of Christ, says that the plan of God was hidden within Him for ages. It was kept a mystery, I believe, because once Satan knows the plan, He will seek to thwart it. Once Jesus revealed His plan to Peter and Peter tried to stop Him, Jesus replied angrily, "Get behind me Satan!" There will be times where God is in the process of revealing some plan, purpose or process to us, Satan will also plant seeds of doubt to try to "undo" your belief in God's revelation. Remember this well, what God reveals, God will accomplish. **Today, rest assured that Satan's greatest effort cannot thwart even God's smallest purpose.**

MAY 13TH

"GOD'S ELEVATION"

1 Peter 5:8 "Humble yourselves, therefore, under God's mighty hand, that he may lift you up in due time."

Hitting homeruns doesn't come without hours of batting practice. The great NBA player, Ray Allen, didn't develop his jump shot lying on his back; he practiced and got better in increments. Stephen Curry often goes into the gym after games are over to hone his shooting. Hard work takes humility. It takes a lot for us not to expect anything to be handed to us. Hard work can be considered stewardship. We use God's gifts to their fullest extent to help others. Life is the same way, there is no "skipping" levels because every level has its own lesson to be learned. When we look for shortcuts and easy routes that displays a lack of faith. God is the one who exalts but we have to trust Him. We cannot seek a quick ascension; we cannot try to leapfrog to the front of the line. There is a lesson on every level and once proven, God will indeed exalt us and move us forward. To trust God at every stage of life and never jump the gun trying to go where God never intended for us to be, takes faith. **Today, remember that God opposes the proud but gives grace to the humble**.

MAY 14TH

"THE ATTITUDE OF CHRIST"

Philippians 2:5 "Have this attitude in yourselves which was also in Christ Jesus…"

At Calvary, Jesus gave us a great example. He could've saved Himself, but He chose not to. His attitude was this: It's not about me; it's about God's glory and doing His will. The Christian life is somewhat altruistic, in that, there is a level of self-sacrifice that is not called for in other religions. There is a level of self-discipline that is not called for in other religions either. The attitude of Christ was totally altruistic. Paul even discusses, in this same chapter, considering others more than ourselves. As Christians, we emulate our Leader and the Author and Finisher of our faith. We strive to be more like Jesus and less like ourselves. **Today, let this attitude be in us that was also in Christ Jesus! Selflessness over selfishness is the only way that we willingly pick up our crosses daily.**

"MAKE UP YOUR MIND"

John 16:24 "Until now you have asked for nothing in My name; ask and you will receive, so that your joy may be made full."

Every day, when we wake up, we have a choice. We have a choice because our Heavenly Father gives us a choice. We can choose to put things into His hands and allow Him to work them out or, we can pout and moan about what we don't have. Jesus, speaking to His disciples, says here that His disciples have not asked for anything in His name. He is teaching His disciples this principle because He would be leaving soon. He says ask in His name, you will receive. What we ask for is inconsequential. God is going to give us what He desires for us to have. The question is, do we have the faith to ask? Here, Jesus commands us to ask! Then, He takes it further and says that when we receive, our joy is made full. The way that full is written, it can be interpreted as "continue to be full." Their joy was full with Jesus with them; He is saying to them, I am not abandoning you just because I'm leaving! The joy of receiving a good and perfect gift is hard to explain. **Today, remember this, before we let someone or something ruin our day: God didn't go to sleep last night, so whatever we encounter, He already knows about it AND has the remedy for it, if we would just ask.**

"DRIVING ON E"

Luke 4:13 "When the devil had finished every temptation, he left Him until an opportune time."

All of us can probably think of a time when we were driving our vehicles with the gas light indicator on. The little yellow light comes on when the tank is almost on empty. It is a warning that most of the time is ignored. I have said myself, "I know my car; we're good." Well, that strategy might work sometimes, but it may not work all the time. As Christians, we don't have a low fuel light that comes on but we do have the Holy Spirit who convicts us and reminds us that we need to refresh and renew. This often entails studying the word of God, diligently. When Satan tempted Jesus in the wilderness, He used Scripture to justify his requests. Jesus, knowing that Satan was doing nothing more than proof-texting and scripture twisting, replied with Scripture of His own to refute Satan. The thing is, Jesus actually had some something in his arsenal. He was not riding around with his fuel light on E; he was on F as it related to scripture. We must adopt this same attitude. In order to fight the devil with scripture, we actually have to know some scripture. It's impossible to make a withdrawal if we have not made any deposits. **Today, let us commit to study our bibles more often!**

"ME AGAINST ME"

1 Corinthians 9:27 "…but I discipline my body and make it my slave, so that, after I have preached to others, I myself will not be disqualified."

Imagine a boxer, shadowboxing. Now, imagine if the shadow of the boxer came to life and boxed back, countering the boxer's every move. Do you think the shadow could win? Of course, it could, because it intimately knows the moves of the boxer. It is as close to the boxer as anyone else in the world. Paul is a master of using analogies to paint vivid pictures and here in this text, he does just that. He paints the picture of an athlete, competing in the ancient Olympics, who must master his own body to make it cooperate with the rigorous training required to compete and win. Here, the athlete's discipline is on display. The crux of the illustration is in verse 27 where Paul says he disciplines his own body, making it his slave, so that his actions are fitting of his vocation. We often compare ourselves to others and use a sliding scale to justify our wrongs. If our actions are not as bad as someone else's actions, we think that we are ok. In reality, walking with God is a competition between you and yourself, not you and others. The shadow analogy is simply to make the point that no one, besides God, knows you better than yourself. **Today, let us focus on self and run the race in such a way that we win.**

MAY 18TH

"DON'T TELL IT, JUST DO IT"

Matthew 6:3 "But when you give to the poor, do not let your left hand know what your right hand is doing..."

In the age of social media, many are looking to go viral. It seems that one of the best ways to go viral is to be seen doing some act of kindness. We see it all the time: homeless people getting hot soup or some articles of clothing, rappers giving away large sums of money in music videos, the president throwing paper towels into a crowd of hurricane ravaged victims in Puerto Rico or bragging about not taking a salary. I could go on and on but I often wonder, how much of this stuff is staged for the exact reason mentioned above? How much of this is real giving from the heart? Jesus gave us the remedy to the seemingly endless desire to go viral. Jesus, in preaching the Sermon on the Mount, tells us plainly, don't tell it, just do it. This is what He means when he says not to let the left hand know what the right hand is doing. Sure, it is more satisfying to get millions of retweets and pats on the back, but in being a blessing to others, don't do it looking for a reward or for glory. Do good works to glorify God, and so that others will see your good works & also glorify Him. **Today, let us remember that what we do in secret will be rewarded openly.**

MAY 19TH

"BE CAREFUL WHEN YOU ASK"

2 Kings 2:9 "When they had crossed over, Elijah said to Elisha, "Ask what I shall do for you before I am taken from you." And Elisha said, "Please, let a double portion of your spirit be upon me."

The relationship between Elijah and Elisha is a very interesting one. Elijah is coming towards the end of his ministry, while Elisha is about to embark on the beginning of his. One man has faced many enemies, fled for his life, lived in the desert and called fire from heaven to demonstrate the sovereignty of the Almighty God. Elisha, on the other hand, was an obscure figure without much fanfare until God sent Elijah to anoint him as his successor. Here in this passage, after crossing over Jordan, a symbolic action reminiscent of the scene that occurred when Joshua took over for Moses, Elisha makes a request. Elisha asks for a double portion of Elijah's spirit. This was a noble request. One of respect. Elisha knew of the great exploits of Elijah and had just seen him part the waters of the Jordan by striking them with his cloak. Elijah says to him, "you have asked a hard thing…" When we look at others and we marvel at how God works through them, we must also consider what tribulation they faced while carrying out God's work. **Today, let us be careful when we ask for a "double portion". With double the apples we also get double the worms.**

"THE STUFF CAN'T TALK"

Mark 8:36 "For what does it profit a man to gain the whole world, and forfeit his soul?"

In American culture, we are preoccupied with stuff. Commercials bombard us with the subliminal messages and tell us that the stuff is the way to happiness. The accumulation of "stuff" only tells others that the accumulator has a deep need to be defined by something or known as something other than what they really are. Gucci doesn't change my character but it gives off the perception that I am somehow special or privileged. Even if I don't have a dime in my pocket or if I am rotten to the core. Unlike DNA, the information contained in the "stuff" that we accumulate will NEVER tell people anything about who we really are. It can only create a perception of who we are which is precisely why we HIDE behind our stuff to protect ourselves in a prideful, image conscious society. In reality stuff cannot define us. Stuff cannot determine our lot in life. Stuff cannot even speak one word as to the content of our character. Often, in the pursuit of stuff, we forget God. In the end, what will the legacy that we leave behind be? Are we going to leave behind a lot of stuff that will eventually rot, break down or become useless? **Today, let us seek to leave behind a more enduring legacy. Only what we do for Christ will last.**

"AN INDELIBLE FINGERPRINT"

Psalm 19:1 "The heavens are telling of the glory of God; and their expanse is declaring the work of His hands."

As a scientist, I'm often befuddled by my colleagues' disdain for God. I know that we always want to have a definitive, empirical answer, but I submit that there are some things that defy empiricism. There is no scientific way to explain why human beings are able to love, feel empathy or desire companionship. Neither is there a scientific way to define morality. God is one of those things that cannot be limited to an empirical test. Yet, in his wisdom, He left clues that the empiricist could see and know that they were not random coincidences. I watch the science channels a lot I am amazed at how atheistic the networks are and how relentless they are to remove God from the equation of life. They often speak about the "laws of nature" removing the need for a "God" but my question is always: "Who created nature?" or "Who set the laws in motion?" We may not need God to explain nature to us, but we see evidence for God in the creation, daily. Paul says in Romans 1:19 that the invisible qualities of God can be observed through His workmanship. **Today, be certain that the utter complexity of the universe, the fact that it had an origin and the complexity of the human anatomy is enough to say, "There is a God."**

"THE TRUTH"

John 8:32 "Then you will know the truth, and the truth will set you free."

Religion and God are not one in the same. God is liberating where religion has often been used to oppress. It is imperative to draw the line. Religion is man's attempt to explain God, but we don't always get it right. The unfortunate thing is, religion is purposefully misleading at times, which causes suspicion when it comes to God and pain for the adherents of that particular religion. If it is done right and, in a Christ-centered way, there is no suspicion, only freedom. The truth is a powerful abolitionist. The truth sets free, where deception and falsehood hold us captive. Jesus, in the 8th chapter of John is laying out a most brilliant argument for Himself as the Messiah and the futility of continuing in an old, error-filled, legalistic religious system that had been corrupted by power-hungry leaders. Jesus says, explicitly that if those who were listening believed and continued in His word, they would know the truth. Jesus gives two commandments, love God and love our neighbors as we love ourselves. The truth is summed up in those two statements. There is no need for legalism or harsh, judgmental rhetoric when we know how to truly serve God. **Today, let the truth set you free from the bondage to manmade systems. Trust Jesus.**

_____

_____

_____

_____

_____

_____

_____

_____

_____

_____

_____

_____

_____

_____

_____

_____

_____

_____

_____

_____

"MASTERY"

Romans 7:15 "For what I am doing, I do not understand; for I am not practicing what I would like to do, but I am doing the very thing I hate."

Dominionism is a popular theology that has taken root more recently in evangelical circles. The belief is that Christians must subdue the earth for God by taking over positions in local, regional and national government. The overall goal is to set up a pseudo-theocracy. Then, and only then, will God exercise His rule in the earth. One of the issues with this theology is the contradiction that it creates when Jesus' statement is unpacked, "repent, for the kingdom of God is near." Jesus inaugurated the earthly kingdom, not man. Jesus never tried to overthrow the secular government. Jesus understood the already-not yet tension that existed between the present kingdom and the coming kingdom. Here is a word of wisdom: first, we must master own selves before seeking to claim some dominion over the earth. Rather than focusing on "dominion" trying to exercise "dominion" in the earth, we need to first exercise dominion over sin so that we might be of TRUE service to God. We are seeking to "conquer" everything except for ourselves. **Today, exercise mastery over sin, through the Holy Spirit. That is a real victory.**

"WORKS DON'T WORK"

Genesis 3:7 "Then the eyes of both of them were opened, and they knew that they were naked; and they sewed fig leaves together and made themselves loin coverings."

Oftentimes, in life, we believe that we can will our way to anything. The belief in self-determination is a double-edged sword. On the one hand, it is important to have self-confidence and belief in what we do. But, on the other hand, how far does too much self-confidence push the need for God out to the edge of our lives? This is why Jesus said it was hard for a rich man to enter heaven. A rich person is confident in his/her possessions. In all honesty, it would seem counterintuitive to promote faith in self and faith in God at the same time. Our efforts are not enough by themselves. We need God! There are some things that we cannot accomplish without God! Adam and Eve sewed fig leaves together but God, by his grace knew that this was totally inadequate and gave them skins instead! He also gave them something else, a preview to the shedding of blood for the remission of sin. Removing our sin is something we cannot do, no matter how hard we try. That's God's prerogative. God covers our inadequacies with His grace. **Today, let us not be afraid to give God free reign to do for us what we cannot do for ourselves.**

"THIS IS IMPOSSIBLE"

Hebrews 11:12 "And so from one man, and he as good as dead, came descendants as numerous as the stars in the sky and as countless as the sand on the seashore."

When Abraham received the promise from God for a son, Abraham was well advanced in years and Sarah was barren. What sounded impossible to them was indeed possible for God. The Bible tells us on multiple occasions that with God, nothing is impossible. So, Abraham had a choice. Believe God or be intimidated by the impossible. He chose to believe and it is said that his faith was credited to him as righteousness. Many who received promises from God were not in ideal positions when they received them. Yet, they still believed God. Moses saw his brothers and sisters enslaved at the hands of Pharaoh when God said to him that he would be their liberator. Peter was in the middle of a storm when Jesus told him to come out on the water. Mary was a poor, insignificant virgin when Gabriel announced that she would be the vehicle for the Messiah to make his earthly entrance. Their lives were what they were, and God was not intimidated by that. He was able to work around and through challenges to accomplish His will. **Today, remember God is not going to make life easy, but possible. Faith makes life possible, not care free.**

"A LIFESTYLE"

Luke 9:62 "But Jesus said to him, "No one, after putting his hand to the plow and looking back, is fit for the kingdom of God."

If Grace is the blanket that covers the bed that we lie on in life, repentance is what keeps the blanket tucked in nice and neat. Jesus makes a hard statement here. But it is a necessary one. There are indeed two kingdoms operating simultaneously in the earth. There is the kingdom of God and the kingdom of the prince of the power of the air. We have to choose who our master will be. In the passage, "looking" can be translated as continually looking back i.e. longing to go back. It's very difficult to plow a straight line if we are looking over our shoulder. When we do look back, it should be to see how far God has brought us, not to desire to go back to a place of bondage. But, in our humanity, we will, most certainly, look back. We should quickly repent and move on with our live, not stare back at past wreckage wondering, "what if?" Repentance is a lifestyle for the Christian because we sin daily in word, thought or action. **Today, let us remember that what is behind us is to be forgotten and what is ahead of us is to be pressed towards.**

"JESUS IS ON THE MAINLINE"

1 Thessalonians 5:17 "...pray without ceasing..."

We are given a command here to pray. The word for pray is written in the imperative mood. There are times when we are too weak to pray. I've been there. There are also times when disillusionment causes us to lose focus and not pray. Prayer is the way that we communicate with our heavenly headquarters. When disrupted, the enemy can not only pounce but frustrate the communication further by implanting his own feedback into the loop. I went through a period, after losing my wife of 16 years, where I couldn't bring myself to pray. It was hard, especially after having prayed so much for her healing and seeing her pass away. That was a catastrophic mistake, but a correctable one, nonetheless. We have to know that 100% of our problems would be solved, or at least ameliorated, by God if we actually took 100% of our problems to God. We cannot spend too much time in prayer but we can certainly spend too much complaining to others. Prayer changes things, including our perception of the things that beset us. **Today, let us commit to prayer, in season and out of season.**

MAY 28TH

"BE TRANSFORMED"

John 3:6 "Truly, truly, I tell you, no one can enter the kingdom of God unless he is born of water and the Spirit."

Jesus, in speaking to Nicodemus, must have seemed a bit off His rocker. When Jesus says that to enter the kingdom of God, we must be born again, Nicodemus was puzzled because He was thinking of natural childbirth. There is a childbirth that must take place. We must become as little children in order to enter and eventually inherit the kingdom of heaven. There is a transformation that must take place. Here, Jesus says that we must be born of water and the Sprit? What does He mean? Ritual baptism only cleanses the outer person (water) but the Spirit cleanses a person's innermost being. God, in His eternal wisdom, does not call us to anything that He will not provide the means to accomplish. God provides the way, through the transformative power of the Holy Ghost, for all of us to go from "caterpillars" to "butterflies". He will indeed wash us clean, make us over and present us faultless, but we must submit to the process of transformation. That process can look different for different people, but, nevertheless, we must all undergo change. **Today, let us embrace the process and the change that comes along with it.**

"MONKEY SEE, MONKEY DO"

1 Corinthians 11:1 "Be imitators of me, just as I also am of Christ."

It is said that imitation is the sincerest form of flattery. When we imitate something, we, in a sense, want to become that thing. We get riotous laughter from comedians who are able to do impressions, especially if they are spot on. When our kids imitate us, it can be quite hilarious, as well. That is because the one being imitated can see something of themselves in the one imitating them. There is also a caveat. When we do things that are wrong or unacceptable, those can be, and often are, imitated as well. This is especially prevalent in children who observe adult behavior intently as they develop their own personalities. As a child, I heard, "do as I say and not as I do" from many sources. Words are hollow when the actions behind those words don't match up. The worst attitude that we can have is "do as I say, not as I do." The more excellent attitude is the one that Paul commands here in the scripture. The Greek word for imitate is mimétés which is where our word mimic comes from. We are to set the example by first being imitators or mimicking what Christ did. The loving, selfless example of Jesus is our template. All other things flow from this. Notice that Paul did not tell his followers to only mimic his words but also his actions. That's because Paul knew that the kingdom was not about words. **Today, let our actions reflect those of Christ.**

"WOLVES AMONG THE SHEEP"

1 John 2:19 "They went out from us, but they did not belong to us."

When the Gospel is preached, it also convicts. The Gospel's first intention is to bring to light the good news of salvation. A secondary consequence of the Gospel is bringing man's sinfulness to the fore. This is what turns many off. We are sinners in need of a savior. Many people do not want to come to grips with the reality that we cannot save ourselves. It is utterly impossible. But the Gospel, full of salvation and the remedy for sin, can empty a church because of its bluntness. So, many have taken to watering it down to appease the masses. The Gospel has been relegated to a feel-good message by those who do not like its abrasiveness. Or, in some cases, it has been scrapped in favor of pop-psychology or self-help doctrine. There are many counterfeit gospels being propagated by counterfeit preachers. Anything that takes the focus off Jesus can be considered a counterfeit gospel. If the focus is on money or possessions or political power, start asking questions. A counterfeit gospel will produce counterfeit disciples, who don't seek Christ, but rather, what that so-called gospel offers. **Today, remember the Gospel message: Christ came to forgive sin, Christ died to save us from sin's penalty and Christ rose again because He defeated sin. It is that simple.**

"PITY THE FOOL"

Psalm 53:1 "The fool says in their heart, "There is no God."

Mr. T was an actor, wrestler and pop-culture icon. Not only was he known for his hundreds of gold chains and pendants, or his signature Mohawk haircut, but he was also known for a popular phrase. He would always say, of someone who disagreed with him or who thought they could subdue him, "I pity the fool!" What exactly is a fool? The Bible describes a fool in many different ways. A fool is one who lacks a sense of morality, one who thinks that immorality will not be punished, one who doesn't think before they speak, one who disregards the wisdom of elders or one who does not believe that there is a God in heaven. There are many in the world who fit the latter description. Not all are atheists, either. Some just live as if there is no God, although they may profess some belief in God or some other higher power. Some tempt fate altogether and live fast lives, anticipating their own demise, often shirking off the wisdom from others to slow down. We have to remember that if we live life at 100 mph, we can expect to have a wreck at some point along the journey. Slow down and listen to God speaking. He sends wisdom and warning from multiple sources. If we continue in disobedience, when the "wreck" finally happens, there is no guarantee that we will survive it. **Today, look for the signs and listen for the sounds that are warning us away from bad situations.**

JUNE 1ST

"BE GRATEFUL FOR WHAT YOU HAVE"

Exodus 20:17 "You shall not covet your neighbor's house; you shall not covet your neighbor's wife or his male servant or his female servant or his ox or his donkey or anything that belongs to your neighbor."

Jealousy is Satan's way of telling us that we are not good enough. Admiration is God's way of telling you that His gifts are given without repentance. There is a reason that God says do not covet; it's simple, the person, thing, or position that you covet may be beyond what you are capable of handling. Not to mention, God has given gifts to each of us. When we are jealous, those emotions can cause us to do things that are out of character. Murder, lying, deceit and greed can all stem from jealousy. Always remember, what God gives us, He did so understanding what we are capable of. If He didn't give something to us, He did so with the understanding of what we are not capable of. If He increases our capabilities then he will also increase our responsibilities. It is a true blessing for us to stay in our respective lanes and exercise the gifts that God gave each one of us. Then there's no time for us to worry about someone else nor is there time for us to listen to the lies of Satan. **Today, let us be grateful to God for what He has given to us and not worry so much about what He hasn't.**

_____

_____

_____

_____

_____

_____

_____

_____

_____

_____

_____

_____

_____

_____

_____

_____

_____

_____

_____

_____

_____

_____

_____

"UNINTENDED CONSEQUENCES"

Acts 7:58 "...Meanwhile, the witnesses laid their coats at the feet of a young man named Saul."

One day, on a walk, I noticed a butterfly romancing a flower. I am sure that the butterfly was there for the nectar but, undoubtedly, some of the flower's pollen got attached to the butterfly. That's how nature works. Sometimes, there are cascades of events that happen from one interaction. There are unintended consequences. That butterfly probably carried off the pollen and gave the flower a chance to multiply. When Stephen was stoned, Saul (Paul) was there to witness it. He actually approved of it. But Saul did not know that he was witnessing a prophetic moment, where his own fate was playing out, right before his eyes. Just as he desired to make Stephen a martyr, he too would become a martyr. His presence was more than just a coincidence. It also propelled the Gospel into other regions. Although he desired to squelch the spread of the gospel, He actually made it spread further by pushing disciples into other places, just as Christ prophesied in Acts 1:8. Oftentimes, what we view as coincidences are actually God-ordained moments in time that serve His providential purpose. Just as the butterfly unknowingly spread the plant's pollen, Saul unknowingly caused a prophecy from Jesus to be fulfilled. **Today, do not be unaware that you are a part of God's plan.**

_____

_____

_____

_____

_____

_____

_____

_____

_____

_____

_____

_____

_____

_____

_____

_____

_____

_____

_____

_____

JUNE 3RD

"YOU SHALL KNOW THEM BY THEIR FRUIT"

1 John 4:3 "…but every spirit that does not acknowledge Jesus is not from God. This is the spirit of the antichrist…"

One afternoon, on my drive home, I was listening to a radio program that dealt with "preachers" who didn't believe in Christ's resurrection. I asked myself, "How can a so-called Christian preacher not believe in the resurrection?" I could understand if it was a debate over a secondary issue. Over 100,000 different denominations exist because of a different interpretation of certain texts. But the resurrection is the primary doctrine of Christianity. No resurrection makes Jesus out to be a liar. That is not possible because the Truth cannot lie. A preacher who discounts the resurrection is nothing more than a motivational speaker! Test everything that comes from the mouth of the preacher, no matter who he/she is. If they are in disagreement over essential Christian doctrines, it may be wise to seek counsel elsewhere. There is a different spirit motivating their speech. John tells us plainly that any spirit who speaks ill of Jesus is not from God, but rather, is the spirit of the antichrist. That is a powerful declaration coming from one who actually walked with the Lord. **Today, let us refuse to get enamored with new doctrine that clearly does not jibe with what we already know to be true.**

JUNE 4TH

"PRISONER OF THE LORD"

Ephesians 4:1 "Therefore I, the prisoner of the Lord, implore you to walk in a manner worthy of the calling with which you have been called..."

We often have a negative image of what it means to be a prisoner. We think about bars and buzzers, clanging cell doors, rage-filled fights and horrible living conditions. We also believe that prison is for criminals. Therefore, to be associated with such a thing would be, and could be embarrassing. But as disciples, we are prisoners too, but in a different sense of the word. We are bound, but not by the world. We are bound to God by our love for Him. We are sometimes hemmed in on every side, but He promises that we will never be crushed. We too lose some freedoms, but we gain liberties. We too are regimented in our devotion to gathering together, to corporate worship, to private prayer time, to studying the word, but we do so out of a desire for a closer walk, not because of a mandate. The thing about being a prisoner is that, oftentimes, their rights get violated or even, stripped away. God does not operate like that. He restores to us the ultimate right, the right to be called His children. Think of it this way, would we rather be prisoners for Christ or hostages of Satan? The two positions are incomparable. **Today, remember this, at least with Jesus, our release date will be better than the day that we started serving time in His house!**

WALK WITH ME: God Seen, God Heard, God Revealed

JUNE 5TH

"WATCH YOUR MOUTH"

Matthew 7:1 "Do not judge so that you will not be judged."

A distinction must be made between judgment and correction. Judgement implies that the sentence has already been levied, whereas correction, especially done in love, could actually spare one from judgment. The phrase, "putting your mouth on someone" is somewhat of an obsession. Does it even matter what someone says about us if it is not true? Let them talk. Jesus said that when they persecute us for the sake of righteousness and they speak evil against us because of Him, we are blessed. Often times when you hear people use the "judge not" defense, it is in reference to correction being offered to someone who may be out of step in their walk with Jesus. The emphasis of Jesus here is not the actual words but whether they are spoken hypocritically. We cannot see a speck in someone else's eye and have a log hanging from ours. That is hypocritical. That is what Jesus is warning us against. Yes, many do often pass unwarranted judgment. But we have to know the difference in judgment and correction. We cannot be uncorrectable or unteachable. The word of God is useful for teaching, reproof, rebuke and training in righteousness. **Today, let us seek the counsel of the word of God for all of our interactions and make righteous judgments in all things.**

"THE STRAIGHT & NARROW"

Isaiah 35:8 "A highway will be there, a roadway, and it will be called the Highway of Holiness. The unclean will not travel on it…"

If you drive a vehicle, you will notice that there are lines on the asphalt to keep cars from veering into opposing lanes. If you drive on the interstate, you might sometimes notice that there are wires or even walls in the median to keep cars from veering into oncoming traffic should they run off the road. Those barriers and lines are there to guide us. There are even signs used to guide us to our destination. But, every now and then, we get turned around or even lose our direction. Even the best of us can lose our way. This highway, that Isaiah speaks of goes to Zion. It is called the Highway of Holiness. When we think of God's holiness, we automatically think of His perfection. When we think of our own holiness, we should automatically know that every day is a day to move closer to God's ideal. This highway, traveled by those who have been made clean by the blood of Jesus is holy because it belongs to God. His grace acts like the lines in the road or the guard rails on the interstate to keep me moving forward. God's grace encourages us not to use it as a hall pass to sin, but to fly straight and to do the things that are pleasing to Him. When we don't hit the mark, grace is there. **Today, let us remember that the kindness of God leads us to repentance!**

JUNE 7TH

"BUBBLE WRAP"

Luke 15:2 "Both the Pharisees and the scribes began to grumble, saying, "This man receives sinners and eats with them."

True evangelism doesn't take place within the four walls of the church. The model for how to deal with people was not set with the Pharisees. To the Pharisees, everyone who was not like them was considered a sinner, even though they too were sinners! This attitude will not only run people away from God, it will make people cynical towards religion in general. Jesus not only fulfilled the prophecy of Moses that God would raise up one from among the people, but also brought God's word in Leviticus 26 to life in that God truly did dwell among his people. We see different ethnic groups or people from different lifestyles and we immediately want to shun them because they don't look like us. The church will not save any souls by covering itself in bubble wrap and praying for protection from the outside world. In order to develop the heart that Jesus had for the people, we must be among the people, in the world but not of the world. The best way for us to develop a real Christology, i.e. learning about the nature of Jesus, is not in a classroom among scholars or stuck inside the church. We need to be out in the world among those whom Jesus told us to love as we love ourselves. **Today, don't settle for simply being a church-goer or a Bible thumper, but rather, a people lover.**

JUNE 8TH

"LET NOT YOUR HEART BE TROUBLED"

Psalm 37:1 "...Do not fret because of evildoers, be not envious toward wrongdoers."

The world often times seems topsy-turvy. We see things that anger us all the time. Sometimes it looks as if people are just getting away with murder. Politicians, criminals and the like seem as if they face no consequences. Furthermore, we can have personal, so-called enemies who dislike us or seek to do us harm for no apparent reason. If we let every seemingly unpunished incident move us to anger or even worse, hatred, we have allowed Satan to win. If we let everyone who has something negative to say about us get under our skin, eventually there will be no room left in there for us. David tells us here not to burn with anger over evildoers or be envious towards those who work iniquity. We have to shake them off and refuse to absorb negative energy from others. We cannot let them alter who we are or cause us to act out of character. What we should all do is submit everything to God in prayer. That is not easy but we must pray and ask the Holy Spirit for His help. David tells us what becomes of the evildoer and the iniquity worker; like the green grass, they will soon be cut down. **Today, let us not ask "how soon, Lord?" but rather, let us say "Thy will be done."**

"LET THERE BE NO DOUBT"

Mark 9:23 "And Jesus said to him, "'If You can?' All things are possible to him who believes."

In Mark's gospel, Jesus has an interesting exchange with a man whose son was possessed. Many say that the young boy had epilepsy that caused him to roll around, foam at the mouth and, at times, throw himself into the fire. The boy's father was obviously very fretful. We cannot pass judgment on him. I have asked this same thing of Jesus during the time when my wife was ill. I've felt the helplessness and the doubt that this man feels in this story. The reply of Jesus tells us everything that we need to know about His ability and the faith that He expects of us. Jesus repeated the man's statement "if you can?" but as a rhetorical question. Can you see the Lord's facial expression? Can you imagine Jesus, sweating a bit, shaking His head from side-to-side, slightly smirking and saying "if you can?" Jesus did not berate the man but told Him where to place His faith. The man's response was key! "I believe, help my unbelief." We have to have a "But Jesus" attitude. If I put the word "but" in front of Jesus, my answer, to whatever my excuse is, is sure to follow. **Today, let us add those two words to our Christian vocabulary and we will surely have a better day today than we had yesterday.**

"WE MATTER TO GOD"

Romans 8:16 "The Spirit Himself testifies with our spirit that we are God's children…"

Being an orphan can be a harrowing experience. Orphans are often abused, manipulated, taken advantage of and neglected. I often worry about that for my own children. If something were to happen to me, with their mother already being deceased, it would be tragic, in my opinion. Of course, God knows best but, in my humanity, I can't help but to consider it. The love of God is such that being an orphan, alone in this cold world, was not something that God desired for us. Instead, He desired for us to have a restored relationship with Him. Enter Jesus. God in the flesh, who came to reconcile us back to Himself. From a spiritual perspective, we were once a part of those who were estranged from God, with no hope in the world. We were enemies of God. Orphans, trapped in the family of the father of lies. The Holy Spirit reminds us that we are no longer strangers but rather, we are sons and daughters! We ought to be thankful to God for sending Jesus to adopt us out of a family of whose head, Satan, is an abusive father who thrives on hate and immorality, and whose end is death! **Today, let us thank Him that we are now a part of Christ's Kingdom of the saints of God in the light and our Father is one of love, grace and mercy!**

JUNE 11TH

"MULTIPLYING WORDS WITHOUT KNOWLEDGE"

Job 26:4 "To whom have you uttered words? And whose spirit was expressed through you?"

Life is one gigantic learning experience. Every day, we are faced with different tests and as we navigate life, we learn more and more. One of the areas that we could all improve is our ability to listen to others. Oftentimes, when others are talking, especially when they are hurting, we tend to moralize, get onto a soapbox and tell them what we would do. God forbid that they lose a loved one, then we start telling them how to grieve, when to cry, when not to cry and otherwise disregarding every word out of their mouth. This was Job's dilemma. He had friends who were great talkers but terrible listeners. They accused him of things that he never did, assumed things about him that the thought they knew and made assertions about his character that were not true. That's because they saw his situation but they did not see him. They saw his trials and assumed that he was being punished. We can learn a lesson from these friends. Although Job referred to them as useless, they are of great use to us. While they each said something that was true, none of it applied to Job's situation. What we learn is to keep our mouths closed until we get all the facts. **Today, remember this: If we are going to speak, let us speak something encouraging and uplifting and let God do the rest**.

"JUST KEEP WORKING"

Nehemiah 4:1 "Now it came about that when Sanballat heard that we were rebuilding the wall, he became furious and very angry and mocked the Jews."

Each of us has a mission in life. Whether small or great, God has a plan for us that we are able to glorify Him through. Sometimes, when we make progress and we start to move forward, setbacks happen. Those traps and roadblocks are sent by the enemy to get us off course and to distract us from God's purpose for our lives. Nehemiah faced this as the Jews faced the daunting task of rebuilding Israel. The wall went up first before the other construction could take place. The enemy tried to distract them. This is a common tactic. You may have heard the phrase "tossing shiny objects into the air" which literally means that as we focus on those objects, some nefarious plot is taking place in another place, unbeknownst to us. The best way for the devil to slip in unawares is to distract those who are supposed to be working on the wall. We must stay focused on what God called us to do. The enemies of progress only get disturbed when progress is actually being made. We must stay mission-minded and sober so that we are able to complete the work! **Today, let us remember that whatever we are doing, we cannot come down from the wall.**

"UNSAVORY INFLUENCES"

Nehemiah 2:17 "Then I said to them, "You see the bad situation we are in, that Jerusalem is desolate and its gates burned by fire. Come, let us rebuild the wall of Jerusalem so that we will no longer be a reproach."

Nehemiah was a man of principle. He was also a man of great wisdom. After receiving permission from King Artaxerxes to go and rebuild Jerusalem, Nehemiah went and inspected everything that was there. The city had been burned down. The wall was destroyed. The few inhabitants were morally defeated. His strategy was very simple. Put the wall back up first. This served a two-fold purpose. First, it would allow them to work safely on the internal parts of the city. Secondly, it would keep unsavory influences out. This is where we find our spiritual gem in this text. Walls served a valuable purpose in Nehemiah's day. A city without a wall was a city under constant siege. As a spiritual defense mechanism, a wall is the perfect way to screen influences and decided what we allow in and what we push away. The world bombards us with constant temptation, people bring drama and Satan sends emissaries to test us, so we need a defense. We need to have our own wall, without breaches and without fissures. **Today, remember that it is up to us what we allow into our lives.**

_____

_____

_____

_____

_____

_____

_____

_____

_____

_____

_____

_____

_____

_____

_____

_____

_____

_____

_____

_____

_____

_____

"THE SILENT TREATMENT"

Nehemiah 2:12 "...And I arose in the night, I and a few men with me. I did not tell anyone what my God was putting into my mind to do for Jerusalem..."

Have you ever had a vision or mission given to you from God? Have you ever shared it with someone who promptly chided you for being crazy or for being too ambitious? When Nehemiah received the vision from God to rebuild Jerusalem, there was really only one person who knew Nehemiah's plans and that was the king, Artaxerxes. He announced his intention to the king to rebuild Judah. Nehemiah reminds his readers that the reason the king said yes is because the "good hand of my God" was on Nehemiah. There was a shift, however, when he actually got to Jerusalem. He went out at night so as not to arouse suspicion of neighbors. He also took some men with him, but he did not tell them what God had given him. His plans were very ambitious and it would require a great deal of faith to start what God sent him to do. The last thing that he needed was discouragement or fear from the inside. He kept this to himself until it was the proper time to reveal it to his cohorts. Today, remember that what God has shown us, he may not have shown those around us. **Today, let us go quietly about our business until it is the proper time to reveal God's plan.**

_____

_____

_____

_____

_____

_____

_____

_____

_____

_____

_____

_____

_____

_____

_____

_____

_____

_____

_____

_____

_____

_____

"REVOLUTIONARY RENEWAL"

1 Corinthians 2:16 "...But we have the mind of Christ."

Having the "mind of "Christ" seems simple until we try to carry out what is necessary to display what it means. Having the mind of Christ means putting the needs of others before ours. It means submitting to God's authority. It means loving our enemies, forgiving others and being willing to hear and act on the truth. This is not for the faint of heart and it takes more than willpower. It actually takes a revolution. It takes a literal rebellion where we must rebel against our flesh and its desires. That rebellion is led by the Holy Spirit. We must follow His leading and submit to His will for us. True revolution causes us to change our thinking and not die thinking the same way. It begins in the renewed mind and is manifested in actions that are decisively different from actions that would occur in our "pre-revolutionary" mentality. The only way to truly be revolutionary is through the renewing of the mind through Christ Jesus. **Today, let the Spirit of renewal be at work within us and let us demonstrate Christlikeness through a renewed approach to life.**

"FINE SOUNDING ARGUMENTS"

Leviticus 19:31 "You must not turn to mediums or spiritists; do not seek them out, or you will be defiled by them. I am the LORD your God."

Unfortunately, the church is under an internal attack. What used to be sacred is no longer sacred. The Bible is nothing more than a prop on the pulpit. As churches move to more of a business paradigm, and they seek to increase numbers, the messages are becoming more watered down, humanistic and, in a sense, life threatening. Many so-called pastors are nothing more than mediums for unsound doctrine and New Age, New Thought concepts. We can never get so "bold" and "innovative" with our preaching that it no longer involves actually using the Bible! Our words are never to be taken as more authoritative than God's word. If the Bible is not being preached, the message is merely being fabricated on the fly. Instead of getting all excited about all of these "-ations". Revel-ation, manifest-ation, delcar-ation, we should, instead, get excited about the ONE (Christ) who makes them all possible. Seek God first before seeking the things of God. **Today, let us prioritize in such a way that Jesus is given the preeminence that He so deserves.**

JUNE 17TH

"SHADOW VS SUBSTANCE I"

Hebrews 10:1 "The Law is only a shadow of the good things to come, not the realities themselves."

Many times, we are hung up on rules and regulations. In church, legalism and religiosity often take precedent over grace. We have constrictions for everything. Too many churches operate like the Pharisees, sometimes stifling worship and even being so legalistic that they cause people to leave the church. Much of what we hold sacred in the church are simply man-made traditions that we cling to for security. The Law, in the same way, although not man-made, definitely caused men to stay stuck in tradition. This is why Jesus was so despised. He was disruptive to their traditions and to their man-made regulations. If only we could understand that the grace of God transcends regulations. The grace of God was made a reality in Jesus Christ. The shadow can accomplish nothing. Why would we cling to a shadow? As soon as the light shifts, so does the shadow. Jesus Christ is the reality. **Today, let us remember that the shadow is not enough. We need the reality that is in Jesus.**

"SHADOW VS SUBSTANCE II"

Colossians 2:17 "…things which are a mere shadow of what is to come; but the substance belongs to Christ."

The apostle Paul battled many heretics who were attacking and seeking to infiltrate the Colossian church. Some were saying that the people needed Jesus and the Law to be justified. Others were saying that there were special festivals and Sabbaths that had to be kept. Still, others were into angel worship and asceticism (harsh treatment of the body). Paul made a clear distinction that we would be wise to heed. He called the Law and the things associated with the Law, a shadow. Meaning that they existed but their source was forthcoming. Anytime a shadow is cast, there has to be something causing the shadow. Often times, we see a person's shadow before we ever see them. That shadow does not give us details, only a partial understanding of the one casting it. Shadows can even exaggerate features like height. That is what the Law was, a precursor to the coming of the one who would fulfill it; a partial understanding of who God really is. Jesus Christ is the body that cast the shadow. He is the fullness of God in bodily form. He is the one who made grace and truth a reality for us. **Today, let us thank God for the reality of Jesus Christ and His revelation of the reality of God unto us**.

JUNE 19TH

"LET MY WORKS SPEAK FOR ME"

1 Samuel 16:7 "But the LORD said to Samuel, "Do not look at his appearance or at the height of his stature, because I have rejected him; for God sees not as man sees, for man looks at the outward appearance, but the LORD looks at the heart."

We spend a great deal of time trying to impress people. It's easy, too. People only see what you show them and therefore, are easily manipulated by outward appearances. There is a reason why confidence (con) men/women are so successful. They take down our natural defenses by appearing as something that they are not. As Christians, there is no conning. While not always readily apparent, insincere faith has a way of exposing itself. In our rush to impress folks, we tend to wear our faith on our sleeves. We buy Jesus bumper stickers, we buy large Bibles, and we condemn those who say Happy Holidays rather than Merry Christmas. None of these things are impressive to God. A sincere heart is, though. David's brothers were all more impressive looking than he was. But God chose David because of his sincere heart. Why waste money on crosses, bumper stickers and holy paraphernalia to say that we are a Christian? Out of a sincere heart, our works will speak for us. **Today, let our lives be what others see and know that we serve the Living God!**

_____

_____

_____

_____

_____

_____

_____

_____

_____

_____

_____

_____

_____

_____

_____

_____

_____

_____

_____

_____

JUNE 20TH

"A KING'S GLORY FOR A SLAVE'S WAGE"

Philippians 2:6,7 "...who, although He existed in the form of God, did not regard equality with God a thing to be grasped, but emptied Himself, taking the form of a bond-servant..."

I think as Christians, we often lose sight of the extravagance of Christ's sacrifice. We have diminished this in favor of more popular teachings or as though we deserved what He did. Scripture says that He existed in the form of God i.e. was God, same in essence as the Father; but He took the form of a bondservant, the lowest servant in the hierarchy. He did not lose an ounce of His divinity in doing this. If you have ever watched Undercover Boss where the boss shows up as an employee; regardless of how he's dressed, he's still the boss. The same is true of the Lord Jesus. Jesus, although He showed up at the worksite (this planet) in overalls, was still God aka the Boss. The largesse of this act lies in the fact that it was voluntary! Would you give up glory to come and be a servant in your own home that you built? Would give your life for those that would not receive you? I can speak for myself and say that it would have been an easy decision...I would have stayed in heaven. **Today, let us thank God that Jesus did not stay and decided, before time began, to come and die for our sins!**

_____

_____

_____

_____

_____

_____

_____

_____

_____

_____

_____

_____

_____

_____

_____

_____

_____

_____

_____

_____

"HE IS STILL WORKING"

Psalm 138:8 "The LORD will accomplish what concerns me; Your lovingkindness, O LORD, is everlasting; Do not forsake the works of Your hands."

We often hear the saying, "God has a plan for your life." We know this to be true. The eternality of God, the finality of His judgments, His omniscience and His Word bear this out. Good works were prepared in advance for us to do. Jeremiah 29:11 is prolifically quoted. God's word cannot return to Him void, but must accomplish that which it set out to do. We've heard all of these things. We should believe all of these things. In the same vein, let us turn our attention to Jesus. Although Joseph, who taught Jesus carpentry, has been out of the carpentry business for thousands of years, Jesus is STILL in the business of smoothing out knots, sanding rough edges and taking raw materials that have no form or use and making them useful! Jesus is still working on us. We are continuous improvement projects. **Today, let us thank Jesus for the work that He has done in our lives, for the knots that He has worked out, for the edges that He has sanded down and for making us useful!**

JUNE 22ND

"BELIEVE GOD"

Luke 8:50 "But when Jesus heard this, He answered him, "Do not be afraid any longer; only believe, and she will be made well."

The story of Jairus could probably be applied to all of us. The starting and stopping. The interruptions to our needs. The anxiety. The unbelief. Life presents us with many dilemmas. There are many junctions in life where we have decisions to make. We have faith decisions and life decisions, which are connected to those faith decisions. At one point during Jairus's journey with Jesus, back to his daughter who was dying, he came into contact with some people who told him that his daughter was dead. They told him to leave Jesus alone. And Jesus gives Jairus some advice that we would all be wise to heed. When Jesus sensed Jairus's anxiety, he simply said, "Do not be afraid any longer; only believe, and she will be made well." A tall order for a man with a dying daughter to whom it was just confirmed that she was actually dead. A tall order for any of us struggling with any issue. But this was God in the flesh telling this powerful man, who had humbled himself to come to Jesus, to be of good courage and believe what I have said to you. **Today, let us remember: 1) God, give me the faith to believe what You say 2) Give me the strength and courage to do what You say and 3) Give me the wisdom and discernment to know that it was You who said it.**

_____

_____

_____

_____

_____

_____

_____

_____

_____

_____

_____

_____

_____

_____

_____

_____

_____

_____

_____

_____

JUNE 23RD

"MOVING ON UP?"

Matthew 26:15 "…What are you willing to give me to betray Him to you?" And they weighed out thirty pieces of silver to him."

Some sects of Christianity teach that moving up is necessarily, positive. If it is an upward move, it had to come from God. The rationale is usually based on Proverbs 10:22 which reads "It is the blessing of the LORD that makes rich, and He adds no sorrow to it." This discounts the thought that a blessing can come in the form of a loss or even a setback. I would venture to say that every promotion is not necessarily from God and every demotion is not necessarily from the devil. Consider getting a promotion on a job, but in being promoted, you work so much more that you lose touch with your family. The paycheck may be bigger, but is it worth it? Sometimes, God does addition by subtraction; He removes the extra baggage for us to get to the goal that He has for us. Sometimes, the devil does subtraction by addition; he adds the extra baggage to keep us from the goal that God has for us. Judas made a decision based on those 30 pieces of sliver. It was upwardly mobile, but look at what it cost him. Let us not be so concerned with going up that we don't recognize who pushed the button on the elevator. **Today, remember this, whenever we have a vertical move (up or down) pending, we should pray for discernment and wisdom!**

JUNE 24TH

"YOU CAN COME HOME"

Malachi 3:7 "...Return to Me, and I will return to you," says the LORD of hosts."

We have a thing in the church where we only believe that God will forgive certain sins. We also put a scale on sin. Some sins are bigger than others. Sexual sin, for instance, is considered more egregious than lying. But, taken in context, lying can potentially have graver consequences. God does not measure sin. In His holiness, no sin is tolerable. But in His grace, all sin is forgivable. That's because God is a redeemer. He is a purchaser of the lost; one who is able to renew purpose and revitalize broken relationships. Nothing is too hard for God. This is the reason Christ was sent, to redeem us and to act as the mediator between God (the Father) and man. Water to wine, no problem for Jesus. Done by only speaking a word. Brokenness to wholeness, no problem for Jesus. The woman with the issue of blood was healed instantly. There is one thing that requires a response. When God offers redemption to us, we have to turn to Him. Repentance is not His problem to fix, it is up to us to turn to Him. He cannot turn for us, we have to respond to his gracious call. **Today, let us remember that God has not moved and He waits with open arms to receive the brokenhearted.**

_____

_____

_____

_____

_____

_____

_____

_____

_____

_____

_____

_____

_____

_____

_____

_____

_____

_____

_____

_____

_____

JUNE 25TH

"LIKE HIM"

1 John 3:2 "Beloved, we are now children of God, and what we will be has not yet been revealed. We know that when Christ appears, we will be like Him, for we will see Him as He is."

We often, and rightly, repeat the phrase "all things work together for the good of those who love the Lord..." When saying this, we must also be cognizant of the fact that the phrase all things doesn't exclude anything. This includes trials, hurt, pain and suffering. God is able to work through all of these things and bring some good from them. That good may be far off in the distance. That is the beauty of God, He sees what we cannot. He knows what we do not. God is always in control. We are becoming what He desires, as we submit to His will. As Christians we ought to reckon ourselves as slabs of marble, life as the chisel and God as the sculptor. He is using the chisel of life to conform us into the image of His Son causing ALL things to work together to produce a holy masterpiece. We do not yet see what we will be. We do not know the length of the process. But, we do know that there is a purpose behind every predicament. **Today, let us remember that as we walk closer to the coming of Christ, and we keep our eyes fixed on Him, we will be as He is, when He comes.**

JUNE 26TH

"EMPIRICAL EVIDENCE FOR THE UNEMPIRICAL GOD"

Psalm19:1 "...The heavens are telling of the glory of God; and their expanse is declaring the work of His hands."

It is amazing to hear some of the arguments against God. One of the most significant arguments is that God cannot be proven empirically. It is true that there is not a way to quantify God. He is not a science experiment. We cannot isolate a molecule of His being in a test tube or determine the mass of a molecule of His being in a mass spectrometer. This is mostly because God, Himself, is a Spirit and cannot be seen. Those who actually saw Jesus were blessed! So are those of us who believe and have not seen Him. But physicists, astrophysicists, chemists, evolutionary biologists and a host of others make up the army of skeptics that are anti-God and, by default anti- anything supernatural. But Scripture tells us clearly that the creation bears the marks of God's handiwork. Scripture also tells us that God, that the invisible attributes of God have been seen since the beginning of time. He has measured the universe by the span of His hand! So, while we cannot put God under a microscope, He can indeed be experienced. He has left traces of his existence, and He did visit us in the person of Jesus Christ. **Today, look for Him in the small things around you. Marvel and wonder at the work of His hands!**

JUNE 27TH

"EMPTY MY CUP"

Mark 12:30 "...AND YOU SHALL LOVE THE LORD YOUR GOD WITH ALL YOUR HEART, AND WITH ALL YOUR SOUL, AND WITH ALL YOUR MIND, AND WITH ALL YOUR STRENGTH.'"

Religious Jews recite the Shema three times daily as part of their devotional life; no Sabbath worship is conducted in the synagogue without its proclamation. When Jesus was asked what the greatest commandment was, he quoted the Shema, which can be found in Deuteronomy 6. If this commandment is followed, all of life flows from it. If we love God like this, by default, what we do, we will do to please Him. Imagine loving God will all of our heart, undivided by the cares and issues of this world. Loving Him with all of our soul, the very part of us that makes us who we are. Loving Him with all of our mind, so much so that our every thought centered on Him! Loving Him with all of our ability, so that every action carried out by us was a reflection of His glory! That would leave nothing in our cups. We'd be exhausted, but in a good way. When we are emptied out, God is able to refill us. **Pray this prayer, today: God, after I have given everything possible, physically and spiritually to You and to others, restore and replenish me so I can do it all over again tomorrow.**

JUNE 28TH

"ILLUMINATED"

Ephesians 1:18 "I pray that the eyes of your heart may be enlightened..."

The book of Ephesians shows the heart of Paul, the pastor and apostle, towards these people. He prayed mightily for them. Here, Paul prays for the eyes of the hearts of the Ephesian believers to be enlightened. It is better translated as "having been enlightened" which points to a past action with present ramifications. The enlightenment, in this case, is an understanding of just how much God loves the saints, and how His power towards the saints was manifested in the resurrection of Jesus Christ. The fact that the enlightenment is written in a passive sense indicates that the enlightenment had to come from an external source. That source is the Holy Spirit. Nothing that God says or does can be discerned, understood or comprehended apart from the revelation of the Holy Spirit. It is the Holy Spirit who gives utterance when prophecy, teaching or preaching goes forth. The Holy Spirit brings all things to our remembrance. The Holy Spirit knows the deep things of God and reveals to us what we are able to withstand. It is the Holy Spirit who opened the eyes of the men in Emmaus as they recognized Jesus in the breaking of the bread. **Today, let us ask for the Holy Spirit to give us enlightened eyes, wisdom and understanding of His ways.**

_____

_____

_____

_____

_____

_____

_____

_____

_____

_____

_____

_____

_____

_____

_____

_____

_____

_____

_____

_____

_____

_____

"TRUE LEADERSHIP"

John 13:12 "When Jesus had washed their feet and put on His outer garments, He reclined with them again and asked, "Do you know what I have done for you?"

When it comes to leadership, there is no shortage of books and seminars that have been released on this subject. Everyone has the winning formula for being a leader. Everyone has the seven steps or the seven thousand steps to being an effective leader of people. Having been in the workforce and having worked in administrative positions, I have come to the conclusion that every so-called boss is not necessarily a great leader and every great leader doesn't have to be the boss. Jesus was a great leader, evidenced by His disciples' willingness to follow Him, although not immediately, even into death. He taught them to serve first. Servanthood always precedes leadership. Many times, when people are thrust into leadership positions without first having served, the results can be disastrous. Serving prepares the heart of a leader, develops empathy, and it develops humility. This is why Jesus led by example and taught His disciples that they must be servant of all, if they ever wished to lead any. Leadership is a lifestyle and a calling. **Today, let us remember that we should lead not with the index finger, but rather with the feet and not ask anyone to do anything that we are unwilling to do.**

JUNE 30TH

"LOVE ANYWAY"

John 3:16 "For God so loved the world, that He gave His only begotten Son..."

Rejection stinks. It is painful and hurtful. It reminds us of our inadequacies. It reminds us that what we offer may not be desirable. Sometimes we are rejected even when we are doing things out of love. Evangelism comes to mind. We evangelize and tell people about the love of Jesus because of our love for them and our desire to see them saved. We give love to our children, to our mates, to those around us and sometimes, that love is not reciprocated. Do not be discouraged. Love anyway. Jesus reminds us that a servant is not greater than his/her master. Scripture tells us that Jesus came to His own, and they did not receive Him. They rejected Him. The religious leaders rejected Him. The people of the Gerasenes rejected Him. His own brothers rejected Him. But Jesus loved them anyway. Unsaved sinners i.e. those who have rejected Jesus are also loved. Surprised? Scripture bears this out plainly: God demonstrated His love in this, while we were yet sinners, Christ died for us. Even with his last breaths, Jesus uttered "Father, forgive them, for they know not what they do." Just as Jesus experienced pain and rejection by freely loving us, if we love unselfishly as God loves, we too will sometimes experience pain and rejection. **Today, let us love anyway, just as Christ loved us.**

_____

_____

_____

_____

_____

_____

_____

_____

_____

_____

_____

_____

_____

_____

_____

_____

_____

_____

_____

_____

_____

_____

"TRANSPLANT RECIPIENT"

James 1:21 "Therefore, putting aside all filthiness and all that remains of wickedness, in humility receive the word implanted, which is able to save your souls."

My late wife was a physician. She was excellent. Part of her excellence stemmed from her ability to do minor procedures in her office and not have to refer patients out to specialists. She had several patients who needed organ transplants, but who were not eligible for one reason or another. That was something that she was not qualified to do. When an organ fails, it must be replaced. When it is replaced, there is always the chance that the body will reject the newly transplanted organ. As you can imagine, this is an arduous process but, one designed to improve the condition of the transplant recipient. God's Word, in the same way, is like receiving a transplant. God places us under the anesthesia of the Holy Ghost and uses the double-edged sword of the Word to continue to do surgery on us. His Word replaces filthiness and wickedness, as James alludes to. It removes what is not like Him in order to put in what is. The discomfort experienced while we are healing helps us to see that God is good and has done a mighty work in us! God, empower us to do Your will. **Today, let us not reject the transplant, but receive it gladly.**

_____

_____

_____

_____

_____

_____

_____

_____

_____

_____

_____

_____

_____

_____

_____

_____

_____

_____

_____

_____

_____

_____

"THE SWORD OF MY MOUTH"

Revelation 2:16 "Therefore repent; or else I am coming to you quickly, and I will make war against them with the sword of My mouth."

Whenever Jesus preached, it was powerful. Large crowds would become small assemblies. Powerful men would become insecure boys, grasping at the straws of pride and hubris to make themselves feel better. Lives were changed. Perspectives were transformed. People were set free. Jesus preached with an uncompromising truthfulness. Not necessarily political incorrectness, but just blunt truth spoken in love. He and John the Baptist preached the same because it was the same Holy Spirit who empowered them. When Jesus references the sword of My mouth it is understood that He is talking about using His words to accomplish something. His judgments are always right, final and exact. Once He speaks, it is finished. This is God talking, after all! The sword of His mouth is very sharp, but it is only as effective as we allow it to be! The Word is only advantageous to us if we are willing to let it crush us, cleanse us and then build us up. It doesn't get real until we realize that what we are reading is for us before it's for anyone else. **Today, let us not despise the rebuke, correction, teaching and training in righteousness that the Word of God provides to us.**

_____

_____

_____

_____

_____

_____

_____

_____

_____

_____

_____

_____

_____

_____

_____

_____

_____

_____

_____

_____

_____

"BROKEN CHAINS"

Colossians 2:14a "…having canceled the debt ascribed to us in the decrees that stood against us. He took it away, nailing it to the cross!"

Wars are often fought for the cause of Freedom. I can recall Operation Enduring Freedom, a war to which my late wife was deployed. It still rages on, today. Wars are intended to have an end, victor on one side and vanquished on the other side. Ideally, the victor fights and wins with the right motives, protecting the greater good, and the vanquished foes are defeated because they wanted to do harm to the greater good. We talk a lot about being "victorious" without realizing that the greatest victory ever, was one that we had nothing to do with, and everything to gain from: Calvary. A Christian's greatest victory on this side is not monetary or material, but rather, spiritual. Christ has secured our place in eternity, our independence from the rule of Satan, our redemption in the eyes of God, and seated us in the heavenly places! Our freedom was paid for with the blood of Jesus. Our debt was paid by the blood of Jesus. **Today, let us celebrate freedom and His victory over our enemies!**

_____

_____

_____

_____

_____

_____

_____

_____

_____

_____

_____

_____

_____

_____

_____

_____

_____

_____

_____

_____

_____

_____

JULY 4TH

"INDEPENDENCE DAY"

Galatians 5:1 "It is for freedom that Christ has set us free. Stand firm, then, and do not be encumbered once more by a yoke of slavery."

One of the most liberating aspects of Christianity is the freedom that comes through Christ. Freedom from legalism. Freedom from bondage to sin. Freedom to do right and not worry about the consequences. Freedom to love God openly and mightily. When Paul was talking to the Galatians, he talked openly about how those Judaizers (those seeking to infuse Jewish customs with Christianity) were pulling the Galatian church back into slavery. If Jesus Christ redeemed us from the curse of the Law, why would we go back to those things? If He redeemed us from the dietary regulations, when and where to worship, the statutes, the sacrifices and the rigmarole of trying to keep every single jot and tittle of the Law why would we subject ourselves to that again? On this particular day, we celebrate the date that America, in its embryonic state, fought and won the battle against tyrannical rule and unjust taxation. Why would we go back to that? We were sold as slaves to sin, and Christ won the victory by going to Calvary and giving His life. That freedom had a cost. It cost Jesus His own life. **Today, let no one take you captive with legalism. Let us celebrate our independence!**

_____

_____

_____

_____

_____

_____

_____

_____

_____

_____

_____

_____

_____

_____

_____

_____

_____

_____

_____

_____

_____

_____

_____

JULY 5TH

"IT'S NOT GOD'S FAULT"

Judges 11:34 "When Jephthah came to his house at Mizpah, behold, his daughter was coming out to meet him with tambourines and with dancing. Now she was his one and only child; besides her he had no son or daughter."

Jephthah was a skilled military warrior who had a faith complex. As is often the case, we tend to depend on ourselves, especially if we see ourselves as a strong person. The story involving Jephthah is a tragic one. He wanted to win a military victory to be accepted by the people. He made a vow to God that if victory was secured he'd sacrifice the first thing that came out of his doors when he returned home from battle. That happened to be his only daughter. Jephthah went through with his vow, but was devastated. Atheists and skeptics use this story often to discredit God, to highlight his mean-spiritedness. "Why would God allow such a thing?" they ask. Well, if we examine the story more closely, we see that the problem lies on Jephthah's shoulders. The time of Judges was a very tumultuous time in the history of the Israelites. Jephthah's painful vow really shows a lack of faith. It begs the question of whether or not he really trusted God, and, therefore, tried to add a safety net in the form of a vow. This dilemma was one of his own making, just like many of the issues that we face. **Today, let us know that God is not responsible for human behavior, humans are.**

JULY 6TH

"REVOLUTION?"

Judges 17:6 "In those days there was no king in Israel; every man did what was right in his own eyes."

What happens when there is no king? What happens in societies where there are no laws? What happens when God is dethroned and self is enthroned? Lawlessness. Anarchy. Greed. Selfishness. Self-centeredness. Relativism. Sound familiar? Sure, it does, because it is what we see around us every day. God is an afterthought. Man is the captain of his own destiny. Man is the penultimate being in the universe. And as such, man will desire whatever man wants, even at the expense of others. We live in a time where even the basic things like gender, facts and truth are open for debate. There is so much confusion in the world. The reason? There is no King. Everyone has decided that their truth is whatever they say it is and everyone has their own version of the truth. This cannot be so. Relative and absolute truth cannot coexist. Something is either true or it is false. If everyone has their own version of the truth, how do we really know what the truth is? **Today, remember this: there is One who is King of Kings. He is also the Truth. Stand on His truth and minimize the confusion of the world.**

_____

_____

_____

_____

_____

_____

_____

_____

_____

_____

_____

_____

_____

_____

_____

_____

_____

_____

_____

_____

_____

_____

JULY 7TH

"NEVER SATISFIED"

Luke 7:33, 34 "For John the Baptist has come eating no bread and drinking no wine, and you say, 'He has a demon!' 34"The Son of Man has come eating and drinking, and you say, 'Behold, a gluttonous man and a drunkard, a friend of tax collectors and sinners!'"

Man is a fickle creature. We have many frailties and many issues that we deal with. Sometimes I wonder if we can ever be satisfied. In this passage, Jesus is dealing with the Jews and He has just testified concerning John the Baptist. Jesus addressed the crowd, many of whom had rejected the baptism of repentance by John. The bible says in John 2:24 that Jesus knows what is in the heart of man. Jesus knew exactly what was in these peoples' hearts. He knew that they could never be satisfied. John the Baptist neither ate nor drank, and they still found fault with him! Jesus came and they found fault with him too! Whenever we are led by our own desires and not by the Spirit of God, we will never be satisfied. The bible says in Proverbs 27:20 that there are three things that are never satisfied: Sheol (the grave) and Abaddon (the pit of destruction) and the eyes of man. Scripture says godliness with contentment is great gain. **Today, let us be satisfied with the provision of God in our lives!**

JULY 8TH

"ARE WE GODS?"

Isaiah 44:6 "Thus saith the LORD the King of Israel, and his redeemer the LORD of hosts; I am the first, and I am the last; and beside me there is no God."

I remember, as a kid, watching the movie Ghostbusters. This is still one of my favorite movies of all times. There was a scene in the movie where the villain in the film, asked Dan Aykroyd if he was a god, to which he rightly replied, no. He was 100% correct, but, there are many churches that teach otherwise. There are churches that teach what is dubbed as "little god theology" based on an erroneous interpretation of Genesis 1:11, 12 and Psalm 82:6. The problem with the Genesis scripture is that while other things reproduce, God actually creates. Therefore, the process is totally different. God can call anything into being that He desires and have complete control over its characteristics. Reproduction does not allow us to control anything. The second issue with Psalm 82:6 is twofold. The interpretation of the word "god" which is taken to mean one who lords over people i.e. earthly leaders or representatives of God is problematic. Secondly, verse seven points to the mortality of said "gods" who were supernatural beings who would be punished with death. One thing is painfully obvious: God is not making copies of Himself so that we can compete for His glory. **Today, be content to be fearfully and wonderfully made. God does not need any help or any competition.**

"THE BODY BEAUTIFUL"

1 Corinthians 12:20 "But now there are many members, but one body."

What if we thought of the body of Christ in a biological sense? The body of Christ, according to the apostle Paul is made up of many members but each member has a different function. So, the hands of the body are people there to touch the world and heal the sick. The arms of the body are people there to be the compassion of Christ, to hug those who are in need of love, and to embrace all who come to Christ out of a dying world. The feet are people who are there to take the gospel to remote nations and to the lost in the world. The feet are shod with the gospel of peace and Scripture says in Isaiah 52:7, How beautiful on the mountains are the feet of those who bring good news, who proclaim peace, who bring good tidings, who proclaim salvation, who say to Zion, 'Your God reigns'! There are also some who are the enzymes in the stomach. When food enters the stomach, enzymes and acids begin to break the food down and convert it into usable things like energy, fat, new muscle, etc. In the same way, there are those within the body of Christ who are used by the Holy Spirit to assist with the transformation of new believers. There are people who are the immune system of the church whose discernment thwarts attacks before they happen. All, through the Holy Spirit's power! **Today, look at God in amazement at how He has equipped His church, and bless His name!**

_____

_____

_____

_____

_____

_____

_____

_____

_____

_____

_____

_____

_____

_____

_____

_____

_____

_____

_____

_____

_____

_____

_____

_____

JULY 10TH

"ANTI-DARWINIAN"

Genesis 1:1 "In the beginning God created the heavens and the earth."

Science has waged war against those whom they label as "creationists" with the singular shout that there is no God; and, therefore, there is no Creator! Many scientists believe that all that we see rose from a primordial ooze that contained all of the genetic material necessary to create every life form on earth. The problems with Darwinian evolution are complex. If everything sprang from the big bang, including the amoeba from which all life supposedly sprang, and the only thing that existed in the beginning was an infinitesimal amount of energy, and that energy was converted into matter, where did the information come from that told the matter what it would become? Informationless energy does not have the ability to become informed matter. Energy and information are two distinctly different things. Yet, we are to believe that planets, cats, dogs, water, rocks, fishes, elements and all else came from the same place? If the amoeba came from the same informationless energy that everything else came from, where did the genetic information within the amoeba come from to tell it to become the entire biological system? Someone had to tell the energy and the matter what to become. **Today, rest in knowing that the someone was God.**

JULY 11TH

"AN UNPAYABLE DEBT"

Job 33:23-24 "If there is an angel as mediator for him, One out of a thousand, To remind a man what is right for him, then let him be gracious to him, and say, 'Deliver him from going down to the pit, I have found a ransom';"

The national debt, the amount of money that the United States government owes to, various creditors, is in the trillions of dollars. If every US citizen was asked to pay a share of the debt, we would immediately owe hundreds of thousands of dollars. That would be a shock to the system of many Americans, many of whom live check to check. Now, imagine an even greater debt than that, payable at once. Every man owes a debt to God because of our sins. But that debt cannot be settled monetarily. Job hints here that a ransom is owed for the soul of a man, but the soul is so costly that man cannot ever dream of redeeming it. The angel in this scripture "finds" a ransom for the soul in peril. He acts as a mediator for the man, who has one foot on the pit and another resting perilously on a banana peel. How marvelous is the wisdom of God! Angelic mediation is an Old Testament biblical concept, but the angels only mediated where God allowed. The wisdom of God sent One who is able to redeem, once for all. Jesus Christ is the mediator who is able to settle our debt fully. **Today, know that He did not find a ransom, He is the ransom.**

_____

_____

_____

_____

_____

_____

_____

_____

_____

_____

_____

_____

_____

_____

_____

_____

_____

_____

_____

_____

JULY 12TH

"YOU DIDN'T KNOW"

Deuteronomy 8:16 "In the wilderness He fed you manna which your fathers did not know, that He might humble you and that He might test you, to do good for you in the end."

"Why am I going through this?" That is a common question that we all ask as we journey towards Zion. This life is fraught with problems and ugly realities that we do not always understand. There are tests of our faith, tests of our desire to do good and tests of our obedience. The Israelites witnessed and experienced all of this. But Scripture informs us that everything that we endure is simply to humble us. Scripture also informs us here that God will do good for us in the end. The problem comes when we cannot see the end. I have struggled mightily with this very idea. I've asked, "God, can you just skip to the good part?" But, if that happened, how would I gain wisdom? How would I gain a greater appreciation for the good? How would I learn who God really is? The end may be far off and the path to it, difficult to endure, but thanks be to God for His grace! During this time for the Israelites, they never went hungry, their clothes never wore out and their feet never swelled, after 40 years in the wilderness. **Today, let us realize that although we do not see the end or know the end, we can be confident that God is working all things out for the good of those who love Him.**

WALK WITH ME: God Seen, God Heard, God Revealed

_____

_____

_____

_____

_____

_____

_____

_____

_____

_____

_____

_____

_____

_____

_____

_____

_____

_____

_____

_____

_____

_____

JULY 13TH

"PRIVATE CONVERSATIONS"

John 12:29 "So the crowd of people who stood by and heard it were saying that it had thundered; others were saying, "An angel has spoken to Him."

There are times when we desperately want to know what God is doing. As human subjects with finite intellects, we see the manifestations of the work happening in the spiritual realm but, we don't always understand what we are seeing. Greeks wanted to see Jesus and the crowds began to celebrate Him and sought to make Him into a pop-culture personality. Jesus prayed for God the Father to glorify the Son. That conversation was interpreted as thunder by some. By others, it was interpreted as an angel having spoken to Jesus. But to John, it was a fully realized conversation between two of the three members of the Godhead. John understood what others misunderstood due to his physical and spiritual proximity to the Lord Jesus Christ. Those conversations between the members of the Godhead are not always readily discernable to us, and sometimes, rightfully so. What we are to do is to accept the outcome of the conversation! Your will be done, Lord! The outcome of the life of Jesus was decided from eternity. Far be it from us to seek to turn Jesus into a celebrity and adore Him with earthly glory, when it was the glory from heaven that mattered. That glory was manifested in His death. **Today, let us realize that when God has spoken, we must accept the outcome, for His glory.**

"THE POWER OF THE TONGUE"

Jeremiah 33:3 "Call to Me and I will answer you, and I will tell you great and mighty things, which you do not know."

David wrote in the 22nd Psalm that the LORD has not despised or detested the torment of the afflicted, He as not hidden His face but rather, He has attended to His cry for help. There is power in the tongue. When there are things that we desire deep insight into, we must use the power of the tongue to call out to God. He instructs us plainly to "call to Me…" That beckoning and exhortation to us to cry out to God is God's call to us, to worship Him. The blessing is that when we call out to God, He answers us! This was a foreign concept, especially in the culture during the time of this writing. Lesser gods were mute, ineffective, immobile and unworthy of worship. God even says so through the prophet Isaiah when He asks, pointedly, "Who is like Me? Let Him answer!" God knew that no answer was forthcoming from any other god because He has no competitor. Yet, God does answer, in His own time. But he still invites us to call to Him, to commune with Him, to be intimate with him. In this intimate relationship, He promises to tell us great and mighty things, which we do not know. There is power in the tongue, not to instruct God or to command God, but rather to call out to Him! **Today, let us call out with the expectation of an answer from the Almighty.**

"HE LEANED IN"

Psalm 40:1 "For the choirmaster. A Psalm of David. I waited patiently for the LORD; He inclined to me and heard my cry."

It is one thing for God to hear us but is another for Him to take a personal interest in our affairs. As a kid, if we got hurt or we fell somewhere in the house, and our parents heard it, they'd come to see if we were ok. We have baby monitors in the rooms of small children so that, if we hear something out of the ordinary, we can go in to investigate. This nurturing aspect of our humanity came to us from the Divinity. God created us in His image and gave us some of his transitive properties, namely, the ability to care and show empathy. So, here, David tells: 1) He waited patiently for the LORD 2) God inclined to him i.e. God leaned in and ministered to him and 3) He heard David's cry. God didn't need to lean in to hear David better; He leaned in for David's sake so that David would be able to sense His presence. Sometimes, sensing the presence of God can be the difference between hope and despair! David gives us wisdom: waiting required patience on the part of David. While praying for patience may not seem a wise thing to do, living a patient life is most certainly wise. David also reminds us that God not only leaned in and listened but He also acted by pulling David from the clay. **Today, know that God hears, sees and will act!**

_____

_____

_____

_____

_____

_____

_____

_____

_____

_____

_____

_____

_____

_____

_____

_____

_____

_____

_____

_____

_____

_____

"GODLY DISCOMFORT"

Ezekiel 4:8 "Now behold, I will tie you up with ropes so you cannot turn from side to side until you have finished the days of your siege."

As the years pass by, our lives change drastically. When we follow God, there are times of extreme discomfort. Ezekiel was asked to prophesy against Israel and Judah by lying on his left side for 390 days and then on his right side for 40 days. This was serious, but Ezekiel was so focused on God that he did not focus on His discomfort. As we continue to walk with God, we have to become much more focused on God. The deeper we go with God, the more intense our lives become. That's because we are in a spiritual battle and the fighting becomes more intense as we become better combatants. This is counterintuitive to the American way. Focusing on God removes our focus from the momentary bouts of discomfort. If this resonates with you, it means that God has called you to something higher than comfort or relaxation. The process of being molded on the Potter's wheel is not comfortable at all but the finished product is what He desires, not always what we desire. **Today, let us die to our comfort seeking selves and pant after the Potter who shapes us, the Master Gardener who prunes us, the Chief Architect who sketches the plans for our lives, the Sculptor who chisels off dead weight to turn us into His masterpieces.**

"NOTHING IS IMPOSSIBLE FOR HIM"

Genesis 18:14 "...Why did Sarah laugh and say, 'Can I really bear a child when I am old? Is anything too difficult for the LORD? At the appointed time I will return to you—in about a year—and Sarah will have a son."

If there is anything in this devotional that is based on any occurrence in my life, it is not embellished. Embellishment and hyperbole diminished the authenticity of any testimony. I once lifted almost 1,500 pounds. It's very true. Now, let me explain. Prior to the documented experience, if you told me that I'd lift 1,500 pounds of anything, I'd laugh at you. But I actually did lift that much weight. I was filling in areas of my yard that were bare and I put down 1,450 pounds of sand in two days; but, I did it one bag at a time. There is a lesson in everything. When we get overwhelming odds or devastating news, we tend to think of everything all at once. God gives us the strength to complete every task, but sometimes we are to do it methodically and over time. It may not be a miracle, but rather a process. The next time you feel overwhelmed, don't panic, just think about what the first step is in overcoming the obstacle and take that ONE step first. After that, then worry about the second step. **Today, let us be reminded that nothing is impossible for God, regardless of how it is accomplished.**

_____

_____

_____

_____

_____

_____

_____

_____

_____

_____

_____

_____

_____

_____

_____

_____

_____

_____

_____

_____

_____

_____

_____

JULY 18TH

"FEAR NO MAN"

Psalm 56:11 "In God I have put my trust, I shall not be afraid. What can man do to me?"

God is supreme over everyone and everything. Once we settle that in our minds, we can know that He is our refuge and our protector. David says here that he has put his trust in God. That means that I am believing what God says, I am looking to God for the answers to hard questions and I have decided that God is the end of all things for me. It also means that I don't live in fear because I know that God is my protector. So, the second part of this psalm is a question that we must ask in all of our daily endeavors: what can man do to me? Is there an enemy made of flesh who is a match for God? A boss? A co-worker? A bully? A potential convert? I think not. **Today, let us remember that men are only flesh and blood, but God is the ultimate authority.**

"ALL FEAR IS GONE"

Revelation 22:12 "Behold, I am coming quickly, and My reward is with Me, to render to every man according to what he has done."

Many people get totally spooked when the book of Revelation is mentioned. The word literally means "to uncover". What is being uncovered, the spiritual wickedness, the world system, the forces at work behind the scenes, can be a bit unnerving. When I was younger, I dreaded the 2nd coming of Jesus. The way it was preached at my church, the way my cousins always talked about the "end of the world" had me shaken. I thought what I would miss, the things that I could no longer do and what it would be like if the "world ended". I later realized that I loved the world and the things in it. I was too shallow to consider the prospect of eternity or where my soul would end up. I was focused only on temporary things! Given the prospect of facing multiple dangers, the state of the world right now and knowing that when Christ returns ALL things will be made right; I agree with John's request at the end of Revelation, "Come quickly Lord Jesus!" **Today, let us not love the world more than we love the appearing of our Lord! Let us pray for the salvation of those who are lost so that when He appears to wipe away every tear, He can wipe theirs away too!**

"I AM THE VINE"

John 15:5 "...apart from Me, you can do nothing."

In this modern age, when travelling, we are usually acutely aware of the need to charge our devices. Once, I was in the airport and I was looking for a seat in the terminal. I looked for one thing, a seat next to a power outlet. Why? We are so dependent on our electronics that we have to have those devices powered up to stay connected to our network. Should we unplug sometimes? Yes, but that's another entry for another day. But, as I searched around, I refused to sit in a place with no power. This is simply an illustration to say that we shouldn't align ourselves with dead stuff but we should always want to be seated next to a power source! Jesus Christ is the vine that supplies the power, nutrients and life to the branches! Christ is our power source! He is SEATED above all rule, authority, dominion and power and IF WE ARE IN CHRIST, we are seated in heavenly places WITH Him. Stay plugged in to the POWER and your batteries will never die! The cross makes us think of a simple question: "At which table am I seated?" If not seated with The Power, Christ, then you're seated at a dead table with no power or life. **Plug in TODAY! Let's be in prayer that someone in a dead situation today will turn and get connected with the Author of Life, Jesus Christ and live!**

"WALKING THROUGH FIRE"

Daniel 3:27 "…in regard to these men that the fire had no effect on the bodies of these men nor was the hair of their head singed, nor were their trousers damaged, nor had the smell of fire even come upon them"

Life is full of furnaces. Life is full of fiery trials. Life is full of pitfalls. Many are the afflictions of the righteous, but God delivers us from them all. There is a lesson in every furnace. Most of the time, the lesson is connected to the indomitable nature of the Almighty God and His ability to turn tragedy into triumph. When Shadrach, Meshach and Abednego were in the furnace, and the fourth man showed up, that was God's reward for their faithfulness. The other reward was their testimony and the witnesses who were there seeing this in real time. They did not even smell like smoke, although the furnace was seven times hotter than normal! The furnace experience was long enough to learn the lesson, but short enough that the smoke or fire had no ill effects. If you're in a hard situation today, keep moving in the name of Jesus! **God will bring you forth as pure gold, with no signs of the hardship. You won't even smell like smoke.**

_____

_____

_____

_____

_____

_____

_____

_____

_____

_____

_____

_____

_____

_____

_____

_____

_____

_____

_____

_____

_____

_____

JULY 22ND

"RALLY IN THE VALLEY"

1 Kings 20:28 "...This is what the LORD says: 'Because the Arameans think the LORD is a god of the hills and not of the valleys, I will deliver all this great army into your hand. Then you will know that I am the LORD."

When we are on the mountaintop, we rejoice that God has given us victory. In the distance, what do we see? Yet another mountain. What does this mean? If we're pessimists, we could dread the impending valley and the ensuing climb. The faithful will not fear the valley or the climb but rather, we rejoice at the opportunity to see another God-given victory! There is strength gained in valleys and spiritual muscles are developed during the climb! Valleys are difficult places to fight for many reasons: shadows and the sun make it difficult to see, the temperature may be different, there's even the danger of falling rocks. The Arameans thought for sure that God was limited to the hills and could not fight in the valleys. What they missed was that God's nature is not bound by circumstances. He is victorious, no matter what. Remember today that the race is not given to the swift nor the battle to the strong. The reason that the race is not given to the swift nor the battle to the strong is because the strong trust in their own strength and the swift trust in their own speed. **Today, know that victory comes when we trust in the LORD and the power of His might.**

_____

_____

_____

_____

_____

_____

_____

_____

_____

_____

_____

_____

_____

_____

_____

_____

_____

_____

_____

_____

_____

_____

_____

JULY 23RD

"WHAT IS FAITH?"

Romans 4:22 "Therefore also "it was credited to him unto righteousness."

Some believe that faith is something we pull out of a drawer when we're in a jam. Faith is not magic. Faith is living with the expectation that God is all sufficient and He cannot lie. Whatever He promised He is well able to deliver. That's how it works. Dusty i.e. unused or underused faith might as well be dead faith. If our faith is not tested and proven, when trouble comes, we can't reach into the drawer fast enough. Our faith must always be active! Trouble comes like a thief in the night, like a burglar. Would you keep your gun in a lockbox if you knew the burglar was outside the window? Exactly! Truth be told, the enemy is always outside the window. Walk by faith at all times, good and bad so that it does not wither and die when trouble comes. It is faith that says to God, "I will trust you with my entire life." **Today, let us be encouraged that God will strengthen our faith and empower us to walk in that faith, to His glory!**

JULY 24TH

"SOMEONE WOULD HAVE SNITCHED BY NOW"

I Corinthians 15:6 "After that, He appeared to more than five hundred brothers at once, most of whom are still alive, though some have fallen asleep."

The resurrection of Jesus Christ has been a point of contention for centuries. What we have to understand is that this is a historically verifiable event. While the resurrection itself was not literally witnessed, Jesus dying on the cross was, the empty tomb was and Jesus was seen for 50 days afterwards! Paul tells us that Jesus not only showed Himself to the disciples but also to a crowd of over 500. If the resurrection was merely a legend being passed off as truth, someone in that 500 would have called the disciples on it after reading about it. Historically, we accept things as truth even if they are written down 500-700 years after the fact. In light of this, the latest gospel account was ~60 years after the resurrection. That's not enough time for a legend to proliferate because there were too many living witnesses who could have refuted it! Someone in that crowd or someone who knew that the disciples were lying would've spilled the beans. **Today, believe what God's word says, He is not a man that He should lie! Jesus got UP! The grave is EMPTY and He is The Prophet, The Priest and The King of Glory!**

"REALLY NOW?"

Isaiah 58:3 "Why have we fasted, and You have not seen? Why have we humbled ourselves, and You have not noticed?" "Behold, on the day of your fast, you do as you please, and you oppress all your workers."

One of the principles woven into the fabric of America is that black people were/are inferior to white people and were therefore justifiably subjugated. That is not a racist statement, it is a verifiable fact. Benjamin Franklin, though later in favor of abolition, once opined that he wished the numbers of Africans in America were decreased and that continent belonged to "white" people because partiality towards white was "natural." Many of the founding fathers were slaveholders. We have called ourselves a Christian nation for centuries, but in all honesty, would a truly Christian nation subjugate and dehumanize people who are also made in the image of God? Isaiah reminds us of the futility of seeking after God when we do not show the love of God to our fellow human being. If we are to be a truly Christian nation, Christ must supersede ideology, politics and institutionally racist systems. **Today, be a difference-maker by following what God has required: do justice, love mercy and walk humbly before Him.**

_____

_____

_____

_____

_____

_____

_____

_____

_____

_____

_____

_____

_____

_____

_____

_____

_____

_____

_____

_____

_____

"BLACK OR WHITE?"

Acts 17:26 "From one man He made every nation of men, to inhabit the whole earth; and He determined their appointed times and the boundaries of their lands."

There is a great episode of Star Trek, season three, episode 15. There were two beings battling for supremacy. Both beings had their faces painted half black and half white. Other than that, they were identical. One said he was supreme because he was "white on the right side" i.e. the right side of his face was white. He proceeds to call the other being a lower form of human for being "white on the left side" i.e. having the left half of his face painted white. Yes, it was that petty, and they were literally willing to kill each other over it; willing to fight to the death because of their hatred for one another. Let's make this as simple as possible, if they (we) slowed down and used some logic they'd (we'd) see that they're (we're) more ALIKE than they're (we're) different! Captain Kirk advised them wisely when he said that mutual destruction was bad for both! When will America wake up and stop using silly stereotypes, foolish preconceived notions, lies and deception that only serve to keep us divided rather than realizing our commonalties? We all came from the same place! Division is of the enemy; a house divided cannot stand. **Today, let's use our platform to promote unity and reconciliation, knowing that God is the Father of all.**

_____

_____

_____

_____

_____

_____

_____

_____

_____

_____

_____

_____

_____

_____

_____

_____

_____

_____

_____

_____

_____

JULY 27TH

"SHUT IT DOWN!"

2 Corinthians 10:5 "We tear down arguments, and every presumption set up against the knowledge of God; and we take captive every thought to make it obedient to Christ."

In 2019, there seemed to be a prevailing sentiment that the truth didn't matter anymore. We were overly preoccupied with presentation and charisma and somehow, unconcerned about the content of one's character. While there were many heretical issues that Paul battled, their core sentiment went against the sovereignty of God. We are fighting the same battle, on a different front, with a different heretical line of thinking. In America, politics and political pundits have somehow seized power, even from the church. Their ideologies are shaping our theology. Their thoughts and their hyper-nationalist musings have somehow, in some way, replaced God's word in many churches. The hatred and division that continues to be preached over the airwaves must be shut down in favor of what God truly desires; love. Those idolatrous issues that keep us at each other's throats must be torn down and demolished. This is a supernatural battle which is why the spread of this type of thinking is so pervasive. **Today, lift Jesus up above every institution, every agency, every official and the world will change for the better.**

_____

_____

_____

_____

_____

_____

_____

_____

_____

_____

_____

_____

_____

_____

_____

_____

_____

_____

_____

_____

_____

_____

JULY 28TH

"NO ARGUMENT HERE"

2 Tim 2:23 "But reject foolish and ignorant speculation, for you know that it breeds quarreling."

We are a culture obsessed with winning. We love to crown champions and celebrate heroes. Winning is not limited to the field of play or the court, however. In our online culture, winning or, the perception of winning, is also a big deal. We spend countless hours arguing and debating with people over minutiae. That is stressful and counterproductive. In addition to being counterproductive, it also pulls us away from having an attitude of godliness to one of selfishness. I am guilty of this myself and I have apologized on multiple occasions to strangers on Twitter. One of the devil's greatest tools is the art of distraction. If we are distracted, then we are also vulnerable to further attacks. The more we occupy our time with mindless behavior, discussing mindless topics and wrangling over words and events that don't contribute substantive results, the less time we actually spend focusing on what's truly important...God. **Today, let's not get caught up in the "pop" culture bubble. Let us remember that we are ambassadors for Christ at all times.**

_____

_____

_____

_____

_____

_____

_____

_____

_____

_____

_____

_____

_____

_____

_____

_____

_____

_____

_____

JULY 29TH

"LIVING THROUGH CHRIST"

Philippians 4:13 "I can do all things through Christ who strengthens me"

As a professor, I have to maintain a certain level of decorum in my classroom. I believe that as important as protocol is, there is also a time and a place to be vulnerable and expose your emotions. When my late wife was ill, I still went to work, every day. I still dealt with the drama of student-professor interactions, parents calling and administrators dropping loads of work on us at the last minute. Many people, however, did not know what I was facing. They never knew that I was really in a bad place. Not to say that I did not share these things with some or, vent to my confidantes, but I did not let my situation show up in the quality of my work or my teaching. It actually pushed me to be an even better preacher, too. A student once asked me how I stay so positive about life. I chuckled because I have down days often, and there is plenty of stuff that makes me angry. But the answer to their question came from what I have learned from dealing with difficult times: 1) Turn every situation over to the Lord 2) Always live with eternity in mind 3) Live one day at a time and 4) Keep stress at a minimum by not worrying over what you cannot control (T.A.L.K). **Today, remember that pain is both a nuisance and a great teacher. It is amazing what harvests we glean from fields sown with trouble.**

_____

_____

_____

_____

_____

_____

_____

_____

_____

_____

_____

_____

_____

_____

_____

_____

_____

_____

_____

_____

_____

_____

JULY 30TH

"DELUSIONAL FAITH"

Romans 5:3 "Not only that, but we also rejoice in our sufferings, because we know that suffering produces perseverance..."

Many times, preachers miss the mark as it pertains to giving people a realistic perception of God. God is both, kind and severe. He is both benevolent and disciplinary. When we only preach his benevolence, we neglect to give a full picture of God or the human condition. The world is a place of suffering because of the effects of sin. That being said, if you feel as if God has let you down you might want to look at who is teaching you about God. Yes, there will be hardships that test our faith and even bring it into question, but we have to come back to the essence of who God is and that if He allows bad, from that, He is able to bring good as well. If ALL you're taught is that it will always be perfect, money will always be flowing, you will have your best life now but you don't see those results; it's not God who let you down, the pastor/teacher has. **Today, pray for discernment!**

_____

_____

_____

_____

_____

_____

_____

_____

_____

_____

_____

_____

_____

_____

_____

_____

_____

_____

_____

_____

_____

"JUST HOLD ON"

Acts 14:22 "...strengthening the souls of the disciples, encouraging them to continue in the faith, and saying, "Through many tribulations we must enter the kingdom of God."

The idyllic, perfect life. We all want it. A white picket fence, 2.5 children and a house with all of the amenities. Barbecues every weekend. No sickness, trouble or anxiety. My, do I wish that this was the case. If we read God's Word for ourselves and pray for discernment, we would know that the Bible dispels any myth of a perfect life. Paul in the reference text is on the run from those who would seek his life. One of our greatest assets in any trial is to have a correct understanding of the context of the situation. Paul's understanding enabled him to strengthen the faith of his fellow believers! It also allowed him to contextualize the moment. To paraphrase, this is what following God looks like! The kingdom will not be preceded by a walk through the tulips. If we survived the trial, God has done His part! **Today, know that God hasn't changed, He's always been faithful and He's always taken care of His people. He's shows His strength perfectly during our times of distress.**

_____

_____

_____

_____

_____

_____

_____

_____

_____

_____

_____

_____

_____

_____

_____

_____

_____

_____

_____

_____

AUGUST 1ST

"WHO'S SPEAKING?"

Acts 16:17 "This girl followed Paul and the rest of us, shouting, "These men are servants of the Most High God, who are proclaiming to you the way of salvation."

The spiritual realm is an amazing phenomenon. We know that it exists. We know that it is compartmentalized. We know that there is a hierarchy of spirits. We also know that there are warring factions within the spiritual realm. God's side and the side of darkness pitted in an eternal struggle that God will ultimately win. In this text, there was a young girl who was suffocated by a spirit of divination. She was being used by men to tell "fortunes" and make money! Following them to the place of prayer indicates the boldness of this spirit. She was shouting and calling Paul and the rest of his cohort servants of the Most High God. What was the problem? The demons spoke of Jesus the same way. This girl predicted future events; however, she was not a prophet. There is a big difference in a prophet and a psychic. Her ability came from the demonic wisdom that exists in what James calls, the worldly realm. She did not speak by the Holy Spirit. We would be wise to pay attention to those who claim some "prophetic" power. We should analyze their words and their motives, and see if they are in agreement with Scripture. **Today, pay attention to who's speaking.**

AUGUST 2ND

"MOTIVATION"

Acts 16:16 "It happened that as we were going to the place of prayer, a slave-girl having a spirit of divination met us, who was bringing her masters much profit by fortune-telling."

Motivation is everything. The Bible warns us that our motives ought to be pure. We ought not be selfishly ambitious, hateful or conniving. The motives of one who follows God, especially one whom is used by God as a mouthpiece, are especially important. Sometimes, we can be hoodwinked into believing that everyone who dons a suit and tie or has a ministry named after them is a legitimate spokesperson for God. One way to know if it is legitimate or not is their motivation for doing it. A calling from God is a joyful burden. Joyful because we know what an honor it is to work in the service of God. Burdensome because we know that it will definitely involve sacrifice and loss. One thing is for certain, not one true prophet or priest or apostle was motivated by money or greed. Whenever someone is selling God to us, their motivation is not salvation, it is money. We know what the Bible says about the love of money: it is a root of all sorts of evil. If the object is to make as much money as possible, the lengths that one goes to in an effort to obtain that money are limitless. **Today, know that God is not for sale but rather, expects us to give freely as He was freely given to us!**

_____

_____

_____

_____

_____

_____

_____

_____

_____

_____

_____

_____

_____

_____

_____

_____

_____

_____

_____

_____

_____

_____

_____

AUGUST 3RD

"PROPHECY OR FORTUNE?"

Jeremiah 1:10 "See, I have appointed you today over nations and kingdoms to uproot and tear down, to destroy and overthrow, to build and plant."

The prophetic office has been hijacked by new age philosophy and ultimately, psychics posing as prophets. We are inundated with ministries that use the prophetic office for illicit gain and for unscrupulous purposes. Prophecy has two basic functions: foretelling i.e. giving an account of future events and foretelling i.e. giving a direct word from the Lord. What passes for prophecy today is literally someone telling people what they want to hear and then asking for a donation for doing it. A true prophet has several distinct qualities: they will not broadcast their title, the LORD will always be the focus, they will not take their office lightly and they will not speak unless prompted by the Holy Spirit. Prophecy is a burden! The prophets of Scripture were all hard pressed as they worked in their calling. A real prophecy from God will be a direct word from the Lord. It will not be for sale. It will align with Scripture. It will not only give the good, but will also chastise the bad. God told Jeremiah to destroy and to build! It will not always be what we want to hear, but rather what God has to say concerning a particular situation, which is why God told Jeremiah not to be afraid! God knew the people would be irritated! **Today, thank God that His word doesn't return void!**

AUGUST 4TH

"HUNGRY FOR RECOGNITION"

1 Kings 17:24 "Then the woman said to Elijah, "Now I know that you are a man of God and that the word of the LORD from your mouth is truth."

The world that we live in is a strange place. We are in a tug of war between what God desires and what the world says is the right thing to do. We live in a competitive society where titles and prestige mean a lot to some people. Interestingly enough, this same mentality has crept into the church. We are obsessed with titles. Everyone wants to be bishop, overseer, right reverend, left reverend, apostle, grand monarch or whatever title is chosen to be indicative of being head honcho. Reading scripture, you see something totally different. In the text here, Elijah comes to Zarephath to a woman's home. He was sent there by God. Notice, he never introduced himself as Elijah the prophet. He never said because I am a prophet, you must listen to me. In actuality, if you study the scriptures, none of God's chosen instruments ever used their position to garner influence or curry favor. They understood that God is truly the sovereign and they were only vessels at His disposal. The woman, however, recognized Elijah's position because of his works. Men can confer many titles, but the authority and the power to carry out the work of God, ultimately come from God. **Today, rather than being obsessed with recognition, let us allow our works to speak for us!**

AUGUST 5TH

"RESTORE GENTLY"

Galatians 6:1 "Brethren, even if anyone is caught in any trespass, you who are spiritual, restore such a one in a spirit of gentleness; each one looking to yourself, so that you too will not be tempted."

The church would do well to get this particular scripture down into our souls. Sin is ever present. As God told Cain, it is crouching at the door waiting to overtake you. Contrary to what is commonly believed, we do indeed sin every day in some form or fashion. Sometimes, it is knowingly and other times, it is unconscious. But nevertheless, we are not in our final form and we are yet being transformed. While we are on our way to Zion, there are any number of pitfalls and traps waiting to cause us to stumble. Hence Paul's admonition that if anyone is "caught" in a trespass. Literally, if anyone is ambushed by sin, caught off guard, makes an error in judgment, they should be restored with a spirit of gentleness. Note, he calls for those who are spiritual. Not those who are religious! Religious people do not let things go and often, have amnesia when it relates to the grace of God over their personal lives. Sometimes, folks spend an inordinate amount of time knocking others down because to help them up, it may actually require the exertion of energy, or a period of reflection on our own mistakes. **Today, encourage someone so that they can endure until tomorrow.**

_____

_____

_____

_____

_____

_____

_____

_____

_____

_____

_____

_____

_____

_____

_____

_____

_____

_____

_____

_____

_____

AUGUST 6TH

"BE THE CHANGE"

Proverbs 22:6 "Train up a child in the way he should go, even when he is old he will not depart from it."

Have you ever noticed how much we complain about subsequent generations? We criticize the way they dress, walk, talk, learn and create. We criticize everything. The problem is not necessarily the criticism because some of it is rightly deserved. But we must also remember that we too were young and rebellious and we too were criticized for being too this or too that. Joe Madison, a popular talk radio personality, always asks complainers "what are you going to do about it?" For every generational hiccup, we have the ability to influence them through correction and loving guidance. We also have a say as to how we raise our own children. If we do not have children, there are scores of young people who need mentors. If we are constantly asking "What's wrong with this generation?" we must also start asking, "What am I doing to contribute to righting the ship?" As cliché as it sounds, we have to be the change that we want to see. We have to start training our sons and daughters to be conscientious citizens and good human beings. Then, the question of what's wrong becomes a non-issue. **Today, don't underestimate your impact on society. You could be a life-changer, just reach back and take someone by the hand.**

"TIME ON LOAN"

Psalm 118:24 "This is the day which the LORD has made; Let us rejoice and be glad in it."

In this era of self-aggrandizement and self-glorification, we forget that the time that we do have is on loan to us. Job said it very simply, "Since his days are determined, the number of his months is with You; and his limits You have set so that he cannot pass." Social media allows us to see the oft-gratuitous celebrations and the "happy birthday to ME" posts that often lead to replies of "this is your day!" Well, technically, it's not our day. In actuality, no day is ours. Everything belongs to Him. When we lose sight of that, it brings to mind what God told Israel on the cusp of the Promised Land, "After you have filled your bellies, you will certainly forget about Me!" Remember when they tell us 'this is your day!' that in reality, everyday belongs to GOD and is on loan to us. Let us glorify Him and not ourselves. **Today, let us rejoice and be glad in the fact that every day belongs to God, in His grace He allows us to enjoy that time!**

"CONSUMER OR PRODUCER?"

1 John 3:17 "If anyone with earthly possessions sees his brother in need, but withholds his compassion from him, how can the love of God abide in him?"

Capitalism is the operative word in America. Politicians laud the "free market" although the market is manipulated daily by those who are in power. We promote the bootstraps, can-do mentality knowing that the true secret to success in capitalism is greed. Keep as much for yourself as possible and make sure the guys at the top eat the most. That's a harsh reality. What is worse is that capitalism somehow views the poor as a drain on society. It deludes proponents into thinking that the poor are the takers and he rich are the producers. In actuality, it is the poor and the lower class that do the work that makes capitalism thrive. God is actually a proponent of benevolence, not usury or greed. So, John cautions his readers and all of us, that we cannot let the prevailing economic sentiment get in the way of doing what is right. We cannot start asking questions about how someone arrived at their station in life. We cannot sit and analyze the circumstances that led to a person's financial demise. If we see someone in need and we are able to assist them, but we choose not to, we have suspended our compassion in favor of the bootstrap mentality! **Today, remember to love those who are in need of being loved, give liberally when possible and always show compassion to those in need.**

_____

_____

_____

_____

_____

_____

_____

_____

_____

_____

_____

_____

_____

_____

_____

_____

_____

_____

_____

_____

_____

_____

_____

AUGUST 9TH

"HIS GLORY CANNOT BE DENIED"

Genesis 1:6 "And God said, 'Let there be an expanse between the waters, to separate the waters from the waters.'"

Skeptics across the globe have tried, in vain, to disprove God. This is an asinine approach for several reasons. The main reason why it is a fruitless attempt is because God is not quantifiable. No man has seen Him (save for those who actually saw Jesus), no man can measure Him, no man can necessarily prove He exists, but by the same token, no man can necessarily disprove that He exists. It cannot be denied that something or someone caused the universe to come into existence. God is a wise God and therefore, He left clues that point to his invisible attributes and His power. A cursory look up into the sky leaves no doubt that everything had to come from somewhere. The clouds, the sun, the distance of the sun from the earth, the order of the planets, the orbits of the planets, the fixed planetary spins on their respective axes are all powerful indicators of a Supreme Being having a hand in the creation and ongoing order within the universe. So, it is really difficult for skeptics to explain God's greatness away. To say that all the order in the universe is random is the greatest oxymoron ever uttered. How can order be random or come from randomness? The heavens declare the glory of God. **Today, know that God is GREAT and GREATLY to be praised!**

WALK WITH ME: God Seen, God Heard, God Revealed

"A RELATIONAL GOD"

John 6:26 "Jesus answered them and said, "Truly, truly, I say to you, you seek Me, not because you saw signs, but because you ate of the loaves and were filled."

In an era of consumerism, it is very easy to mash God up into the mix of one to be consumed. We make everything else consumable, why not make God consumable too? We've been conditioned to have a give to get mentality and in doing so, we simply become consumers. We look to God for what He can give us. We pray for cars and don't even have the means to maintain them. We pray for larger houses but won't clean the ones that we have already. We pray for more and more stuff, not understanding that although God is the giver of good and perfect gifts, the giver is more important! The gifts will fade and crumble and the one who gave them will be right there still, eternal in the heavens. So, when Jesus confronts the followers in this large crowd with their true motives, it is not surprising. These people wanted more bread and did not realize that they were in the presence of the True Bread of Life! Jesus is relational, and no solid relationship is based on possessions. The signs were meant to draw crowds and validate the ministry of Jesus. From there, a relationship is formed! **Today, remember, if there is no real relationship with Christ, when the signs and miracles run out...so will our faith.**

WALK WITH ME: God Seen, God Heard, God Revealed

AUGUST 11TH

"PERFECT LOVE"

Deuteronomy 6:5 "You shall love the LORD your God with all your heart and with all your soul and with all your might."

At first glance, this scripture in Deuteronomy seems lofty and unattainable. When Jesus quoted this as the first commandment, he said it in a particular context. Someone asked Him what the greatest commandment in the Law is. Note, this commandment is not even a part of the Law. It actually supersedes the Law. It is a call for us to, as cliché as it sounds, put God first. So when Jesus says this is the greatest commandment, it literally is because there is nothing more important than God being first in everything. What makes this difficult for most of us is how so many things we have competing for our attention and our devotion! We have our jobs, our families, our social engagements and myriad other things that are pulling on us. It doesn't help that we often relegate God to the back pew of our spiritual sanctuary and allow some other interest to take the pulpit. It is not an unattainable command, but it is one that takes discipline and one that takes commitment. **Today, after we have given everything possible, physically and spiritually, to You and to others, let us ask God to restore and replenish us so we can do it all over again tomorrow.**

AUGUST 12TH

"ENOUGH"

1 Peter 1:18,19 "For you know that it was not with perishable things such as silver or gold that you were redeemed from the empty way of life you inherited from your forefathers, but with the precious blood of Christ, a lamb without blemish or spot."

God, as complex as He is, does things very simply. He uses this simplicity to relate to our finite understanding. There is no way that we could possibly understand God's magnificence. There is no way that we could understand God's mind. Only the Holy Spirit knows the deep things of God. It's odd because we overcomplicate Christianity with so many rules and doctrines, much of it being man-made. Here is the blessing of the simplicity of God: everything in God is summed up in Jesus. All of the promises of God are "yes and amen" in Jesus. With Jesus, there was one purpose: to die for the sins of humanity. With Jesus there was one main proof of His identity: His resurrection. So, it makes it easy to understand that Jesus specializes in 'enough'. His grace is enough to see us through, His blood is enough to cleanse us from all sin and faith in Him is enough to save! He is the all sufficient One. **Today, let us magnify God for being enough, even when the world tells us that we need more.**

_____

_____

_____

_____

_____

_____

_____

_____

_____

_____

_____

_____

_____

_____

_____

_____

_____

_____

_____

_____

_____

AUGUST 13TH

"THE PERFECT PERSON"

1 John 1:9 "If we confess our sins, He is faithful and just to forgive us our sins and to cleanse us from all unrighteousness."

There is no such thing as a sinless human being. I don't care how perfect we are, we will never be perfect. There are some whose piety is impressive, but even then, sin is still there in some form or fashion. We may not be practitioners of sin, but we live in a broken world and are born into sin. This is why Jesus was and is necessary! When John says "if we confess" this is what is called an if/then clause. If we confess, then He will forgive. There is a cause and effect happening here. Confession means that we own up to our wrongdoing and we turn from it. Confession means that we recognize that we have sinned against God. Sin is as inevitable as breathing. Not all sins are the same, not all sins are the same magnitude, but in God's sight, sin is sin and there is only one way that is can be forgiven; the blood of Jesus! On our journey toward Zion, we often take detours, pit-stops, have wrecks and even give up. **Today, remember this, we can be confident that the blood of Jesus will forgive every misstep and if we accept God's correction, He will restore us AND put us back on the path.**

AUGUST 14TH

"UNDERESTIMATED GRACE"

Micah 7:8 "Don't rejoice over me my enemy, though I fall, I will rise. Though I sit in darkness, the Lord is a light for me."

The prophet Micah gives us sage advice here in this passage of scripture. God is indeed a God of redemption; however, many rejoice when human beings fail. Especially if they view that human being as someone who does not follow their agenda. Society is agenda and trend driven. When we go against what is popular, as Micah and many other prophets did, and somehow, we fall down, spectators see that as a victory for themselves! They see your demise as one who stands for truth and for God with glee and adulation. People want to see God fail because people need a reason not to believe in God. However, God cannot and does not fail. God is a forgiving God and when we do fall, His grace is sufficient. Although Satan takes every opportunity to throw fiery darts; especially at those who live for God, we have the shield of faith. Micah gives good advice for these moments to those who doubt God: 1. Save your celebration because God will redeem me, 2. Yes, I have fallen but my story is not over, and 3. The Lord is the best source of light because He is light! **Today, remember that God has you in the palm of his hand!**

AUGUST 15TH

"TIME TO GO"

Luke 9:30,31 "Suddenly two men, Moses and Elijah, began talking with Jesus. They appeared in glory and spoke about His departure, which He was about to accomplish at Jerusalem."

The life of Jesus was a remedy sent to correct the failures of Israel. What they could not accomplish as a nation, He did. He is the true Israel of God. After His birth, his parents hid Him in Egypt and He left Egypt free to symbolize Israel's exodus. He spent forty days in the wilderness, but did not yield to the temptation of Satan, to symbolize, and rectify, Israel's 40-year long wandering in the wilderness. Good news for every believer, Jesus actually had a second exodus in which He would prove, again, that nothing could hold Him hostage. During the transfiguration, Jesus talked with Moses and Elijah about His departure [exodus]. Not only did He accomplish His second exodus from death, He made a way for every believer to do the same! **Today, give Him thanks for leading our exodus out of a spiritual Egypt, out of the hands of Pharaoh Satan, parting the sea of sin and iniquity and giving us a chance to walk to salvation on dry land! He is our Elijah who brings our attention back to God and gives us the opportunity to no longer limp between two opinions.**

AUGUST 16TH

"BAD COMPANY"

1 Corinthians 15:33 "Do not be deceived: "Bad company corrupts good morals."

Sometimes, we really think that we are above being influenced by our surroundings or the people in them. Subliminally though, we do take in what surrounds us. One of the things that can be affected is how we view God. Many times, those who are outside of the will of God will make excuses or minimize God to make their shortcomings seem less egregious. When we hear this constant din of the minimization and hearing God deemphasized, it can negatively affect our view of Him. We too can begin seeking a God of our own creation. Paul tells us plainly that we are not to deceive ourselves. Bad company i.e. bad relationships with people who are toxic to our spirituality will cause our own morality to shrivel up and die. Am I saying that we are to cut everyone and everything off? No. Paul teaches us that to avoid sinners we would basically have to leave the planet. But what I am saying is to be mindful of who has access to your ear and your heart. Make sure your friends and associates have a proper theology before accepting or implementing their advice. If they don't see God as all powerful in their lives, how will they see Him in yours? **Today, ask God for discernment and for courage to move away from anything that has the potential to corrupt us.**

AUGUST 17TH

"WHO MOVED?"

James 4:8 "Draw near to God and He will draw near to you. Cleanse your hands, you sinners; and purify your hearts, you double-minded."

Isaiah teaches us that God desires to reason with us. That word reason literally means to argue a case. So picture you in a courtroom with God, God having all kinds of discovery evidence, your secrets, but being gracious enough to allow you to reason and give an account of why you should win. Now, picture that same God saying that the evidence against you is so damning that you are stained with sin but, I will wash you clean and make you as white as snow. This is the God of the universe who says "come". There are many theories about whether God can move or does move, but the prevailing sentiment is that God does not move. If He invites us to come, it must be that we moved far from him. James commands us here to draw near to God. Think of it as someone standing at the top of the Washington Monument beckoning you to come. As you walk towards the monument, the monument suddenly seems a lot closer than it was before you started making your way to it. This immovable object seems to be moving towards you, but in reality, you are moving towards it! **Today, let's remember that God did not move, we did and in His immovable nature, there is abundant grace for the one coming closer to Him!**

_____

_____

_____

_____

_____

_____

_____

_____

_____

_____

_____

_____

_____

_____

_____

_____

_____

_____

_____

_____

_____

_____

AUGUST 18TH

"JUST KEEP WALKING"

Psalm 23:4 "Even though I walk through the valley of the shadow of death, I fear no evil, for You are with me; Your rod and Your staff, they comfort me."

I marvel at people who have endured hard trials and situations. I know that God says that His grace is sufficient, but it is still amazing to see people come out of trials and continue to live and glorify God! The Psalmist, David, was a man who dealt with much adversity which began the moment he schemed to make Bathsheba his wife. The sword never departed from his house. Amazingly, David knew that it was his own doing, but He also knew that God was a gracious God! So, in this 23rd Psalm, David gives us great encouragement to know that the beneficence of God most certainly outweighs any trial that we might face in life. So here, speaking in terms of a sheep being guided by a shepherd, David said "Yea though I walk through the valley..." He had to walk because there was a lesson in the valley. He couldn't run because he might have missed it and he couldn't camp out and stay because the valley was too terrifying. The shadow of death loomed over him. So, David just kept walking. **Today, if you're in a hard situation, keep moving in the name of Jesus! Don't camp out, don't have a pity party and live in expectation that the shadow of death will give way to the Light.**

_____

_____

_____

_____

_____

_____

_____

_____

_____

_____

_____

_____

_____

_____

_____

_____

_____

_____

_____

_____

_____

"THE AROMA OF LIFE"

2 Corinthians 2:15, 16 "For we are a fragrance of Christ to God among those who are being saved and among those who are perishing; to the one an aroma from death to death, to the other an aroma from life to life."

We have a smell, as Christians. Thanks be to God, we don't smell like the furnaces that we've been in. But rather, we smell like the sweet aroma of knowing Him. To ones who are on the same journey upon which we walk, we smell like life to each other. Nothing is more pleasant or invigorating than to have a fellow Christian speak life to us, especially when we have endured much trouble. A kind word is like cool water to a parched soul! But to others, who are perishing, we smell like death. We smell like what God desires from them but what they are unwilling to give. That's ok. Even from that smell of death, life can come if those who are perishing make a decision to follow the same road that we travel. **Today, let us pray for the strength to witness to the perishing and for the Holy Spirit's persuasive power to change their sense of smell, overcome them and lead them from darkness into the marvelous light.**

_____

_____

_____

_____

_____

_____

_____

_____

_____

_____

_____

_____

_____

_____

_____

_____

_____

_____

_____

_____

_____

_____

AUGUST 20TH

"DRINK UP"

Isaiah 55:1 "Come, all you who are thirsty, come to the waters; and you without money, come, buy, and eat! Come, buy wine and milk, without money and without cost!"

Thirst can cause many side effects. It can cause dry mouth, hallucinations, and in extreme cases, death. It's amazing that the body can survive without food for three weeks but can only go one week without water. That's because the processes in the body and the organs are all dependent on water. Spiritual thirst is also real. Spiritual thirst is the desire for something, anything to fill the void in our lives created by having eternity in our hearts, but only a finite understanding of the One who is able to fill that void. That's why we resort to all types of behaviors and seek all types of things. In reality, there is only One who is able to quench this thirst, the Almighty. And, his thirst quencher, unlike Gatorade or PowerAde or other popular sports drinks, is 100% free and it is also unlimited. He beckons us here in this passage that if we are thirsty, we should come to the waters. Even if we cannot afford it. Come buy and eat because everything that God offers he does so freely from His own grace! The whole world is dehydrated because of sin and yet many refuse to drink the free water that Christ offers! **Today, let us rejoice that we have received the living waters!**

"JEHOVAH JIREH"

Genesis 22:14 "Abraham called the name of that place The LORD Will Provide, as it is said to this day, "In the mount of the LORD it will be provided."

Have you ever been in a situation where the resources to carry out what God commanded did not match your expectations? In the current text, Abraham had the resources but, unbeknownst to Isaac, he would be the sacrifice. Isaac was not crazy. Even he knew that if they were going up the mountain, they needed something to take with them to place over the fire that would burn when they lit that bundle of wood that he was carrying. Abraham was not even wrestling with God's decision because Abraham knew that God was faithful. He knew that limited resources do not diminish God's power or provision. Abraham had bound Isaac and was getting ready to cut his throat when the Angel of the Lord spoke to him and told him to stop. Just then, Abraham saw a ram caught in a thicket and that became the sacrifice in the place of Isaac. We should never doubt God's ability to provide. God is able to put springs in the desert; can He not do something miraculous our lives? **Today, look for the ram caught in the thicket, God knows what we need.**

AUGUST 22ND

"THERE IS A GOD"

Romans 1:20 "For since the creation of the world God's invisible qualities, His eternal power and divine nature, have been clearly seen, being understood from His workmanship, so that men are without excuse."

To deny the existence of God is to deny our own existence. Surely, we did not create ourselves! Surely, there are things so irreducibly complex that there is no other explanation for them except that a creator designed them! The human eye, for instance, is multifaceted and each part is unique. The Cornea has five layers and focuses light, the pupil monitors the amount of light entering the eye, the iris is used to adjust the size of the pupil and to control light flow and the lens- controls focus. ALL of this happening in this organ at the same time, every waking hour. But what is the difference in the eye and the liver? There are major differences! So, how did the cells that became the liver know to become the liver and the cells that formed the eyes know to become the eyes? Some would say, oh, it was just random. But, to say that is to disrespect the orderliness of the Creator! The cells were pre-programmed to become what they would become, but who programmed them? Who put the information into the cell? Better yet, who differentiated the cells so that they know where to go? **Today, rejoice that there is indeed a God whose handiwork is the universe, who crafted us and whose image we bear!**

AUGUST 23RD

"GOD DOESN'T TAKE ORDERS"

Acts 17:25 "...nor is He served by human hands, as though He needed anything, since He Himself gives to all people life and breath and all things..."

It is conspicuously evident that men have lost respect for God. The term "God-fearing" doesn't carry the same weight as it used to. Partly because we've, in effect, become our own gods. Partly because, we've been taught, even in the church, that God is only here to serve our needs and desires. A.W. Tozer is quoted as saying that whatever comes into our mind when we think about God is the most important thing about is. In other words, our theology matters. It is much better to view God as sovereign rather than seeing Him as a puppet. He does not need us and definitely cannot be commanded by us. We lower His status by believing that we can command Him! Demons are subject to the commands of men, not the Almighty. The minute that puppet god doesn't obey then it is no longer our god and we lose confidence in its ability to help us. However, when we know that God is sovereign, as scripture clearly teaches, we can be absolutely certain that all of His answers (yes and no) are divinely designed to meet His purposes and we are blessed to be included. He gives life and breath to all things. We are not able to do that. If we minimize His power and His sovereignty, we may as well just make God one of us. **Today, recognize His sovereignty and ascribe greatness to Him!**

"LET GOD FINISH HIS WORK"

Ezekiel 37:3 "He said to me, "Son of man, can these bones live?" And I answered, "O Lord GOD, You know."

Imagine the shock of the prophet Ezekiel, looking out over a valley full of the bones of dead people. Ezekiel lived during the Babylonian exile and saw death, disobedience and destruction all around him. He is in a situation where God seemed distant and looking out over this barren and dystopian landscape, God asks him a question: Can the bones that you see live, Ezekiel? God knew the answer, Ezekiel turned the question back to God and before his eyes, God raised the bones up and began putting flesh on them and gave Ezekiel the order to prophesy breath into the bodies that were standing before him. Imagine if the bodies just took off before the breath came? We do not become living beings until the breath of life is breathed into us! We have to always remember that if God is working in our lives, we must allow Him to complete the process. In the valley of dry bones, the bones got up with flesh but they had no breath! We must stay put and let God FULLY revive us before we jump off His operating table! Without His breath, without His Spirit we are nothing more than walking shells, spiritual zombies headed to nowhere! **Today, let us be patient and faithful while Jesus is doing His work in us.**

_____

_____

_____

_____

_____

_____

_____

_____

_____

_____

_____

_____

_____

_____

_____

_____

_____

_____

_____

_____

_____

AUGUST 25TH

"ALL THINGS WORK TOGETHER"

John 6:7 "But He was asking this to test him, for He knew what He was about to do."

As any good teacher would, Jesus tested the faith of His disciples often. Many can attest to the fact that when we were in grade school and the teacher piled work up on us, we complained. We groaned and griped not understanding what the teacher understood: learning can be built through repetition. They had a reason for the work and the lessons which they added on to what we were already doing. I will testify that God is our Teacher and He knows what He is doing! Jesus, putting Philip in this predicament was yet another example of Jesus testing the faith of His disciples. I have to be honest, I have grumbled and complained because I lost sight of the fact that the Teacher is teaching me something that only time and repetition will allow me to master. For everything God has a purpose. Lord, forgive our grumbling! It gets hot in this furnace some days! Renew our strength Lord as we continue to wait for You faithfully and filled with hope. You ARE what we are not. You ARE in spite of what we are. You ARE the Great I AM. **Today, let us rest in that.**

AUGUST 26TH

"NOT EMPIRICALLY PROVABLE BUT CERTAINLY CONSCIOUSLY KNOWABLE"

Isaiah 40:12 "Who has measured the waters in the hollow of his hand, or marked off the heavens with the span of his hand? Who has held the dust of the earth in a basket, or weighed the mountains on a scale and the hills with a balance?"

Scientists disapprove of what they consider a God-of-the-gaps mentality. There is a line of thinking in science that a mystery explained by invoking God only creates a "bigger mystery." This is where some scientists are mistaken. The mystery exists to force us to think beyond our whiteboards, telescopes, petri dishes and computers. God is definitely a bigger mystery but He is also a knowable mystery. The true gap exists between the evidence for God and the unbeliever's refusal to acknowledge it. Atheists are silly enough to believe the sun just magically positioned itself 93,000,000 miles from us and not one mile closer (we'd burn up) or one mile further away (we'd freeze) but claim that Christians are silly for believing in the One who hung the sun in its place. **Today, let us remember that kind of stuff doesn't just randomly happen folks.**

AUGUST 27TH

"NOTHING IS IMPOSSIBLE FOR HIM"

Genesis 18:12 "So she laughed to herself, saying, "After I am worn out and my master is old, will I now have this pleasure?"

If you told me that I'd lift 1500 pounds of anything, I'd laugh at you. I am not the strongest or most muscular person in the world. I am ok, but not nearly in a position to lift 1,500 pounds. But, one day, I did just that. I put down 1450lbs of sand in my yard, in two days, but I did it one bag at a time. There is a lesson in everything. It sounded overwhelming, just like when God told Sarai that she'd have a son. She laughed and sarcastically said, I'm old and nooooow I'll have a baby? When we get overwhelming odds or devastating news we tend to think of everything all at once. God gives us the strength to complete every task, but sometimes we are to do it methodically and over time. Next time you feel overwhelmed, don't panic, just think about what the first step is in overcoming the obstacle and take that ONE step first. After that, then worry about the second step. **Today, let us thank God for the lessons taught, one step at a time.**

AUGUST 28TH

"SLAYED, FRAYED, AFRAID BUT NOT DISMAYED"

2 Corinthians 4:8 "...we are afflicted in every way, but not crushed; perplexed, but not despairing; persecuted, but not forsaken; struck down, but not destroyed..."

In life, there are going to be things that hit us so hard that we get broken into pieces. The direction that those pieces fall will determine how we handle the onslaught. There are only two directions, away from God and toward God. Paul reminds us here that our jars of clay will be hard pressed, but they will not be crushed. We will have issues with no answers to them, but we will not despair. We will be persecuted but God will not forsake us and although we will be struck down, our problems will not destroy us. Knowing this, we can hold on to the Word of God and draw strength from the keeping power of God! As Job reminded us, when we come out of the furnace, we will come forth as pure gold. Pure, with the trial having removed some impurity or imperfection from us! **Today, let us pray the pieces will always fall towards God. Only He can make peace from the pieces!**

_____

_____

_____

_____

_____

_____

_____

_____

_____

_____

_____

_____

_____

_____

_____

_____

_____

_____

_____

_____

_____

_____

"MAN DOWN"

1 Peter 5:9 "But resist him, firm in your faith, knowing that the same experiences of suffering are being accomplished by your brethren who are in the world."

One of the most effective tricks of the enemy is to have us think that we are isolated and that God has abandoned us on the battlefield. Elijah complained about being the only prophet left. He didn't realize that Obadiah hadn't sold out and that Obadiah also hid 100 prophets in a cave who hadn't sold out. ALL of these prophets were in the same predicament as Elijah. Peter reminds us here to resist the roaring lion, Satan, and stay rooted in our faith knowing that many are also suffering for the name of Christ. Not just in our circle, but in the whole world! In trial, it is very easy to believe that you're the ONLY one going through. Nothing is further from the truth. We must do our level best to avoid the pity party and remember that the whole world is under bondage to sin and people are suffering everywhere. **Today, let us remember that there is power in community!**

AUGUST 30TH

"SEASONS DON'T LAST FOREVER"

1 Kings 17:7 "It happened after a while that the brook dried up, because there was no rain in the land."

Solomon tells us that for everything under heaven, there is a season. It is also helpful to understand that seasons are prescribed times. They are programmed to occur when they occur. Winter gives way to spring, spring to summer, summer to fall. Seasons can be harsh or plentiful. That's God's prerogative. Many of us have endured or are enduring a hard season. God has a simple message for us today. We must live in the season until it passes. We cannot avoid it. Elijah had to endure 3.5 years of drought in Israel. When his resources at the brook dried up, God moved him. The drought was still in effect but Elijah survived because God provided, even in a hard season. God hasn't changed and His methods are still effective. He will provide what you need, even if it is from an unlikely source. Remember, whoever hopes in the Lord will NEVER be put to shame. **Today, let us remember that hope does not disappoint, that tribulation builds patience and that patience builds proven character!**

AUGUST 31ST

"CONTEMPORARIES MATTER"

2 Corinthians 10:12 "For we are not bold to class or compare ourselves with some of those who commend themselves; but when they measure themselves by themselves and compare themselves with themselves, they are without understanding."

If we compare ourselves to Jesus, we soon find out that we leave a lot to be desired. But, we are often encouraged to look at one another and do our comparisons that way. Especially with the advent of social media, we get to pick and choose who is the devil and who we will forgive. Here is a newsflash; anyone can call themselves great if they are around others in whom they can readily spot deficiencies. But in another place, Paul tells us to judge ourselves by ourselves and if we think we are something we are nothing, we have succeeded in deceiving ourselves. Greatness is not about judging superiority based on others' inferiority. That is the easy way out. Jesus said greatness is shown when we make ourselves like the least of these; the servant of all. Jesus took the form of a bondservant, the lowest of all slaves. So, we ought to emulate him and not be comparing ourselves to our neighbors. **Today, let our evaluation be based on the person in the mirror, not the person next to us.**

SEPTEMBER 1ST

"THE BENEFITS OF THE CROSS PART I: DROPPED CHARGES"

Romans 8:1 "Therefore there is now no condemnation for those who are in Christ Jesus."

In the eighth chapter of Romans, Paul lays out a treatise on the Christian life. Romans is said to be his finest work. Here, we will focus on the theme of being justified. Imagine facing a criminal court case and all of the evidence is stacked against you. I know people who have faced decades in prison and it is not a pretty picture to see your life disintegrate before your eyes. But Paul tells us that there is a way to have the case dismissed and the charges dropped, even if we are guilty! He says that in Christ Jesus, there is no condemnation. There are, however, a host of benefits. There is emancipation in that we are no longer slaves to sin and death. There is transformation in that we now walk in a way that is pleasing to God and there is rejuvenation in that the Holy Spirit will quicken both our physical and spiritual bodies. This sounds like a sweetheart deal to me. We know that we are all guilty of sin, but the blood of Jesus covers our sin and gives us access to the forgiveness and the mercy of God. **Today, thank God for His grace, His mercy and His full payment of our sin debt.**

_____

_____

_____

_____

_____

_____

_____

_____

_____

_____

_____

_____

_____

_____

_____

_____

_____

_____

_____

_____

_____

_____

SEPTEMBER 2ND

"THE BENEFITS OF THE CROSS PART II:

SET FREE FROM DEATH"

Romans 8:13 "For if you live according to the flesh, you will die; but if by the Spirit you put to death the deeds of the body, you will live."

Death is scary to many of us. I have been afraid to die, not because of what awaited me but because of the thought of my children being without both of their parents at such a young age. I still struggle with that, but in all honesty, I think we all do. Another benefit of the cross is that death no longer causes fear. Death was defeated at the cross. Death and the flesh go hand-in-hand. Paul instructs us that if we live according to the flesh, we will die. Period. And that covers the first death as well as the second death. But, if we live by the Spirit of God and, through the Spirit of God, we put those deeds of the flesh to death, we will live. This covers both this life and the life to come! Notice that Paul did not say that we have to put the deeds to death ourselves. It is way more complicated than that. He says put them to death by the Spirit. What he is saying is that we must yield to the conviction of the Holy Spirit when He speaks and when He gives us the way of escape from sin. There are other benefits: we become God's children, we become intimate with God, we are affirmed as God's children when the Spirit testifies with our spirit and there is the glory of being joint heirs with Christ! **Today, thank God that through the cross, we received the Holy Spirit!**

"THE BENEFITS OF THE CROSS PART III: EAGER EXPECTATION"

Romans 8:18 "For I consider that the sufferings of this present time are not worthy to be compared with the glory that is to be revealed to us."

I recall, as a little boy, going to church with my mother and family. Going to church was not the goal for me, it was what I knew would happen after church. We'd go to one of three places, Duff's, Western Sizzlin' or Burger King. Either place was fine with me because I loved Whoppers and Veal Parmesan sandwiches from Burger King, I loved the steak at Western Sizzlin' and Duff's was a buffet. I got up and got dressed with those places in mind, eagerly expecting to visit one of them as soon as we left church! Expectations (hope) can propel us and give us strength to endure things that we consider unbearable. Paul tells us here that although we are suffering during our tenure on earth, there is a glory that will be revealed in us, through God's hand, to which the suffering cannot compare. We can expect relief from the sin-sickness of the world in which we live! We can expect that the full glory of God will be revealed. The glory of God, in all of its magnificence, will overcome all darkness and the whole world will behold it! All of this produces hope in us as we wait for God's plan to unfold. **Today, be excited that God is working behind the scenes for us, to redeem us from this evil world.**

_____

_____

_____

_____

_____

_____

_____

_____

_____

_____

_____

_____

_____

_____

_____

_____

_____

_____

_____

_____

_____

_____

_____

SEPTEMBER 4TH

"THE BENEFITS OF THE CROSS PART IV:
DIVINE INTERCESSION"

Romans 8:27 "And He who searches our hearts knows the mind of the Spirit, because the Spirit intercedes for the saints according to the will of God."

As a young man, I had a lot of fights. Some of those fights required some intervention. There is nothing like doing the fight dance, where you get shoulder to shoulder and walk in a circle to see who would throw the first blow and, out of nowhere, someone steps in says, "If you fight him, you have to fight me too." That would immediately change the calculus of the situation and many times, mitigate the fight altogether. So it is with God's intercession in our lives, through the Holy Spirit. The Holy Spirit changes the calculus of our fight with the devil. Because of this divine intercession, we have power in prayer as the Holy Spirit takes our words to God and converts them into what we need. The Holy Spirit aligns us with God's will as He intercedes for us according to the will of God; a necessary caveat for any believer because we do not always know what is best. We have situational engineering as God works all things out for our good. There is also, as Douglas Moo has termed, the golden chain of salvation: We are foreknown, predestined to be conformed into the likeness of Christ, we are called, we are justified and we will eventually be glorified! **Today, let us thank God for the assurance of salvation through divine intercession!**

_____

_____

_____

_____

_____

_____

_____

_____

_____

_____

_____

_____

_____

_____

_____

_____

_____

_____

_____

_____

_____

SEPTEMBER 5TH

"THE BENEFITS OF THE CROSS-PART V:
ETERNAL INTIMACY"

Romans 8:39 "…neither height nor depth, nor anything else in all creation, will be able to separate us from the love of God that is in Christ Jesus our Lord."

Natalie Cole had a song, Inseparable, that was a ballad dedicated to the significant other in her life. One part in particular says that, "there's no way we can break up, no words can make us…" and in another part of the song, she says "it's so wonderful, to know you will always be around." I marvel at love songs because they speak as if we are eternal beings, knowing that we are finite and temporal creatures incapable of loving the way the songs proclaim. However, there is One who is able to love like this! He is eternal and He is everlasting and therefore, whatever He gives must have these same attributes. One of the benefits of the cross is that the ones who are in Christ will never be separated from God's love, which was lavished on us in the person of Christ Jesus! This love is an eternal, undying love that is incomprehensible to the human imagination. It's stronger than any power or principality, higher than any height, lower than any depth and so tightly bound that nothing in creation is able to pull us away from it. God will never stop loving us and this love was demonstrated in that while we were yet sinners, Christ died for us. **Today, thank God that through Christ Jesus, we have this eternal intimacy with Him that He loves us through everything.**

SEPTEMBER 6TH

"EVERY MORNING"

Lamentations 3:22,23 "Because of the LORD's loving devotion we are not consumed, for His compassions never fail. They are new every morning; great is Your faithfulness!"

It is a blessing that we serve a merciful God who is slow to anger and abounding in lovingkindness. We all make mistakes, daily. The beautiful thing about God is that He doesn't love us any less because of our mistakes. If there is breath in our bodies, we can still repent and ask for forgiveness. God's great faithfulness is demonstrated by this: with each sunrise we receive a new day and new mercies! If you can hear the birds chirping, see the sun rise or even simply inhale/exhale today, it means that God has extended His breath and His hand of mercy to you once again. While we slept, he kept us. Enjoy this day which He has made, rejoice and be glad in it. Take advantage of this day. Let us bless someone as God has blessed us. Let us forgive someone as God has forgiven us. Let us love someone as God, in Christ, has loved us. **Today, let us remember the unfailing mercy of God and extend mercy to those around us.**

_____

_____

_____

_____

_____

_____

_____

_____

_____

_____

_____

_____

_____

_____

_____

_____

_____

_____

_____

_____

SEPTEMBER 7TH

"I DON'T SEE ANYTHING"

Matthew 21:21 "'Truly I tell you,' Jesus replied, 'if you have faith and do not doubt, not only will you do what was done to the fig tree, but even if you say to this mountain, 'Be lifted up and thrown into the sea,' it will happen."

Time is relative. Sitting in one spot all day, it seems as if time drags by very slowly. Get up with a to-do list, and it seems as if there are not enough hours in the day! Some scientists even believe that time is a part of a fabric and is interwoven with space. It doesn't matter because when we are in critical situations, we want the Lord to act quickly. We see the dilemma, we have analyzed the consequences and we want God to rip the fabric of time just like he ripped the veil in the temple. It is in these moments where we must slow down as ask, why is God dragging this out and is there some nugget of wisdom that I can gather from it? Sometimes we panic because we pray for the mountain to move and it doesn't. What we don't realize is that some mountains are moved immediately while others are moved one rock at a time. The end result is the same, the mountain gets moved and God gets the glory! **Today, hold onto your faith and know that God is always working!**

_____

_____

_____

_____

_____

_____

_____

_____

_____

_____

_____

_____

_____

_____

_____

_____

_____

_____

_____

_____

_____

_____

_____

SEPTEMBER 8TH

"BABBLING"

Matthew 6:7 "And when you pray, do not babble on like pagans, for they think that by their many words they will be heard."

Jesus is a great teacher. He taught us how to live, how to love one another and how to carry our crosses. One critical teaching of Jesus was his teaching on prayer. We have turned prayer into a show. Associate ministers in churches often use prayer time as their showcase. They turn prayers into sermonettes. Jesus taught us to keep prayer simple. He says that pagans believe that the more they talk, the more likely it is that they will be heard. The word babble literally means "vain repetitions", just saying the same thing over and over again. This is written as a very strong denouncement of this practice. Instead, Jesus reminds his listeners that God already knows what we need so the babbling is unnecessary. He taught us to pray Our Father, who is in heaven, hallowed be Your name, Your kingdom come, Your will be done, on earth as it is in heaven. Give us this day our daily bread and forgive us our debts, as we forgive our debtors. Lead us not into temptation but deliver us from evil. For Yours is the kingdom and the power and the glory, forever, amen. Don't be deceived about prayer. It does not always have to be a dissertation. Sometimes a sentence will do, sometimes even a single word will do. **Today, let us remember that God already knows what we need!**

SEPTEMBER 9TH

"TWO MASTERS"

Matthew 6:24 "No one can serve two masters; for either he will hate the one and love the other, or he will be devoted to one and despise the other. You cannot serve God and wealth."

Wealth is often a goal in the lives of many. There is no shortage of get-rich-quick investing schemes, Ponzi schemes, network marketing schemes or myriad other ways to supposedly grow wealth in America. Money is indeed an idol god. Mute, deaf and blind, but able to exercise great control over people. The O'Jays once sang "for the love of money, people would rob their own brother..." Churches lure people into giving their last with the promise of God granting an overflow or increase based on how large of a seed is sown. But Jesus recognized that money, which he called a master, can come into direct competition with God. If money is our God, then our worship will consists of constantly seeking more, stepping on your brother/sister to get more, refusing to give to the least of these and bowing down to profit rather than reason. A man cannot serve God and money. We have to choose. Does our bottom line supersede our ethics? Do we care more about being rich in possessions or rich in God's grace? The answers to these questions will tell us where our hearts are. **Today, let us choose which master we will serve.**

_____

_____

_____

_____

_____

_____

_____

_____

_____

_____

_____

_____

_____

_____

_____

_____

_____

_____

_____

_____

_____

_____

"VANITY OF VANITIES"

Ecclesiastes 12:8 "Vanity of vanities," says the Preacher, "All is vanity."

We naturally gravitate toward what we chase. If we chase money, we like to hang around people with money. If we chase sex, we like to hang around places where sex is easily available. If we chase power, we want powerful people in our circle. Solomon tells us in the book of Ecclesiastes that at the end of everything, it is all vanity. The money, the excess, the debauchery, the pleasure, all of life is vanity, like chasing after the wind. Satan knows how to bait trails so that all we do is chase, but we are rarely, if ever, satisfied. This is why David says that his soul panted after God as a deer pants for water. The question is, why are we moving away from Jesus? It's because we do not chase Him. We do not gravitate towards him because we are born programmed to sin and programmed to move in the opposite direction. We run away from Him for fear of picking up that big, heavy cross and having to carry it for the rest of our days. But at the end of the cross carrying, there is a crown of righteousness stored up for us. The pursuit of God is a noble and necessary one. Solomon told us what the end of the matter was: to fear God and to keep His commandments. **Today, out of reverential fear, let us ramp up our pursuit for God and leave vanity behind!**

_____

_____

_____

_____

_____

_____

_____

_____

_____

_____

_____

_____

_____

_____

_____

_____

_____

_____

_____

_____

_____

_____

SEPTEMBER 11TH

"COUNT IT ALL JOY"

James 1:2 "Consider it all joy, my brethren, when you encounter various trials..."

The hardest part of the Christian walk is being in intimate relationship with an all-powerful God, but not being buffeted from the physical and emotional effects of this broken world. The Bible does not teach us that we are exempt from tribulation, but rather that we should expect it. We endure countless trials in this life and it hurts. It is easy to spout off platitudes and say churchy things, but if we are honest, life can be very painful. But there is hope in that one day the pain will be remedied, eased, by God Himself. We have to remain cognizant that the turbulence has a reason. Sometimes, our trees bear fruit on high limbs and the only way to get that fruit to fall down, to be used in the service of God is for the wind to blow. Just as God intends (allows), the fruit that falls from your tree will be a blessing to someone else. Take comfort in knowing that the devil does not shake empty trees, he shakes trees with fruit on them because a fruit bearing tree is a threat to his earthly dominion. A fruit bearing tree brings glory to God. Empty trees don't get shaken. They get chopped down by the Vinedresser. **Today, let us be thankful that the fruit on our tree can and will be used to bless someone else and glorify God through that blessing!**

SEPTEMBER 12TH

"THE ABSENCE OF HOPE"

Psalm 71:1 "In You, O LORD, I have taken refuge; let me never be put to shame."

Many skeptics discount hope. They say "you Christians can keep that pie in the sky rhetoric." Let's be honest and real in light of skyrocketing suicide rates: hope can be the difference in putting a .45 to your head or getting up and continuing to fight! Hope is joyful expectation and whoever hopes in God will never be put to shame. Hold on to the hope that everyone else is skeptical about. Hold on to Jesus and He will deliver what He promised. Don't ever lose hope. When they question you for being hopeful, give them an answer for the hope that is within you. Tell them it comes from God, it is stirred by His Spirit and it belongs to all believers! Life is very difficult. Even the strongest, most faithful men and women of God have breaks and times when they get overwhelmed. It's not a sin to feel overwhelmed. It's definitely not a sin to cry. Let it out, don't internalize it! Have a heart to heart with God. He already knows that we are but dust and he is mindful of the afflicted. We can't walk around like we have all the answers. We don't, but our God does. **Today, remind yourself of the hope that God inspires within each and every believer.**

SEPTEMBER 13TH

"A LOVE SUPREME"

1 John 2:2 "…and He Himself is the propitiation for our sins; and not for ours only, but also for those of the whole world."

God's love is unfathomable. The depth, breadth and height cannot be comprehended apart from His own revelation of these qualities to us. Know this, God loves everyone! His love is not predicated upon our station, condition, works or personality! Man's feelings can quickly fade based on changes in the object's appearance or sometimes a lack of incentive but God needs no incentive to love. God is love. Jesus loves us despite what our background check turns up. That's real love based on His grace and not our performance. He loved us first! As Christians, even if we disagree with others, we are still compelled to love them. Jesus is the Savior of the whole world. Not just a few, not just white evangelicals, not just Jews, not just black people, not just Calvinists, but literally the whole world. It's not the marred, broken, sin-stained image that matters, it is the fact that we're all made in God's image that does. **Today, let us beckon God to teach us to love like Him!**

"A TRAINED HEART"

Matthew 7:15 "Beware of the false prophets, who come to you in sheep's clothing, but inwardly are ravenous wolves."

Satan is a master at counterfeiting which is why so many churches are in disarray. Just like fake bills can be spotted with a marker, fake spirits can be tested and shown not to be of God. We MUST sharpen our discernment skills through knowing God's Son, studying God's word, living God's mandate and not being afraid to tell or accept the truth. This situation will not improve. It will get worse. Jesus warned us that not only will it get worse, if the time isn't cut short; the deception would be effective enough to fool even the elect. Let us be vigilant and always be willing to test everything. Those things that are legitimate, we keep; those things that are meant for ill will, we push away. Jesus said plainly, "My sheep know My voice." **Today, let our hearts not answer to or go after another shepherd, but only to the Good Shepherd.**

SEPTEMBER 15TH

"DOWN GOES SATAN"

Revelation 12:9 "And the great dragon was thrown down, the serpent of old who is called the devil and Satan, who deceives the whole world; he was thrown down to the earth, and his angels were thrown down with him."

Sometimes, it can seem as if God is asleep at the wheel. It can seem as if God does not see or know what is going on. The world can seem like a scary place. The violence, apathy, nihilism, death and destruction on a daily basis can be overwhelming, even for the most seasoned Christian soldier. But there will come a time when the accuser of the brethren, the great dragon, the one who accuses us day and night before the Lord, the cosmic prosecutor, and the third of the angels whom he has coopted, will be thrown down to the earth in defeat! He is the prince of the power of the air and he has a time to have dominion over the earth, but do understand that Satan exercises influence from the heavenly realms (see Ephesians 6:12). His influence will be no more when he is cast down by the Almighty Himself. Be steadfast, be encouraged and be vigilant, knowing that the roaring lion who prowls looking for those whom he may devour will be no more and the armies of heaven, and Jesus, who is called Faithful and True, will mount up and establish His peace forevermore! **Today, let us rejoice that when time is no more and history has recorded its last deed, we will be on the side of the Lord!**

_____

_____

_____

_____

_____

_____

_____

_____

_____

_____

_____

_____

_____

_____

_____

_____

_____

_____

_____

_____

_____

_____

_____

SEPTEMBER 16TH

"PERSPECTIVE IS EVERYTHING"

Luke 7:39 "When the Pharisee who had invited Jesus saw this, he said to himself, "If this man were a prophet, He would know who this is and what kind of woman is touching Him—for she is a sinner!"

Those in the church who strain out a gnat to swallow a camel usually end up "choking" when the game is on the line. The game was on the line when Jesus was invited to Simon the Pharisee's home. He wanted to inspect Jesus and he wanted the prestige of eating with the new guy in town. But Simon did not believe. Simon questioned the prophetic office of Jesus. But it wasn't because Jesus missed the mark on a prophecy. No, it was because Jesus did not away a prostitute who found out where He was. She came in and cried so much that she wet his feet with her tears. He actually did know she was a sinner, but rather than casting her out, he forgave her. In contrast, Simon did not even offer to wash Jesus' feet, a common practice in this culture. What Jesus was saying was that her praise was proportional to her victory. He gave her victory over her sinful life through His forgiveness. Simon did not see the need for forgiveness because he thought he had it together! He missed the mark. **Today, let us praise God for His forgiveness because we are all guilty of sin!**

"OUT OF DARKNESS"

1 Peter 2:9 "…a holy nation, a people for his own possession, that you may proclaim the excellencies of him who called you out of darkness into his marvelous light."

Once I was out on an afternoon walk and the sun (Son) taught me something profound. As I walked, I looked to my right and I noticed my shadow. Everywhere I went, my shadow went. A shadow is generated when light hits an object and what's not absorbed by the object or transmitted through the object is blocked by it. The light from the sun hit me and my frame caused a shadow. What's the spiritual connection? If Jesus is the Light, and I am the object, it took His light to expose my second self! God revealed to me that my shadow represents my old self, the darkness in me, exposed only by the light of Christ. He has a way of exposing us. He also told us that men love darkness, because in darkness, our deeds and our true selves are not exposed and thus are unavailable to be transformed. The old me was not a pretty sight. And honestly, we all still wrestle with the old self. But, we thank God for His light and for His word that is sharper than any two-edged sword, knows the thoughts and intentions of the heart. We also thank God for the new self, shaped in His image, being conformed day by day. Every day is a battle between flesh and spirit. **Today, we bless God that we will lose some, but we will also win many through the power of the Holy Spirit.**

"KEEP LOOKING"

1 Kings 18:43 "He said to his servant, "Go up now, look toward the sea." So he went up and looked and said, "There is nothing." And he said, "Go back." seven times."

It is faith that makes the unseen visible. After all, the Hebrew writer tells us that it is the evidence of things not seen. I will be the first to admit that the kind of faith that allows us to look into a distant future and believe that God has already worked all things together for our good is not easy to come by. Faith is built by repetition. We go into storms, and God brings us out of storms and we trust Him more and more. It is a cycle of testing and testifying. Elijah pronounced a drought that lasted for three-and-a-half years in Israel. When the drought was about to end, God told Elijah, who had to deliver the message to Ahab, who had been seeking his life. After meeting Ahab and pronouncing an end to the drought, Elijah sends his servant to the sea to look for any sign of rain. The servant made eight trips. Not only was Elijah's faith tested during this time but the faith of his servant was also being built! On the eighth trip, the servant saw a cloud the size of a man's fist. From that small cloud, the entire nation would be revived and refreshed. **Today, let us believe God for whatever He has promised! Sometimes, we just have to keep looking.**

SEPTEMBER 19TH

"SMELLING SALTS"

Psalm 27:13 "I would have despaired unless I had believed that I would see the goodness of the LORD In the land of the living."

No doubt that you have seen a movie with one of the actors woozy and in a state of duress with another actor lightly slapping their face trying to revive them. The one doing the slapping would probably be repeating something like, "C'mon, get up, get up!" Then, when all else fails, you see them break out the smelling salts and wave it around the nose of the person in distress. Often, they are revived immediately. Smelling salts consists of ammonium carbonate and other ingredients and can be sniffed as a restorative. The ingredients combine to release ammonia gas which triggers an inhalation response. It is a way to revive a person who is suffering from the effects of some event that caused them to get weak or pass out. God specializes in delivering the smelling salts to His people! We often go through tribulation. Our trials inflict mental and physical damage as well. Sometimes we are near the point of giving up. David was when he penned this psalm. But his smelling salts moment came when his faith said that the goodness of God would be experienced on this side of heaven! He didn't say how long he had to wait, but we know that waiting on the Lord results in the renewing of our strength! **Today, let us praise God for renewed strength and real revival.**

_____

_____

_____

_____

_____

_____

_____

_____

_____

_____

_____

_____

_____

_____

_____

_____

_____

_____

_____

_____

_____

_____

SEPTEMBER 20TH

"THE WHITE MAN'S RELIGION?"

John 4:24 "God is spirit, and those who worship Him must worship in spirit and truth."

Here is a point to ponder. Many like to say that Christianity is a "white man's religion" without even acknowledging that if Christ is the branch from the root of Jesse, Christianity has its roots in Judaism. There was no "white" in Judah or Jerusalem. Jesus was from the tribe of Judah, not Europe, which is common knowledge. When the prophet Isaiah wrote "though your sins are scarlet, they shall be as white as snow" he was, in no way, referencing white as it relates to the white race. The sins being made white refers to God's forgiveness and is not racial at all. Snow is actually white, you know? It is a literary device, not a racist tool. The white is clean, black is bad stereotype began much later than when Isaiah was written. That negative stereotype has its roots in the early exploratory and imperial missions of Europeans into Africa. They began using cultural differences to create their belief of racial superiority. As a matter of fact, the concept of white, as we know it, did not exist during the time that the Bible was written; only righteous and unrighteous. Righteousness doesn't have a color. **Today, when someone questions what you believe, and doesn't invite you to question what they are using to supplant your beliefs, start asking questions.**

"KEEP YOUR GUARD UP"

Nehemiah 1:3 "And they told me, 'The remnant who survived the exile are there in the province, in great trouble and disgrace. The wall of Jerusalem is broken down, and its gates are burned with fire.'"

Weeds can pop up out of nowhere. You can have the most well-manicured lawn in the world and you will eventually have weeds. The reason is simple. Many times we think it's the grass that is bad. I once learned from a master gardener that the wind blows seeds, spores etc. from everywhere and they land wherever they please. He said, "There is really no way to stop it". That made me feel powerless but it brings a great point to light. Weeds also crop up in our lives. Jesus even taught us that weeds can choke the gospel out of our lives. The point is, it may not be the grass that's the problem; it may be the undue influences that have been allowed to land on our grass. We cannot control what the wind blows onto our physical grass, but we most certainly can control what infiltrates our spiritual lawn. We can stop the wind from blowing some things our way that aren't good for us. AND we can definitely use some "weed" killer to root those things out if they so happen to land on our grass! Nehemiah knew this and was adamant about erecting the gates around Jerusalem. **Today, let us refuse to let the weeds grow on our lawns where they don't belong. Root them out.**

SEPTEMBER 22ND

"YOU HAVE BEEN MADE NEW"

John 3:8 "The wind blows where it wishes and you hear the sound of it, but do not know where it comes from and where it is going; so is everyone who is born of the Spirit."

Born again people are new creatures. The Bible is full of examples of God's regenerative power. He can turn the hearts of kings, use the hands of prostitutes to tie red threads in their windows, turn blasphemers into apostles and use ordinary people to do extraordinary things. No one understands how God is able to do this and many will analyze our past lives to try to understand our present state of grace. Jesus teaches this to Nicodemus in a very simple lesson. Now, with modern technology, we can actually track the direction of the wind, but do we really know the origin of the wind? That's a bit more difficult. But Jesus says the wind blows wherever it wishes to blow and we hear it but we don't know the origin or the destination. The same can be said for those of us who are born again. We do not know how the Spirit does what He does, we do not know the mechanism of His action but we do know that once we are born again, there are visible and tangible differences in our lives. **Today, let us not be concerned about the origin of our change, but let us rejoice that it happened!**

_____

_____

_____

_____

_____

_____

_____

_____

_____

_____

_____

_____

_____

_____

_____

_____

_____

_____

_____

_____

_____

SEPTEMBER 23RD

"IN THE MIDST OF IT ALL"

Jeremiah 29:11 "For I know the plans that I have for you,' declares the LORD, 'plans for welfare and not for calamity to give you a future and a hope."

The period in the history of Judah in which they were under Babylonian captivity was a dark time. Their sin and their rebellion against God brought this punishment on. False prophets prophesied that the time would be shorter. The people did not heed the warnings of God through His true prophets. However, even in the midst of the calamity, God's grace was revealed. Jeremiah 29:11 comes in the midst of God reminding His people that they would spend 70 years in Babylonian captivity. It's like a parent saying "you're grounded" but still preparing dinner and carrying on as usual because, obviously, being grounded doesn't mean that you are unloved. The chastisement was out of God's love! We have to understand that even as God's people we will encounter difficulty. Sometimes, the difficulty comes as a result of our own disobedience. We have to trust that in the difficulty, God is not absent but ever present to guide, teach and protect us! David said even darkness is light to God so trust that our dark moments do not scare God, He saw them coming and planned for the outcome to glorify Himself and to build our witness. **Today, let us be encouraged that in the midst of it all, God never fails.**

SEPTEMBER 24TH

"WRESTLING IN PRAYER"

Colossians 4:12 "Epaphras, who is one of your number, a bondslave of Jesus Christ, sends you his greetings, always laboring earnestly for you in his prayers, that you may stand perfect and fully assured in all the will of God."

Epaphras was a Colossian man who was an understudy of the apostle Paul. He is referred to, in this scripture, as a bondslave of Jesus. That is a pretty powerful title, especially coming from Paul. Paul writes that Epaphras was contending or "wrestling" in prayer for the Christians in Colossae. He was standing in the gap for those who were Christians like himself, that they would stand complete and fully assured of the will of God for themselves! We too can stand in the gap for our fellow believers. A simple intercessory prayer could ask God not to let our deceptive hearts lead us astray from what He desires, to remove the stumbling blocks from our own life and the lives of those whom we know and love, and finally, we can pray that when the Holy City comes down, that we have all accepted Jesus so that we can see each other again. **Today, bless God for the day of rejoicing that will come at the coming of His glory!**

"NO ALTERNATIVE"

John 6:68 "Simon Peter replied, "Lord, to whom would we go? You have the words of eternal life."

When Jesus taught about being the Bread of Life, many deserted Him. This was a hard teaching, telling those who followed Him that they had to eat His flesh and drink His blood. It was really Jesus hinting at the intimacy of the relationship between Himself and those who followed Him. He is also pointing to the Lord's Supper where we remember His sacrifice on our behalf. After the crowd thinned out, Jesus asked those closest to Him if they wanted to leave too. They replied, "Where will we go? YOU have the words to eternal life." As His disciples, when hard things occur, this must be our response to the option to quit that will most certainly be presented by the enemy! The enemy will always give us every reason to walk away. We must ask ourselves, "Where will we go?" The answer: There is nowhere else TO go except into the arms of Christ! **Today, let us be determined to walk with Jesus each and every day.**

SEPTEMBER 26TH

"THE CHOICE IS YOURS"

Job 2:10 "But he said to her, "You speak as one of the foolish women speaks. Shall we indeed accept good from God and not accept adversity?" In all this Job did not sin with his lips."

I dare not minimize the suffering of any saint. We all deal with our issues in different ways. There is an old saying that sometimes we have to "shut up and deal." In today's hypersensitive environment, that would seem harsh. Saying it doesn't mean that you won't receive support from those around you, it is simply a conscious decision to accept what God is doing and trust Him to bring us through it. You don't learn to shut up and deal until you have to shut up and deal. Sometimes, we complain about the minutiae when others are suffering much worse. We have to stop complaining about trivialities. We whine about a toe stub but the diabetic amputee is just happy to have one foot. We complain about the weather when there are folks who are shut in and wish they could feel rain on their skin. We complain about our jobs but never think what it would be like to be living under a bridge. Job teaches us that we must accept both the good and the adversity that God allows into our lives. In doing so, he did not sin by speaking against Him. **Today, let us be grateful for our time, health, finances, children, job, career, food and every other blessing bestowed upon us.**

_____

_____

_____

_____

_____

_____

_____

_____

_____

_____

_____

_____

_____

_____

_____

_____

_____

_____

_____

_____

_____

_____

"PEW MEMBERS"

John 12:6 "Judas did not say this because he cared about the poor, but because he was a thief. As keeper of the money bag, he used to take from what was put into it."

Judas' role in the ministry cannot be underestimated. We know that he was called the son of perdition and Jesus said that he was destined to be lost. That is a teaching for another time, and a difficult one at that. But judging from the actions of Judas, it is almost as if he never opened his heart to be transformed. Scripture reveals to us that he was a thief who loved money. He also was willing to sell out Jesus for thirty pieces of silver and hand him over to the religious leaders to be crucified. This is an amazing observation. Judas was in the very presence of Jesus and still stole, lied and cheated. The presence of Christ had no effect on him! If there is no real change in the fruit that we bear, can we really call ourselves Christian or are we just in the crowd? Yes, we have all sinned and fallen short of His glory but we have to get back up. Judas attended every event and yet he left the same way that he came. We must be mindful that attendance alone doesn't change us, repentance does! Not a good look for Judas or for us. **Today, let us make every effort to never hear the four words, "I NEVER KNEW YOU."**

_____

_____

_____

_____

_____

_____

_____

_____

_____

_____

_____

_____

_____

_____

_____

_____

_____

_____

_____

_____

_____

"BE SOMEONE'S GATORADE"

Proverbs 25:25 "Like cold water to a weary soul, so is good news from a distant land."

Gatorade is a very popular thirst quencher. They have a marketing machine behind them that is second-to-none and most major sporting organizations have incorporated Gatorade into their sports training regimens. They claim to replenish electrolytes and other nutrients lost during rigorous exercise. Have you ever thought that life can sometimes be considered equivalent to rigorous exercise? Life can be deflating, it can deplete us and rob us of our joy and happiness if allowed, and life can be extremely difficult. So, when we come across people, we should always be considerate of the fact that they may just be going through some turbulent times in their life. Solomon teaches us that bringing some good news to a weary soul is like giving them cold water! Whether that good news is the Gospel of Jesus Christ or simply a kind word or gesture, we can be a momentary thirst quencher for someone who crosses our path. **Today, let us remember that we can be difference makers through the gift of kindness to others! The world definitely needs it.**

_____

_____

_____

_____

_____

_____

_____

_____

_____

_____

_____

_____

_____

_____

_____

_____

_____

_____

_____

_____

_____

_____

_____

SEPTEMBER 29TH

"BROKEN FOR THE BLESSING"

Acts 9:4 "He fell to the ground and heard a voice say to him, "Saul, Saul, why do you persecute Me?"

If you know the story of the apostle Paul, you will know that he was not always an apostle. Paul was rigorously trained in the ways of the Pharisees and had an impeccable Jewish pedigree, was affluent and well versed in the Law. But with all of these perceived blessings, Paul (Saul) was woefully inadequate when it came to having a true relationship with God. He had, as he penned to Timothy, a form of godliness but he denied its power. So, before he became Paul, he was on his way to Damascus to persecute Christians. On the road, he encountered Jesus. He had a letter from the high priest giving him permission to hunt and punish those who were disciples of Jesus Christ. Jesus pointedly asked him amidst a flashing light from heaven, "Why do you persecute Me?" Jesus later spoke to a man named Ananias and told him that Paul was his instrument and that Paul must also suffer for the sake of Jesus. He had to break Paul before He could bless Paul with years of service to Him. Many of us have experienced this breaking. It may have come in a different form, but the Lord had to put us on the potter's wheel and smooth out some lumps before blessing us and calling us into service! **Today, let us give thanks that God is a God of grace who not only breaks us, but also blesses us!**

SEPTEMBER 30TH

"QUICKSAND"

Psalm 1:1 "Blessed is the man who does not walk in the counsel of the wicked, or set foot on the path of sinners, or sit in the seat of mockers."

My neighborhood was drug and crime infested. I lost many friends either to prison or to the coffin. As I grew older and the opportunity to escape that environment came, I took it. But, I never forgot from whence I came and I am still friends with many of the guys who survived that struggle. I do not judge anyone. But when I go home, I know how long to stay and fraternize. I do not linger because anything can happen at any time. I've seen it way too often. This Psalm is a great reminder of knowing when to leave! Sin is just like quicksand. The longer we stay around it, the more prone we are to slipping up! There is a distinct progression that the author gives us here. First, we walk in the counsel of ungodly people and the descent begins. Then we stop walking and start standing in the place of sinners. Then we get comfortable and we sit down in the seat of the scornful. Once seated, it's a wrap. Walking slows to standing which slows to sitting. That is not the progress that we want! **Today, let us stay around positive people who walk the same path that we walk, who stand for the things we stand for and who long to sit in God's presence. Today, let our lives reflect His glory.**

"THE POINT OF IT ALL"

Proverbs 1:7 "The fear of the LORD is the beginning of knowledge, but fools despise wisdom and discipline."

Solomon's proverbs teach us a lot. I like to think of proverbs as pro-verbs. Verbs are action words and to be pro- anything means to be an advocate of that thing. So, pro-verbs means to be proactive about turning words into action. To be doers of the word and not just hearers. The summary of the purpose of proverbs is here in the very first one. Solomon writes that the proverbs are for the readers to know wisdom and understand insight, receive advice for wise living, justice and equity, to give prudence to the simple i.e. the uneducated, to teach knowledge and discretion to the young who always need guidance. So, we are admonished to listen and gain instruction, wise counsel through the use of these proverbs and parables. Is this not the goal of the whole counsel of God? To teach us, instruct us, rebuke us, reprove us and to train us up in righteousness? Solomon gives us clear understanding in this scripture. The very first step to knowledge is to fear the LORD. Once we know that and once we put that into action, everything else is governed by that reverence for Yahweh. **Today, let us take the necessary steps towards the fear of the Lord be led by that in all of our endeavors.**

_____

_____

_____

_____

_____

_____

_____

_____

_____

_____

_____

_____

_____

_____

_____

_____

_____

_____

_____

_____

_____

_____

_____

"A LIFELONG QUEST"

Proverbs 2:4,5 "…if you seek it like silver and search it out like hidden treasure, then you will discern the fear of the LORD and discover the knowledge of God."

James teaches that if anyone lacks wisdom, they should ask God and the Father of Lights will liberally grant it from above. What is wisdom? There are numerous definitions but the simplest definition is applied knowledge. Knowledge is obtained through experience and the more we learn, the wiser we should become. Once something is learned, it is stored until an opportune time and the applied to a situation. That is the exercise of wisdom. The writer gives sound advice for all in this passage. Wisdom is gained or passed down from those who have experienced what we haven't. We must listen to sound counsel in order to benefit from that wisdom being passed down. The author then places the onus on the seeker. We must call out to God and ask for wisdom. God gives insight, God gives understanding and God gives wisdom to all who ask. But we must seek it out. Every experience offers us something upon which we can build. But we have to be seekers. We have to seek out wisdom and understanding and knowledge like it is a hidden treasure. That's a fitting analogy because there is great treasure in wisdom! **Today, let us follow Christ's advice by asking, seeking and knocking in our quest to become wiser every day!**

"WHAT'S THE PURPOSE?"

Proverbs 2:9 "Then you will discern righteousness and justice and equity—every good path."

Have you ever done something or sought something but didn't know why? College graduates sometimes get degrees in fields that don't match their skillset or passion and end up asking "why did I study this?" There must be a purpose for everything that we do. So what is the purpose of seeking wisdom? Why is it such a treasured asset in the eyes of God? And before we get to the answer, there are certainly two types of wisdom. James teaches us that there is worldly wisdom that comes from demonic sources and there is godly wisdom that comes from God. So, why do we seek wisdom from God? It is the same reason why we consult a GPS on a journey in which we have no idea how to get to the destination. Wisdom from God will allow us to discern what is right, what is just and what is equitable! Why is this important? Because we also coexist with other people made in God's image and should govern ourselves accordingly. Wisdom will also help us to discern which path to tread as we move closer to glory. **Today, let us be thankful to God for the dispensation of wisdom to all who seek it out.**

OCTOBER 4TH

"I DID IT MY WAY"

Proverbs 3:7,8 "Do not be wise in your own eyes; fear the LORD and turn away from evil. This will bring healing to your body and refreshment to your bones."

Music has a way of communicating thoughts and ideas that are difficult to grapple with through conventional conversation. Frank Sinatra, famed Rat Pack singer and probably one of the largest music icons in the history of music, communicated a very simple message with profound implications. But as great as the song was, it is antithetical to a biblical worldview. His song, I Did It My Way, was a smash and the basic premise of the song was that he lived life according to his own rules. There were not many regrets or inhibitions, just life and living. Ironically, the song's introduction says that he's facing the final curtain i.e. he's about to die. What a chilling thought to be nearing death and saying, nothing else matters, I did it my own way. Solomon advises us not to lean on our own understanding but rather, to trust in the Lord and let Him direct us. He instructs us that to use our own worldly wisdom is not the correct way to live life. We ought not think of ourselves and our way as the correct way, unless that way is being directed by God. If we fear Him, turn away from evil, God will restore health and wellness to us! The pursuit of evil will always lead to issues!

_____

_____

_____

_____

_____

_____

_____

_____

_____

_____

_____

_____

_____

_____

_____

_____

_____

_____

_____

_____

_____

_____

OCTOBER 5TH

"BE WELL"

Proverbs 3:27 "Do not withhold good from the deserving when it is within your power to act."

If we are able to do good we should do it. There is no rationalization necessary for doing good. If it is within our power, do it. This scripture begs the question, "who is deserving?" I always lean on the encouragement of the Holy Spirit. Many situations arise in which we are faced with decisions to help or not to help. If we are in a position to give a hard worker a raise, why would we deny that raise? As a college administrator, many students come into my office seeking financial assistance. What good does it do me to have money in my budget for such assistance, have the power to distribute such money at my discretion, and not do it for a deserving student? If we see someone being mistreated and we have the power to intervene, why would we not intervene? If we see a poor person on the street who is hungry, and we have the means to provide food, what good does it do us to withhold such means to uphold some worldly principle of "every man for himself"? It is plain, as James teaches us, that we cannot simply wish someone without a coat to be warm; especially, if we have the means to provide a coat. God does not withhold any good thing from those who walk uprightly. **Today, let us be mindful to emulate God if we are in a position to help someone!**

_____

_____

_____

_____

_____

_____

_____

_____

_____

_____

_____

_____

_____

_____

_____

_____

_____

_____

_____

_____

_____

"NO VISITORS, PLEASE"

Proverbs 4:23 "Guard your heart with all diligence, for from it flow springs of life."

The heart is an important organ and literally keeps us alive by pumping blood and oxygen to places within our bodies that need those things. The heart, in ancient thought, is also seen as the seat of our emotions and passions. Jeremiah said that the heart is deceitfully wicked and cannot be understood. Ezekiel inferred that the people to whom he prophesied had hearts of stone. This is why the heart must be guarded, as the writer instructs. Springs of life flow from our heart. What does that mean? Let's create a chain. First of all, if the heart is where our emotions and passions are seated, it must be protected such that it is not corrupted by unrighteousness. Jesus tells us that it is from the overflow of the heart that the mouth speaks. The writer says in another place that life and death is in the power of the tongue. So, if we do not guard our hearts, what comes out of our mouths may be detrimental to those who are around us! So, keeping our hearts pure and our motives pure will result in us speaking life rather than death. Our motives will be to build up rather than to tear down. Therefore, we have to control what visits our hearts and keep negative influences out. **Today, let us ask God to put a hedge of protection around our hearts and make them follow after Him!**

"FLATTERY WILL GET YOU..."

Proverbs 5:3,4 "Though the lips of the forbidden woman drip honey and her speech is smoother than oil, her end is bitter as wormwood, sharp as a double-edged sword."

Depending on our perspective on life, flattery will either get you everywhere or nowhere. Flattery can be a powerful tool in the hands of an enemy seeking our destruction. Sin does not always show up dressed in dirty clothes and looking like sin. Sometimes, sin shows up in a beautiful outfit, with curves (or muscles), looking exactly like what we desire. The forbidden woman in the scripture is Folly. She leads men to their death, oftentimes through flattery. Her lips drip honey. Honey is sweet to the taste and sticky to the touch. Her speech is smooth. She will tell us everything that we want to hear, whatever it takes to get us off the pathway of wisdom and life. That's the problem with sin. It may taste good going down, but the end is death. The writer says that the end of this forbidden woman is as bitter as wormwood. That imagery, in the minds of ancient readers, brought to mind something so bitter that it was inedible. The writer instructs the reader multiple times in this and many of the other proverbs to stay on the path. We must turn away from sin and turn to God. **Today, let our hearts not be susceptible to empty flattery but may they be stayed on the Lord!**

_____

_____

_____

_____

_____

_____

_____

_____

_____

_____

_____

_____

_____

_____

_____

_____

_____

_____

_____

_____

_____

_____

"GIFTED TO WORK"

Proverbs 6:6 "Walk in the manner of the ant, O slacker; observe its ways and become wise."

As you can imagine, things have changed a lot since the biblical days. As we have transitioned from an agrarian economy to a more technological economy, the conditions for work have also changed. We live in a time now where tech jobs call for employees to sit at a desk and type code all day long. What hasn't changed is work ethic. A hard worker can work hard, no matter the type of work. There are several keys to having a great work ethic. The Bible tells us that God gives us the ability to create wealth i.e. He gives us the ability to work and make money. Solomon instructs us to consider the ant. The ant has a tireless work ethic because a lazy ant is a dead ant. So, the ant can teach us a lot! The ant doesn't have a master and yet it works every day. That means that the ant is self-motivated, a key to having a great work ethic. The ant prepares for winter in summer. That means that the ant is a planner. A good plan makes work smoother and allows for goal setting. The ant gathers its own food at harvest. That means that the ant takes responsibility for its own well-being. How much less complicated would our lives be if we gathered our own harvests instead of waiting on someone to do it for us? **Today, let us learn from the ant and use the gifts that God has given us!**

_____

_____

_____

_____

_____

_____

_____

_____

_____

_____

_____

_____

_____

_____

_____

_____

_____

_____

_____

_____

_____

"THE THINGS THAT GOD HATES"

Proverbs 6:16-19 "There are six things that the LORD hates, seven that are detestable to Him: haughty eyes, a lying tongue, hands that shed innocent blood, a heart that devises wicked schemes, feet that run swiftly to evil, a false witness who gives false testimony, and one who stirs up discord among brothers"

We have been taught to believe that God cannot hate because God is love. However, when we consider the context, God can indeed have a strong aversion to something. He has an aversion to sin! So much so that it cost the Lord Jesus His life at Calvary. He was the sin offering required to satisfy God the Father's requirement of blood to atone for sin. So, God can hate. The writer here tells us that there are seven things that the LORD hates. God hates arrogance (haughty eyes). God hates lying (a lying tongue). God hates injustice (shedding innocent blood). God hates hearts that are only set towards evil (devising wicked schemes). God hates those who seek out evil deed in which to participate (feet that run swiftly to evil). God hates a false witness who gives false testimony (see the trial of Jesus). God hates one who is an instigator (stirs up discord). Is there a remedy? Yes! Repentance. We can or may have been guilty of some or all of these things but God offers forgiveness to those who see the error of their ways and turn away from evil. **Today, let us flee evil and seek God!**

"WISDOM IS LIFE"

Proverbs 8:35 "For whoever finds me finds life and obtains the favor of the LORD."

It is no secret that Solomon asked for wisdom when God offered him whatever he wished. He asked for wisdom to rule God's people in a way that was pleasing to God. So, his affinity for wisdom is displayed in his writing. He writes about wisdom because he understands that wisdom also brings forth understanding, discretion, empathy, just dealings and other actions upon which God looks favorably. Wisdom keeps us grounded and keeps us on God's path which He set for our lives. Solomon says here that whoever finds wisdom finds life. How is that possible? Is wisdom really that important? Here is a practical example. If you had a friend who was going to rob a bank, wisdom would tell you not to get into the car, to consider the consequences, to stay back and not run into that trap. Folly on the other hand would have you counting the money before you even get into the car. Now, imagine going through with the robbery and getting shot by the guard, and dying. Can you see how wisdom and life go hand in hand? Wisdom will keep us from making dumb mistakes and help us see trouble before it happens. Finding wisdom and acting on wisdom also results in God's favor. **Today, let us seek the blessings and favor of the Lord by seeking wisdom from above.**

_____

_____

_____

_____

_____

_____

_____

_____

_____

_____

_____

_____

_____

_____

_____

_____

_____

_____

_____

_____

"LEAVE ME ALONE"

Proverbs 9:8 "Do not rebuke a mocker, or he will hate you; rebuke a wise man, and he will love you."

"You really shouldn't be doing that." Have you ever heard that? We all have. Our reaction to that admonishment tells a lot about what our mental state is at the time of the commission of the act. Teens, tweens and sometimes adults, look at the person offering correction and scoff. "Why are you in my business?!" Rapper Lil' Wayne was adamant that people should mind their business as it related to his consumption of codeine syrup mixed with soda aka "Drank" . "Don't worry about what's in my cup!" he'd say. Keep in mind, his drug use almost killed him, more than once. But one who is a mocker, who refuses instruction, will not tolerate a rebuke. Their reaction lies in their inability to process that although all things are permissible, all things are not beneficial. We are free beings, but everything has a limit. A wise man will have a different reaction. The author intimates that even a wise man can get off track and make mistakes. But when they are rebuked, they appreciate the rebuke; when someone is trying to help them get back on course. Our parents were right when they were chastising us and giving us wisdom to live by, we were just too immature to understand it at the time. **Today, let us thank God that there are people around us with our best interests at heart.**

_____

_____

_____

_____

_____

_____

_____

_____

_____

_____

_____

_____

_____

_____

_____

_____

_____

_____

_____

_____

_____

_____

_____

"A LASTING LEGACY"

Proverbs 10:7 "The memory of the righteous is a blessing, but the name of the wicked will rot."

One of the things that I least like to discuss is death. Although we will all die and we will all have to meet God for ourselves, I do not like thinking about it. I want to grow old and die at a ripe old age. I want to experience having grandkids and telling them stories about their parents. But, it is appointed to every man once to die and after that, the judgment. So, the question is, how will you be remembered? Will those who remember you reminisce fondly on how you touched their lives? Will they wax poetic about your virtues? Will they smile and remember what a blessing you were? If you lived a righteous life, then the answer will probably be, yes. Righteous, in this sense, simply means one who desires to do right by others. I've preached eulogies where the focus had to be on Jesus because there was really nothing that I could say about the deceased. I couldn't pepper the message with intimate details of their life or legacy because there wasn't much good to talk about. The author is telling the truth. The name of the wicked will rot because there is nothing to sustain it. The legacy will forever be tainted. How will the world remember us? **Today, let us ask God to give us the strength to live a righteous life so that we can leave a lasting and positive legacy!**

"HUSH UP"

Proverbs 11:13 "A gossip reveals a secret, but a trustworthy person keeps a confidence."

There is an old saying that we use to describe people who gossip. We would say, "You can't hold a cold potato." I still say it. My late wife Danielle used to get upset with me because there were certain things that I would not divulge to her. If someone asks me to keep something in confidence, I will. I do that because I want people who confide in me to know that they can trust me. I do not like having so much information about so many things. In fact, it can be quite overwhelming. But, I do my best to keep those things under wraps. A gossip, on the other hand, does not. When I hear people gossiping, I go the other way. If they gossip about others in front of you, what makes you think they aren't gathering intel about you to take to someone else? Gossiping is one of my least favorite activities. Some people live for the "tea" but not me. We have enough problems trying to mind our own business! Why do we need to mind someone else's? Listen to the writer. When someone trusts you enough to place their confidence in you, don't betray them by telling their secrets to someone else. James says that we ought to confess our faults to one another. The problem is, sometimes that confession becomes the topic of the day at the water cooler! **Today, let us guard our lips and our speech!**

_____

_____

_____

_____

_____

_____

_____

_____

_____

_____

_____

_____

_____

_____

_____

_____

_____

_____

_____

_____

_____

"THIS IS BENEATH ME"

Proverbs 12:26 "A righteous man is cautious in friendship, but the ways of the wicked lead them astray."

Unfortunately, we must be careful who we call friend. We cannot ascribe that title to everyone because everyone does not have our best interest at heart. Many times, the people who we call friends are corrupt company who lead us into all manner of ungodly behavior. Solomon tells us that a righteous man is cautious in friendship. A righteous person will employ discipline, discernment and diplomacy with all people. That is because a righteous person will exercise wisdom in all of their dealings. Solomon compares the righteous and the wicked a lot and there is always this dichotomy so that we can glean the wisdom that he is trying to impart. The wicked will call anyone friend and be led astray because they do not operate by the same principles as the righteous. **Today, let us not be so quick to call every person a friend. Let time reveal them as a friend or an associate.**

_____

_____

_____

_____

_____

_____

_____

_____

_____

_____

_____

_____

_____

_____

_____

_____

_____

_____

_____

_____

_____

_____

"WHAT A TIME TO BE ALIVE"

Proverbs 13:7 "There is one who pretends to be rich, but has nothing; another pretends to be poor, but has great wealth."

The social media age is upon us. I consider it a low point in human history. Not because of the technology but because of the use of the technology to mask our true selves. On a social media platform, we can be whoever we want to be. Read some of the profile names. Some are catchy; others are reaching for something beyond. One of the things that social media has given rise to is the faux rich generation. We call it many things, perpetrating, flagin' (i.e. camouflaging), fronting, faking the funk, faking it 'til you make it, flexing, stunting and there are many more adjectives to describe what Solomon points out. There is nothing new under the sun. People have been pretending for a long time. The only difference was they couldn't take selfies while holding a stack of money up to their ear pretending that it was a telephone. Many of these so-called rich social media posters are nothing more than imposters. You'd never see Bill Gates doing that. He wears modest clothing and simple accoutrements, and yet he's worth billions of dollars. The Lord knows the truth. I'd much rather be rich and thought of as broke than to be broke and thought of as rich. Let that sink in. **Today, let us resist the urge to put up any fronts and be our authentic selves!**

"THE FINAL ANALYSIS"

Proverbs 14:13 "Even in laughter the heart may be in pain, And the end of joy may be grief."

You have undoubtedly heard the expression, laugh now, cry later. It is true and it is a sobering thought. In context, it depends on what we are laughing at and what is bringing us joy. God does not turn laughter into pain or joy into grief unless our laughter and joy are connected to those things apart from His will. Someone who is living in sin may look to be having the time of their lives. In all honesty, many of us lived that same lifestyle. The lasciviousness, the derogatory language, the partying, the debauchery and the frenzied life of sinful indulgence had many of us trapped. We had a wonderful time if we judged it by the world's standards, but there were probably some tears shed as a result of our actions. Maybe an illegitimate child was conceived, maybe someone's feelings were wrecked, maybe an addiction surfaced, maybe we lost our way for a time. That laughter ended in pain. The joy of the moment ended in grief. Thanks be to God that we can forget those things that are behind us and press forward towards the mark of the high calling of Christ Jesus! **Today, let us thank God that He is also able to take the tears and grief of a repentant heart and turn them into joy and laughter for His own glory!**

"A PIECE OF MY MIND"

Proverbs 15:1 "A gentle answer turns away wrath, but a harsh word stirs up anger."

You're at the store. The cashier makes a mistake. You correct her and she proceeds to become rude and indignant with you. You have two choices in that moment. You can proceed to give them a piece of your mind or you could choose the high road and not revile back, but rather be the bigger person. Taking the high road is not as popular as it used to be. Everyone is ready to "turn up" at a moment's notice. Everyone is ready to unload, but when will Christians get back to the Word of God? Solomon says that a gentle answer can quell a potential storm. A gentle answer can stop wrath in its tracks. A gentle answer takes into account that the person on the tirade could very well have other issues that we are not aware of. If we want to inflame the situation, the easiest thing to do is to spit fire right back at the offending party. But, that is the easy way out. **Today, let us ask God to give us a gentle answer to have ready for every potential fire.**

_____

_____

_____

_____

_____

_____

_____

_____

_____

_____

_____

_____

_____

_____

_____

_____

_____

_____

_____

_____

_____

"PERCEPTION VS REALITY"

Proverbs 17:28 "Even a fool, when he keeps silent, is considered wise; When he closes his lips, he is considered prudent."

What exactly is a fool? The definition of the word used here is one who despises wisdom, one who will not accept correction. Solomon talks much about folly and being a fool and he does so in contrast with the wise or one who exercises wisdom. But how do we tell the difference if both a foolish person and a wise person are together in the same place at the same time? There is really no way to tell the difference unless we observe their actions or their words. Solomon gives us excellent advice here. We do not know a fool until they reveal their foolishness. Our speech and our behavior oftentimes can be indicative of our character. So, one of the best things that we can do is to keep silent when silence is called for. Even a fool can be mistaken for a prudent man if they keep their mouths shut. **Today, let us ask God to know when to speak and when to listen so that our actions and words reflect His glory.**

"GOD OPENS DOORS"

Proverbs 18:26 "A man's gift opens doors for him, and brings him before great men."

God is an amazing gift giver. He has gifted each and every one of us with something in which we are uniquely great. We are gifted with the use of our hands, the use of our intellect, the use of our energy and talents and it all comes from God. The author states that the gift belongs to us, but we all know that God gives us our ability. We have the ability to create wealth. We have the ability to build, to create, to innovate and to push the envelope of human ingenuity. Daniel's gift brought him before King Nebuchadnezzar. Joseph's gift brought him before Pharaoh. Paul's gift brought him before King Agrippa. The question is, when our gifts make room for us and bring us before dignitaries, who will get the credit? Will we smile and demure with faux humility and say "Aw shucks, thanks." Or, will we ascribe glory to God first? **Today, let us remember that all of our gifts emanate from the Most High God!**

"ALWAYS DO GOOD"

Proverbs 19:17 "Kindness to the poor is a loan to the LORD, and He will repay the lender."

Have you ever been driving and you passed by a homeless person, only to get that gut feeling in your stomach and end up turning around to offer food or assistance to that person? Have you ever gotten a phone call from someone who is truly in need and you had the means to help, but didn't because you felt like you were being played? There are multiple opportunities to show God's kindness to people each and every day. Solomon teaches us plainly that when we are kind to the poor it is almost like we are storing up favor with God. If you read the story of Cornelius in Acts 10, one of the reasons that God sent Peter to Cornelius was because of the generosity that Cornelius had shown to poor Jews who had been under Roman oppression. We don't know how the poor arrived at their station in life. Some of us have been poor ourselves. I know that I have. And this is by no means intended to foster a give-to-get mentality. It is intended to remind us that God desires us to show kindness to those who are less fortunate and that our kindness is not forgotten by the LORD. **Today, let us show kindness and generosity to those around us, especially those who are in need.**

"DON'T SPARE THE ROD"

Proverbs 19:18 "Discipline your son, for in that there is hope; do not be party to his death."

We've all heard the phrase "spare the rod and spoil the child." It is true. Discipline is a necessary element to prudent living. God disciplines us when we get out of line. He does so out of His love for us. Growing up, I am certain that we've all seen kids who never got in trouble for staying out all night, using drugs or doing whatever they wished. I grew up with many guys like that and most of them ended up in prison or dead. As parents, we have to walk the fine line between friend and disciplinarian. But we have to remember that being a disciplinarian is a blessing to our children. We don't have to be overly strict or harsh and mean-spirited. Being a disciplinarian simply means that when there is an infraction, it is dealt with. I don't advocate physical punishment, but I am not totally against it in certain cases. The writer tells us what a lack of discipline leads to, a life that will not end well. We teach our children boundaries. We teach them how to address elders, how to conduct themselves in public and how to be respectful of others, including us. It is up to us to instill values in them from an early age and not be party to their demise by not putting up some guard rails for them. **Today, let us remember that there is hope in discipline and we thank God for that.**

_____

_____

_____

_____

_____

_____

_____

_____

_____

_____

_____

_____

_____

_____

_____

_____

_____

_____

_____

_____

_____

_____

_____

_____

"RECIPROCITY"

Proverbs 20:4 "The slacker does not plow in season; at harvest time he looks, but nothing is there."

Reciprocity is a biblical concept. It is not meant to be twisted, as many preachers have done, so that people develop a "give to get" mentality. But, there is a general understanding that you get out what you put in. Or, as the apostle Paul said, if we sow sparingly then we will reap sparingly. So, Solomon teaches us here that a slacker, a lazy person with no drive, will not plow when it's time to plow. Plowing prepares the ground for seeds to be sown into it. If he's not plowing then he has no intention to sow any seeds. So, the outcome is inevitable. When it is harvest time, there is nothing in the field. Ironically, why would he even look in the field, knowing that nothing was sown? Many operate on that principle. It is very disheartening when people expect something for nothing. And this is about more than monetary blessings. If we want to make good friends, we must sow good friendship. If we want to raise empathetic kids, we have to sow empathy into them. If we want to raise godly kids, we have to sow godliness into them. We cannot expect to reap where we haven't sown. **Today, let us vow not to be slack out of season so that there will be a harvest waiting for us during harvest time!**

"LEADERSHIP"

Proverbs 21:1 "The king's heart is a waterway in the hand of the LORD; He directs it where He pleases."

The Bible instructs us to pray for our leaders and those in authority over us so that we might lead peaceful lives. Recent political events have made this ever so critical. We often fret over who is in power in the White House, but we must always remember that the ultimate King is Jesus. When leaders are installed, God allows that leader in that position. If the leader is a despot or a good man, they are allowed by God. Some are allowed by God as judgment against sin, others are allowed by God to bring nations out of bad places. At the end of the day, the "king's heart" is in the hands of God. If God raised a leader up, God is also going to direct the actions of that leader. It may not seem so at times, but God is always in control. If a leader is not what they should be, pray for God to turn their hearts. **Today, take out some time and pray for those in leadership, whether you agree with them or not, pray that God would order their steps.**

_____

_____

_____

_____

_____

_____

_____

_____

_____

_____

_____

_____

_____

_____

_____

_____

_____

_____

_____

_____

_____

OCTOBER 24TH

"STOP BEEFING"

Proverbs 22:2 "The rich and the poor have this in common: the LORD is Maker of them all."

There is a dichotomy in the world: the rich and the poor. Politicians exploit this all the time. Conservatives point out that the rich use their wealth to create jobs and invest in infrastructure and, as a result, that wealth will trickle down to the poor if we only give those at the top really good tax breaks. Liberals point out that the poor deserve more and that the way to get it to them is to tax the bejeezus out of the rich. So, here we are pitted against one another and the very ones doing the pitting are also getting wealthier and wealthier. Here is a fun fact: no matter how rich someone is, they can't take any of that money with them. By the same token, there is no longer poverty in death either and one who has lived a life to God and accepted Christ will inherit the eternal riches that God promised to every believer. We cannot afford to despise one another due to our socioeconomic status. Both rich and poor must meet the same Maker. Both rich and poor must answer the eternal question, "What did you do with your talents?" Both rich and poor belong to God. Before we were formed in the wombs of our mothers, we were neither rich nor poor. Naked we came into the world and naked we shall return. **Today, remember that God is not interested in our bank accounts, He wants our souls.**

OCTOBER 25TH

"AVOIDING THE RAT RACE"

Proverbs 23:4,5 "Do not wear yourself out to get rich; be wise enough to restrain yourself. When you glance at wealth, it disappears, for it makes wings for itself and flies like an eagle to the sky."

I have a saying that I always use: "If you chase money, you will always end up out of breath." It is a trustworthy statement. I've ended up hospitalized trying to chase a dollar. The problem in America is that we have a powerful media that thrives off of advertising. The advertising feeds us images of rich people living the life, exotic vacations, dream cars and dream homes, but those advertisements never say how we can acquire those things. So, we do what is natural: we work ourselves to death. We work doubles, overtime, weekends and holidays to accumulate enough money to afford what the media has influenced us to believe that we need. Solomon, who was very wealthy, writes here that the pursuit of riches will indeed wear us out because wealth is fleeting! Yes, we all want to be comfortable, but we must ask ourselves, is this money worth my health and my time that I can never replenish? Maybe instead of trying to live up to the idyllic scenes of rich people sitting beside a pool sipping mimosas, we should learn to be content with what we have. **Today, let us just bless God for what we already have!**

"GOD IS ALWAYS WATCHING"

Proverbs 24:10-12 "If you faint in the day of distress, how small is your strength! Rescue those being led away to death, and restrain those stumbling toward the slaughter. If you say, "Behold, we did not know about this," does not He who weighs hearts consider it? Does not the One who guards your life know? Will He not repay a man according to his deeds?"

This is not a platitude. But, we know that Scripture says that the one who endures until the end will be saved. Endurance means that we will have to go through something. It means that there must be something to actually endure. When calamity strikes, it often does so unannounced, but the Lord is never unaware of the events in our lives. This is all the more reason for us to hold on to our faith. Although we do not know when or where these things will happen, God does and He is the One who guards our lives. He is the One who weighs our hearts and motives. He is the One who protects us in the day of calamity. He is the One who raises a standard when the enemy comes in like a flood. He is the One who give us our just recompense. **Today, let us thank God that in His watching, He has also provided a ram in the bush for us in the time of trouble.**

"MUDDY WATERS"

Proverbs 25:26 "Like a muddied spring or a polluted well is a righteous man who gives way to the wicked."

We must be careful who we give access to. Access equals influence. Influence equals actions. Have you ever found yourself trying to compromise your morals and your values to appease those who do not view the world the same as you? Have you ever placed your faith in your back pocket so that someone wouldn't get offended? This is what it looks like to give way to the wicked. We allow the wicked to prevail in our presence. In doing so, it is possible to be corrupted by their influence. We become muddled springs or polluted wells. What does that matter? No one drinks from a well that has been polluted, and a muddled spring does not produce clear water, so it is useless. This is why we must guard our hearts and our minds against unrighteousness. This is why we cannot stay in the presence of wickedness. If we are to be of use to God, we cannot allow anything to muddle our waters. **Today, let us ask God to keep us clean and surround us with righteousness so that we are able to be used by Him.**

"MUZZLED"

Proverbs 26:4 "Do not answer a fool according to his folly, or you yourself will be like him."

How many times have we thought: "I just need to give them a piece of my mind!"? Retaliation to a slight is a common human response. Honestly, sometimes it feels good to retaliate, too. It relieves stress, but in the end, our consciences usually eat away at us because that retaliation usually results in us acting out of character. Solomon tells us here that a fool is going to always be out of character and their words and actions are going to be according to their own foolishness. While it may seem advantageous to answer back, it will only result in frustration. Foolishness and fools go hand in hand. By the same token, if they are operating in foolishness, then they will not heed wise counsel nor will they respond to reason. So, we have two choices: we can respond and be like the fool or we can apply wisdom and walk away. We cannot allow our pride and our egos to goad us into an unwinnable argument or dispute. Besides, the energy expended arguing with a fool could be used on more productive things, like, breathing, or laughing or walking away. **Today, let us remember that there is only One who is capable of changing the heart of a foolish person. We put it all into His hands.**

"TOOT, TOOT"

Proverbs 27:2 "Let another praise you, and not your own mouth— a stranger, and not your own lips."

Pretentiousness, haughtiness, arrogance, boastfulness, pride, avarice, gloating, self-absorption and self-promotion are not descriptions befitting a Christian. Even Jesus did not testify about Himself. Although He had every right, and His works spoke for Him, He did not go around bragging on His abilities. In an era of shameless self-promotion, excessive "self-love" and branding, how do we avoid tooting our own horns? It's not easy. But we have to remember three things: 1. God's horn is bigger than ours, 2. People respect you more when you let your actions speak for you, and 3. Self-promotion is really a way of masking deficiencies. Have you ever seen one of those old movies where a snake-oil salesman comes to town promising health and wealth and touting himself and his magic elixir? Are we really willing to put ourselves into that class of persons? Are we simply concerned with flattery and self-aggrandizement? It is better to let others pat us on the back than to pat ourselves on our own backs. Let others speak well of you rather than coming in announcing how marvelous we are. **Today, remember that God honors our good works and His favor is really all that matters.**

OCTOBER 30TH

"STAND UP FOR WHAT'S RIGHT"

Proverbs 28:1 "The wicked flee when no one pursues, but the righteous are as bold as a lion."

Lions are very bold animals. They lie around sleeping in broad daylight. They sleep in savannahs with all other types of predators prowling around them, but they do not live in fear. Even their most staunch enemy, the hyena, cackles and roams the very same savannah, but the lion, in all of its boldness, sleeps soundly while the wind blows through the grass. Lions are bold because they are able to vigorously defend their position. The hyena, on the other hand, is always jumpy, nervous, paranoid and easily startled. They are a much lesser predator on the food chain. So, to make this applicable to us, are our positions and our principles defensible? Are we able to vigorously defend our faith and our actions? Are we able to stand up for what is right? If the answer is yes, then we may sleep when predators prowl about because we cannot be shaken from our stances. When we stand on the Word of God, we cannot be easily moved. If our motives are suspect and our actions are unrighteous, we are easily spooked. I've been there before, like a hyena, looking over my shoulder, wondering who saw me and wondering when or if I'd get caught. That's a weak person's position! **Today, let us thank God for His righteousness and His strength that makes us able to stand.**

OCTOBER 31ST

"CLOSED MINDS, CLOSED EYES, OPEN MOUTHS"

Proverbs 30:12 "There is a generation of those who are pure in their own eyes and yet unwashed of their filth."

This proverb is very powerful and reminiscent of Jesus' parable of the log in the eye or the parable of the Pharisees straining out a gnat or swallowing a camel. This generation of relative truth is full of people who cannot see their own filth but are quick to point out everyone else's filth. If you need a good example of this, simply go to Twitter, a 24-hour bash session for whoever has said something offensive to the masses. While people pound their keyboards and launch crusades against trolls, they miss the fact that they too have their own skeletons, but they are not exposed because the issue about which they are raging doesn't open that door of their closet. Bands of people pile on when someone says they are not in agreement with homosexuality, but the same bands demand tolerance. How can you demand tolerance when you won't even tolerate someone's dissent? A lack of self-awareness is characteristic of this generation who prides themselves on being self-aware. We are witnessing a generation whose eyes are closed to their own sin, whose minds are closed to entertaining different perspectives; yet, their mouths are open to cast judgment on all who would dare disagree with them. **Today, let us seek God for wisdom to not be conformed to the ways of this world.**

_____

_____

_____

_____

_____

_____

_____

_____

_____

_____

_____

_____

_____

_____

_____

_____

_____

_____

_____

NOVEMBER 1ST

"EXERCISE CAUTION, APPLY WISDOM 1"

John 7:1 "After these things Jesus was walking in Galilee, for He was unwilling to walk in Judea because the Jews were seeking to kill Him."

There comes a time where we must use caution. In our hyper masculine, face first, macho culture, caution is sometimes viewed as fear. Fear, in and of itself, is not always a bad thing. It is an emotion given to us by God so that we do not simply live buckwild lives. We should fear no man, but there are times when fear is an appropriate response. Fear and caution often go hand in hand. Many times, when God tells us to "fear not" it is because He already has seen the end of the thing to which He has called us. Jesus was not afraid, but even Jesus exercised caution. His brothers tried to goad him into going to Judea. They were somewhat condescending towards him telling him to go to Judea and show off His powers. Jesus, ever the wise, did not take that bait because Jesus knew that the Jews in Judea wanted to kill Him. He did not try to prove a point to his brothers, He did not go into Judea on a suicide mission, He did not walk into a trap trying to be big and bad, He simply laid low until it was His time. That is ok. If we sense danger, why would we run to it? **Today, be mindful of the fact that caution is not wimpy, it is using wisdom to know when to move and when to stay put.**

_____

_____

_____

_____

_____

_____

_____

_____

_____

_____

_____

_____

_____

_____

_____

_____

_____

_____

_____

_____

_____

_____

"EXERCISE CAUTION, APPLY WISDOM 2"

1 Kings 18:2 "So Elijah went to show himself to Ahab. Now the famine was severe in Samaria."

Elijah was, by all accounts, a man's man. He was gruff, he was a precursor to John the Baptist; he wore camel's hair and lived in the wilderness. If any prophet would be considered macho, it would be Elijah. He was probably a bit like the Daryl character from the Walking Dead TV show. He was rugged. But Elijah was no fool. Once he pronounced drought in Israel, God sent him to hide out by a brook of water in a place called Cherith. Ahab searched high and low for him but could not find him. Elijah stayed at the brook until it dried up, after which, he went to Zarephath and lived with a widow. As macho as he was, even Elijah understood that his life was in danger and that the entire kingdom was looking for him to turn him in to Ahab and Jezebel. To reveal himself before God told him to would have been foolish. So, he did not emerge for three-and-a-half years! When he did emerge, he showed himself to Ahab who called him "the troubler of Israel." He showed himself when the drought was at its peak. And yet, not one second before God sent him. He did not grandstand and dare Ahab to come after him. If we sense danger, why would we run to it? **Today, be mindful of the fact that caution is not wimpy, it is using wisdom to know when to move and when to stay put.**

"EXERCISE CAUTION, APPLY WISDOM 3"

1 Samuel 21:13 "So he disguised his sanity before them, and acted insanely in their hands, and scribbled on the doors of the gate, and let his saliva run down into his beard."

David was not what we'd call, in modern times, soft. He was a warrior. He killed Goliath and was more courageous than every other soldier who was there when Goliath was taunting God. David killed a lion and a bear with his bare hands, according to his own accounts. If anyone was fit to walk up to Saul and stand toe-to-toe with him, it was David! And yet, here David finds himself in Gath, after leaving Nob, running for his life from Saul. He was not afraid of Saul. He did not want to kill Saul because he understood, however flawed Saul was, God still chose him as king. In Gath, the people recognized him and started bragging and singing the same song that made Saul jealous of David, that he had killed tens of thousands in battle. The bible records that David got scared! He feared for his life before King Achish. To get out of this jam, he feigned insanity and slobbered all over himself such that the king would dismiss him as a madman, which he did. David sensed danger, why would he run to it? **Today, be mindful of the fact that caution is not wimpy, it is using wisdom to know when to move and when to stay put.**

_____

_____

_____

_____

_____

_____

_____

_____

_____

_____

_____

_____

_____

_____

_____

_____

_____

_____

_____

_____

_____

_____

_____

_____

_____

NOVEMBER 4TH

"EXERCISE CAUTION, APPLY WISDOM 4"

2 Corinthians 11:33 "...and I was let down in a basket through a window in the wall, and so escaped his hands."

Paul knew a lot about persecution. He was a persecutor himself. He jailed Christians, followers of The Way, he terrorized families and he singlehandedly set the disciples in Jerusalem on a world tour, causing them to flee to the ends of the earth, when he came breathing out threats against them. He was a violent aggressor, in his own words, and he was one who sought to destroy the church. If I had to compare Paul to a modern day character, I would probably use Christopher Walken's character from King of New York. Subtle, quiet, but lethal when pressed. But once he was converted, the persecutor became the persecuted. He was hunted by Jews and sought by kings, who wanted to kill him. His life was in danger at every turn. At no time in his ministry did Paul puff his chest up and say "come and get me!" No, he exercised caution and in this instance, Paul, was under the threat of being arrested by King Aretas. Rather than taunt the king or brag about his faith, Paul, with the help of some other Christians, escaped arrest by the skin of his teeth, being lowered in a basket through a hole in the wall. Paul sensed danger, why would he run to it? **Today, be mindful of the fact that caution is not wimpy, it is using wisdom to know when to move and when to stay put.**

NOVEMBER 5TH

"EXERCISE CAUTION, APPLY WISDOM 5"

Judges 11:17 "Then Israel traveled through the wilderness and bypassed the lands of Edom and Moab."

Moses was a rugged shepherd. He was a man of great physical prowess, once beating and killing an Egyptian for mistreating a Hebrew. Moses was a man of great might. The people respected him and revered him. He made due in the desert. He dealt with scores of people and personalities within this band of an estimated 2.4 million people that he was leading out of Egypt. But when the people left Egypt and wanted to pass through Edom, the king of Edom said no. As a matter of fact, the king sent troops to let them know that they could not nor should they even try to pass through his kingdom. The Moabites had a similar response. Moses, a man of great understanding and an underrated military tactician, simply had the people turn around and go a different way. He did not try to bargain or reason with the king because he understood that there were many lives that would have been lost if he had continued or protested the king's wishes. Moses did what was in the best interest of the group, not try to be prideful and make war with a nation that he could not defeat. Moses understood that danger was imminent. Why would he run to it? **Today, be mindful of the fact that caution is not wimpy, it is using wisdom to know when to move and when to stay put.**

"GIVE US EYES TO SEE"

2 Timothy 4:3 "For the time will come when men will not tolerate sound doctrine, but with itching ears they will gather around themselves teachers to suit their own desires."

As we continue into history, we will see a shift of the "church" into a more worldly and accommodating position. We will see the church move away from the truth of God's word and into error and heresy. We are warned multiple times in scripture that we are to resist this shift and continue steadfastly following God; even if it means death. People have already begun to water down the Scriptures. We have already seen churches who have adopted practices that are contrary to Scripture. Churches and entire denominations are fractured because one side is listening to scripture and the other side is listening to their deceitful hearts. Let us not be afraid to call those erroneous teachings out when we hear them. Remember, if it doesn't square with scripture, it must be rejected. In times like these when preachers preach out of their own minds and not the Bible, preach with the bible closed or better yet, give motivational speeches on Sunday rather than sermons, we must be even more diligent to seek out the rightly divided Word of God. **Today, let us pray for discernment in order to be able to detect those false teachers and their teachings.**

NOVEMBER 7TH

THE RIGHT TO REMAIN SILENT

Acts 5:20 "Go, stand in the temple courts and tell the people the full message of this new life."

The apostles were jailed on multiple occasions. Peter and John were jailed on the account of preaching Jesus and the resurrection. The Sanhedrin, which was comprised of the Pharisees and the Sadducees (who don't believe in resurrection), was highly upset because of their teachings. Once, the apostles were healing and preaching and the council got so upset that they threw them in jail again, but this time, an angel unlocked the jail and sent them right back to the spot where they had been arrested and told them, keep preaching! They could have remained silent to avoid persecution, but they did not. We are often in this same predicament. We are often reprimanded for speaking about Jesus. We have a choice to remain silent or to proclaim the Name. When arrested by law enforcement, we are given the right to remain silent. When it comes to Jesus however, we ought to give that right up and confess Him before the world. Some worry about being ostracized but we have to live with eternity in mind. Would we rather be ostracized here or in heaven? We should desire God's approval and not man's fickle, insignificant approval. Refuse to be silent when those who are popular in society threaten to remove you from their social circles. **Today, let us unashamedly confess Him before men so that He confesses us before the Father!**

NOVEMBER 8TH

"WELL DONE"

Matthew 25:34 "Then the King will say to those on His right, 'Come, you who are blessed of My Father, inherit the kingdom prepared for you from the foundation of the world.'"

If we did an honest self-assessment, how would we score ourselves? If we did it honestly, some of our scores would be dismal. I know that some of my scores would be embarrassing. We should ask ourselves, now and then, how we are doing as disciples of Jesus Christ. Truthfully, the disciples depicted in the Bible gave up much more than we could even imagine. That being said, they were not perfect. They still struggled with their faith and they often bickered over who would be the greatest. However, the crucible of their suffering and persecution developed their faith and they were all martyred for the cause of Christ, save for John who was exiled to Patmos. There are two words we want to hear when we reach eternity: "Well done!" There are also four words that we don't want to hear when we reach eternity: "I never knew you." **Today, let us prayerfully approach our walk as disciples and pray for strength from Jesus to continue to press toward His heavenly calling.**

NOVEMBER 9TH

"ETERNALLY MINDED"

Hebrews 12:3 "For consider Him who has endured such hostility by sinners against Himself, so that you will not grow weary and lose heart."

Jesus is the author and finisher of faith. Jesus endured the cross and despised its shame. Jesus was tempted in every way and yet He was without sin. He is our example. He came here to show us how to live righteously. We, as believers must know that there is a better land that this one. An eternal land, a temple not made with hands. As believers, we must live with eternity in mind! We must live with the understanding that we cannot mortgage the future blessings for short term, fleeting pleasures. Everything that we see is all temporal. The money, the houses, the cars, the relationships, the status and positions, it is all dung. None of these things will persist in the coming Kingdom of God. When we read scripture, we understand that there were many who did not live to see the promises that God made to them come to fruition. Many died before ever receiving what God had for them. But there were many who did see what God promised, and it was glorious. **Today, let us not lose heart! God has a plan and we must remind ourselves of this constantly.**

_____

_____

_____

_____

_____

_____

_____

_____

_____

_____

_____

_____

_____

_____

_____

_____

_____

_____

_____

_____

_____

_____

"WHO ARE YOU FOOLING?"

Isaiah 1:13 "Bring your worthless offerings no longer, incense is an abomination to Me. New moon and Sabbath, the calling of assemblies—I cannot endure iniquity and the solemn assembly."

It is impossible to fool God. He is all wise, all knowing and all seeing. He knows our inner workings, our minds and our thoughts. He created the very mind and intellect that we often try to use to outsmart him. It is the equivalent of a computer engineer creating a circuit board. That engineer is going to know every detail about that board. He will know every ridge, the location of every capacitor and every resistor. Therefore, when we come to God we must be honest and forthright. We cannot come into the presence of God with the intention of deceiving Him! He already knows our motives. What we don't want is to delude ourselves into thinking that we can defraud God of anything: worship, praise, giving, works of righteousness; all that we do must be done with the proper motives and motivation! **Today, let our desire to be for God to always hear us and consider us as He considered David, as people after His own heart!**

"EL SHADDAI"

Exodus 15:11 "'Who is like You among the gods, O LORD? Who is like You, majestic in holiness, Awesome in praises, working wonders?"

El Shaddai, translated into English, means God Almighty. It is an all-encompassing name. It literally connotes the omnipotence of God, the sufficiency of God and the power of God. The Old Testament saints got to see this God up close and personal. They got to witness His miracles in person. Manna from heaven, the plagues in Egypt, the sea parting, the rock bringing forth water, bitter water turned sweet, enemies cut down. After the exodus, Moses praised God with this song and asked, "Who is like You, O LORD?" Even the word LORD has a powerful meaning behind it. It is translated from the word Yahweh (Supreme God), which ancient Jews thought so holy that they wouldn't say it and they removed the vowels and left four letters, YHWH. We need to reflect on the majesty and the awesomeness of God and let that color our worldview. The thought of how powerful and mighty God is ought to bleed into every aspect of our lives. Isaiah saw this greatness; Peter, James and John witnessed the splendor; Moses' face shone like a light when he beheld the beauty of God. **Today, let us be encouraged that this God whom we serve is not a mystery or a galactic vapor, He is real, He is ever present and He loves us!**

NOVEMBER 12TH

"THE ACCOMPLISHED WORD"

Isaiah 55:11 "So will My word be which goes forth from My mouth; It will not return to Me empty, Without accomplishing what I desire, And without succeeding in the matter for which I sent it."

God has never made a promise that He has not kept. He is a God of His Word and His Word never returns void. Many things in our lives occur because God has already ordained our steps and our paths. This does not necessarily mean that every single second of our lives is predetermined but God's will is always accomplished, regardless of the detours that we take. God can work around our mistakes to accomplish His will! He did that throughout the Old Testament as the lineage of Christ made mistake after mistake. God promised Abraham that the world would be blessed through his seed [the seed is Christ] and from that promise, God's plan was implemented and carried out over centuries of time. The plan was both accurate and timely, regardless of how poorly those who were executing the plan messed up. **Today, let us be reminded of this for our own lives, whatever God has purposed for us, God will bring it to pass.**

_____

_____

_____

_____

_____

_____

_____

_____

_____

_____

_____

_____

_____

_____

_____

_____

_____

_____

_____

"SUNRISE"

Psalm 30:4,5 "Sing praise to the LORD, you His godly ones, and give thanks to His holy name. For His anger is but for a moment, His favor is for a lifetime; Weeping may last for the night, But a shout of joy comes in the morning."

Jesus endured much hardship in His life on earth. He participated readily in the pain that life presented. His friend Lazarus died. The sisters of Lazarus were so devastated after losing their brother that it made Jesus weep. There was much in-fighting among the disciples so much so that it grieved and frustrated Jesus. His family did not believe in Him. To add to this, Jesus faced constant pressure from the religious establishment and ultimately He faced death, undeservedly so, in order to atone for the sins of even the very ones who put Him to death. Thankfully, God put a comma where Rome and Jerusalem put a period, and we know that Jesus Christ was resurrected on the third day and now sits at the right hand of Glory. The point is, we will all face difficulty in this life but we must do so with the understanding that trouble does not last forever and God will bring good out of even the worst of situations. **Today, let us be still, be of good courage and be well aware that the sun will rise again.**

"A LAMP ON A DARK PATH"

Psalm 119:105 "Your word is a lamp unto my feet, a light for my path."

A timely word is fitting. Sometimes we think that words are not enough. Sometimes, our situations can be so grim that words may seem like empty rhetoric. The words of man sometime fit into this category. We spout off platitudes of unknown origin or repeat something we read in a book thinking that somehow a word will change things. Well, man's word may be empty but God's Word is not only full but it is rich. God's Words are His promises to us and when we study God's Word and internalize God's Word we begin to realize that He's speaking to us plainly. God's Word can be taken at face value and is always appropriate and He knows exactly what to say to us in our times of need. His Word and His promises are guaranteed to us because He cannot lie. If you are struggling with an issue, ask God to speak to you through His word. **Today, be sensitive to the Holy Spirit's communication and trust that whatever God says is so.**

"HE THAT HAS AN EAR"

Psalm 138:3 "On the day I called, You answered me; You made me bold with strength in my soul."

Hearing from God in crucial situations is a vital part of Christian survival. What is Christian survival? It is the ability to persevere through tragedy, toils and trouble. You can also call it by its more proper name, faith. Not believing faith, but what I like to call working faith, or faith in action. Many times, we feel like we are only holding on by a thread. Rest assured that God is holding on to us much more tightly! Those times when life gets difficult, remember that God will speak peace to the storm. It will come through His Word as we study it and He continues to reveal Himself to us. It could come through a song that you hear that somehow speaks directly to you. It could come through a person coming up to you confirming what God has already said to you. It could come through a sermon at church or on the radio. By any means necessary, God will always communicate with His children to comfort us. Be confident that whatever God promises, God will deliver. **Today, let us stand on His Word when there is nothing left; believe God even when it looks as if all hope is lost.**

_____

_____

_____

_____

_____

_____

_____

_____

_____

_____

_____

_____

_____

_____

_____

_____

_____

_____

_____

_____

_____

_____

"THE LORD IS AWESOME"

Psalm 145:1,2 I will extol You, my God, O King, And I will bless Your name forever and ever. Every day I will bless You, And I will praise Your name forever and ever.

Today is a day that the Lord has made. It's a day that we will never see again. It's a day that came with all of its own contents: joy, pain, peace, laughter, mercy and grace. God ordained all days from the beginning. Knowing that this is our God, all-powerful, all-sufficient and all-knowing, let us give Him the praise that He is due. He has provided everything for us. He provided the food that we consume. He provided the possessions that we enjoy so much. He provided the homes that we dwell in. He even provided the air that we breathe in every time we inhale; and he provided the trees and plants to consume the carbon dioxide that we exhale! How awesome is God? Awesome enough to deserve all of our praises! Not only does he deserve the praise, He is WORTHY of them. **Today, let us give Him praise and honor God with the fruit of our lips.**

_____

_____

_____

_____

_____

_____

_____

_____

_____

_____

_____

_____

_____

_____

_____

_____

_____

_____

_____

_____

_____

"HAVE A FLASHBACK"

Psalm 150:1-6 "Praise the Lord; Praise God in his sanctuary; praise Him in His mighty heavens. Praise Him for his acts of power; praise Him for his surpassing greatness. Praise Him with the sounding of the trumpet, praise Him with the harp and lyre, praise Him with timbrel and dancing, praise Him with the strings and pipe, praise him with the clash of cymbals, praise Him with resounding cymbals. Let everything that has breath praise the Lord."

I know that you have probably been to churches where it's noisy and loud. There was a lot of shouting and the musicians were going bananas on their instruments. I know that some of us were raised in churches that it was thought to be offensive to even say, "Amen." But, when we consider the majesty of God, He is worthy of our shouts and our adoration! Praising God does not take imagination, just memory. Think about a time when you truly needed God and He provided! Think about an illness that God brought you through. Think about when you got saved, which is the most praiseworthy moment in the life of any believer. God is worthy of the praises of His people. Scripture says that He is enthroned on our praises! He is the ONLY God and beside Him there is no other. Praise Him with the fruit of your lips. Praise Him with the strength of your limbs. Praise Him through your service to humanity. **Today, let us praise Him because He deserves it.**

_____

_____

_____

_____

_____

_____

_____

_____

_____

_____

_____

_____

_____

_____

_____

_____

_____

_____

_____

_____

_____

"A PLAN OF ACTION"

Ephesians 3:8-11 [NLT] "This was his eternal plan, which he carried out through Christ Jesus our Lord."

It is often said that one who fails to plan, plans to fail. This euphemism is true. Serendipity sometimes brings us things that we have not planned for, but by and large we must always have a plan prior to any action that we take. We plan because we are made in God's image and God is a planner. Even in creation, God was planning things out in His mind before He arranged them in the way that they should be. The Bible says "then God said" and after He spoke, those things which began in His mind were created by His Word. Just as God planned creation, God also planned for the redemption of man. God foreknew that man would sin and therefore had to have a plan in place for the reconciliation of His most prized possession. This is why the Bible refers to Jesus as the lamb slain from before the foundation of the earth. Had God not planned, we would be ruined, trapped in our sins with no hope for redemption. **Today, let us all thank God for always having a plan and for including us in it and for carrying that plan out with the best possible solution, Jesus Christ!**

"HE KNOWS"

Hebrews 4:14-16 [NLT] "Therefore, since we have a great high priest who has ascended into heaven, Jesus the Son of God, let us hold firmly to the faith we profess. For we do not have a high priest who is unable to empathize with our weaknesses, but we have one who has been tempted in every way, just as we are—yet he did not sin. Let us then approach God's throne of grace with confidence, so that we may receive mercy and find grace to help us in our time of need."

Oftentimes we think of Jesus as an ethereal being who hovers above the earth and sits on His throne beside God the Father. We feel disconnected from Jesus because we tend to forget that He was human! Jesus was 100% God and 100% human. That's what biblical scholars term as the hypostatic union. The point is, in His humanity, Jesus experienced everything that we experience. His disciples betrayed Him, His family doubted Him, the religious leaders wanted to kill Him, His best friend Lazarus died; every human emotion that we experience Jesus experienced it. There is no way that we can ever say "Jesus doesn't understand this." He understands the human existence because he was made like his brothers and sisters in every way. He was made complete through his suffering. This is good news. The better news is that he did not succumb to the temptation! **Today, let us have confidence that He loves us and He understands what we endure while in the flesh.**

"THE TELESCOPE OF TIME"

Isaiah 25:1 "O LORD, You are my God; I will exalt You, I will give thanks to Your name; For You have worked wonders, plans formed long ago, with perfect faithfulness."

Being an eternal entity means that time has no constraints on God. Time is a manmade construct. Time was invented by us when we noticed patterns in the sunrise, sunset, seasonal changes and other noticeable events in nature. Time and planning go hand-in-hand. There is nothing too hard for God nor is there anything that can bind his hands when it comes to accomplishing His will. When we think of God, we have to be mindful that He does not plan haphazardly nor does He plan on the spot. He has looked down the telescope of time from His eternal abode. His plans are from before time and creation. How can God do such a thing? God is all-knowing, all-seeing, all powerful and everything has been planned according to His will. Most importantly, God planned the method of our Salvation, Jesus Christ dying on a cross, from eternity. Sin would not have the chance to claim what God created. Instead, God laid out a plan to eradicate sin, thwart sin's power and save us from sin's penalty through Jesus Christ. **Today, let us be grateful that Bethlehem was not the starting point, but that Jesus is the "Lamb slain from the foundation of the world" whose purpose, from eternity, has always been to save.**

NOVEMBER 21ST

"THE AGONY OF VICTORY"

Luke 22:44 "And being in agony He was praying very fervently; and His sweat became like drops of blood, falling down upon the ground."

The most agonizing moment of Jesus' human life was probably at Gethsemane. Scripture records that Jesus was in agony. That word has an interesting background. It was used to describe gladiators or athletes prior to a match. Imagine a football player sitting and brooding in a locker room prior to a football game. This was the fourth quarter for Jesus and the game was on the line. Luke records that Jesus was so stressed in Gethsemane that his sweat was like drops of blood! Even that is a verifiable medical condition called hematidrosis. Jesus understood His destination and the pain and torture that awaited Him. His prayer says everything about how we should respond to crises that arise in our walk with Him. He says to the Father "Your will be done..." He sacrificed His own comfort and even His life in order to glorify the Father. When we are in dark moments that are being used for God's glory, we should have the same attitude in ourselves that was also in Christ Jesus. We must submit our wills to God and let Him get glory, even from our pain. **Today, let us be assured that the outcome of surrendering our wills to God will always be one which produces great joy in us, and bring joy to the Lord.**

_____

_____

_____

_____

_____

_____

_____

_____

_____

_____

_____

_____

_____

_____

_____

_____

_____

_____

_____

_____

_____

"HIGH AND LIFTED UP"

Hebrews 1:3,4 "And He is the radiance of His glory and the exact representation of His nature, and upholds all things by the word of His power. When He had made purification of sins, He sat down at the right hand of the Majesty on high, having become as much better than the angels, as He has inherited a more excellent name than they."

Jesus Christ is exalted above ALL. The reasons for His exaltation are 1. That He was/is God incarnate and exists in eternal equality with the Father and the Holy Spirit and 2. He carried out the mission of reconciliation through His death on a cross. There is no heavenly power higher than Jesus and there is certainly no earthly power higher than Jesus. He is the creator and sustainer of the universe with everything being held together in Him. Now, imagine for one second that this exalted Jesus wants to live in relationship with you. What an awesome thought! Not only did He condescend and come to us, He desires a relationship with us! Think of the most famous person that you know and how it would be virtually impossible to meet them. Now, think about Jesus who is more glorious than any human being and how easy it is to meet Him! **Today, know this, that if you've never met Him, He's waiting and He loves you.**

"FROM NOTHING"

Psalm 118:22-24 "The stone the builders rejected has become the cornerstone; the Lord has done this, and it is marvelous in our eyes. The Lord has done it this very day; let us rejoice today and be glad."

You have heard many times that God can take nothing and turn it into something. Countless times, we see God working miracles with little to no resources. God also does the same thing with people. He takes people of low status who are humble and obedient and exalts them for His own glory. Moses, David and Jesus are examples. God opposes the proud but He gives grace to the humble. Scripture says that God chooses the foolish things of the world to shame the wise and the weak things of the world to shame the mighty. He even created the entire cosmos from nothing, ex nihilo. God does this to demonstrate His power. By exalting the things that men despise or reject, God glorifies Himself and reminds men that He does not operate by the principles of this world. Jesus Himself was born into meager conditions, looked down upon, despised and rejected yet God exalted Him because of His obedience. God still operates under this same principle. If we humble ourselves He will exalt us. If we are obedient, He will bless us. If we are rejected by men, God can still use us for His glory. **Today, let us bask in God's glory that shines through every circumstance.**

_____

_____

_____

_____

_____

_____

_____

_____

_____

_____

_____

_____

_____

_____

_____

_____

_____

_____

_____

_____

"CAN'T PLEASE EVERYBODY"

Mark 2:10,11 "But so that you may know that the Son of Man has authority on earth to forgive sins..." He said to the paralytic, 'I tell you, get up, pick up your mat, and go home.'"

Jesus once healed a paralytic. But it wasn't immediate. He first forgave the man's sin. But when the Pharisees heard this, they were indignant because they didn't feel as though Jesus had the authority to forgive sin. This led Jesus to healing the man's physical malady, in front of the Pharisees. He knew what they thought in their hardened hearts. They tried to use the Sabbath as an excuse for their indignation. But it was just a front. They were upset rather than praising God for the man being able to walk again or the man having his sins forgiven. Jesus teaches us a valuable lesson about doing good. There is never a bad time to do good. It is always appropriate. Some people will be happy about it. Others will not. But God will always be glorified by our good works! If you put 1,000 people in a room, at least one of them will be unhappy about something. Here is a trustworthy statement worthy of full acceptance...we will never make everyone happy, so why continue trying? **Today, let us focus our love and energy where it belongs, toward pleasing God and accomplishing His will.**

"HIDDEN CRACKS"

Job 10:11 "You clothed me with skin and flesh, and knit me together with bones and sinews."

God made us. God knows our innermost thoughts and desires. He formed us from the womb. God knows us intimately. Every one of us has obvious things that everyone can see. But we also have those things that only God knows about. Here's the problem with that: when our cracks aren't visible, we can sometimes get haughty. Some of our cracks are visible. Some of us go through very public, very ugly issues. It's easy to get on a high horse and become overly critical and judgmental. But the problem is, we all have cracks in our vessels. Just because your cracks aren't visible doesn't give you any right to judge someone whose cracks are readily apparent. It is better to be the sinner praying at the wall rather than the Pharisee praying next to him. We should be thankful for the grace of God and for the mercy of God that keep our "stuff" from being exposed to everyone. **Today, let us be mindful that only the Lord is righteous.**

_____

_____

_____

_____

_____

_____

_____

_____

_____

_____

_____

_____

_____

_____

_____

_____

_____

_____

_____

_____

_____

"OUR GOD IS AWESOME"

Isaiah 44:6,7 "Thus says the LORD, the King and Redeemer of Israel, the LORD of Hosts: "I am the first and I am the last, and there is no God but Me. Who then is like Me? Let him say so! Let him declare his case before Me, since I established an ancient people."

Who is like God? He asks that rhetorically in this scripture, knowing that the answer is, unequivocally, no one. Sometimes we need a reminder of this truth. I pray that God will show us something today that will remind us all that HE is the sovereign Creator of the universe. We wait with expectation at the revelation of Your glory through events both big and small. We look UP, knowing that all of our help comes from You. We look around knowing that as You help us, we should be ready and willing to help others who are in need. We look down, knowing that the two feet that You have given us are not to stand still but to move forward to proclaim Your gospel and Your greatness. **Today, God, let us reflect on Your glory and wonder at Your magnificence. Now unto Him, who is able to keep us from stumbling, be glory, honor, dominion and power both now and forever. In the mighty name of Jesus, it is so.**

NOVEMBER 27TH

"FULL POTENTIAL"

Ephesians 6:7 "Serve with good will, as to the Lord and not to men…"

We often define success using terms created by "successful" people i.e. people who have accumulated many worldly possessions. In actuality, we should define success by asking this: Have I served God to my fullest potential? Recall the parable of the talents. Each one received according to their ability, but only two of them maximized their potential by working with what they had to the best of their abilities. That is the true definition of success. Defining success in this way requires a great deal of humility. It takes a great deal of humility to refuse to chase the worldly ideal of success. But God gives grace to the humble and God will give more to the one who takes what was given and multiplies it. We often pray for success without praying for the humility or wisdom to handle that success. **Today, let us endeavor to give God our best and use the gifts that He has given us not to accumulate, but rather, to distribute such that God is glorified.**

"MY FORTRESS"

Psalm 144:2 "He is my loving devotion and my fortress, my stronghold and my deliverer. He is my shield, in whom I take refuge, who subdues peoples under me."

Avalanches are natural wonders. Avalanches have different triggers, but one thing is certain, you do not want to be on the receiving end of one. If you've ever seen an avalanche, you know that as it continues downhill, it accelerates, collects more snow and increases in size. There is seemingly nothing that can stop it. In life, we can actually be on the receiving end of an avalanche. There's an old saying, "When it rains, it pours." That's how it feels sometimes. But Scripture tells us that God is our fortress, our stronghold and our deliverer! He is a place where we may take refuge. So, that avalanche that Satan keeps pushing trying to overtake you; that keeps getting bigger and bigger does not stand a chance against our God! Sometimes life can beat the happiness out of us but thank God that His JOY is our strength! **Today, let us be steadfast and know that whatever the obstacle is, we must keep pushing. God is listening!**

NOVEMBER 29TH

"PATIENCE IS A VIRTUE"

Luke 21:19 "By your patient endurance, you will gain your souls."

I grew up in a house where we cooked, a lot. My mother would cook huge meals every day. I've heard from my sisters that she was a regular Betty Crocker when they were younger. She didn't bake much during my own childhood, but my sisters did. They baked cakes all the time. One of the biggest lessons that I learned about baking cakes is that you cannot take them out before they are done. If a cake is removed from the oven too early, it will sink. It may still be edible, but it won't look like much. Sometimes believers think the Lord is slow. Slow to fix problems, slow to act, slow to bring justice etc. It seems slow to us because we look at calendars and clocks while God operates outside of time. We must be aware of the fact that God is sovereign and in His sovereignty He controls how long, how fast and how much AND in His grace He equips us to endure for that season of time. Think back on what was learned from a trial. Sometimes, if a trial ends prematurely, the lesson won't stick. God is all about teaching and developing us. We have to honestly ask: If the lesson was cut short, would we have learned what God was trying to teach us? **Today, let us remember that seasons don't last forever but God's grace and mercy do.**

"AN INTEGRATED HEAVEN? YEP."

Revelation 7:9 "After this I looked and saw a multitude too large to count, from every nation and tribe and people and tongue, standing before the throne and before the Lamb. They were wearing white robes and were holding palm branches in their hands."

It is interesting how we allow manmade issues to divide the church. One of the things that the church often struggles with is the issue of race. Let's face it, racism is a man-made construct. American racism is the repugnant residue of slavery put in place by colonial settlers. The ramifications of slavery were never considered, but here we are over two hundred years after the Revolutionary War and we are still struggling with race. God has a prescription for this. Remove the barriers and impediments that man created. Scripture speaks here about a "great multitude" that was incalculable, multi-ethnic and singularly focused on worshipping God. When will the Christians in America realize that this is God's model and the Church should be the last place on earth that's segregated? Equality is a requirement from GOD Himself! We must focus on worship and do so in kinship with our brothers and sisters in Christ. **Today, let us focus on living Christ centered, God-glorifying lives instead of looking for reasons to stay divided.**

_____

_____

_____

_____

_____

_____

_____

_____

_____

_____

_____

_____

_____

_____

_____

_____

_____

_____

_____

_____

_____

_____

"BORN TO DIE"

Matthew 2:11 "After coming into the house they saw the Child with Mary His mother; and they fell to the ground and worshiped Him. Then, opening their treasures, they presented to Him gifts of gold, frankincense, and myrrh."

As we enter into the season of celebrating the birth of Jesus, his death is also put into perspective. It is important not to fall victim to the commercialization of the holiday season, but rather, use it to reflect on the fact that the Word was made flesh for a purpose. The wise men, who were pagans, worshipped the Lord Jesus because they understood what the star in the sky meant. The word worship literally means to kiss ground that feet are on. They traveled over 600 miles and in addition to their worship, they offered gifts. They brought gold because Jesus was royalty. But, they also brought frankincense and myrrh, both death spices, to a baby. Frankincense was the incense used in the holy of holies and is the only incense permitted on the altar, which acknowledges the holiness and divinity of Jesus. Myrrh was the principal ingredient in anointing oil; also used to anoint dead bodies. It was often mixed with wine and given to those who are crucified as a sedative. This was to acknowledge the eventual suffering and death of Jesus. **Today, let us thank God for sending the Savior for the purpose of saving!**

WALK WITH ME: God Seen, God Heard, God Revealed

_____

_____

_____

_____

_____

_____

_____

_____

_____

_____

_____

_____

_____

_____

_____

_____

_____

_____

_____

_____

DECEMBER 2ND

"A LIFE OF SERVICE"

Luke 2:34 "Then Simeon blessed them, and said to Mary His mother, "Behold, this Child is destined for the fall and rising of many in Israel, and for a sign which will be spoken against..."

Every one of us has a purpose and every one of us can offer up service to God! God gives us examples to follow. Mary and Joseph were servants! Mary received the news of being the carrier of the Messiah and she called herself the bondservant of the Lord. Joseph, hitched to a pregnant woman whose baby was not his biological son, had to remain in place so that he could lead them to Egypt to hide from Herod. Simeon, here waiting in the temple for the baby Jesus to be dedicated, was a prophet with a message for Mary about the service that Jesus would render unto the Father. Jesus' service would be to cause the fall and rise of many! He was destined, appointed for this very reason, to reveal the hearts of mankind. He was destined to be the crossroads that every human must encounter and make a decision to serve Him or reject Him. His ultimate service would be at Calvary where He would die so that believers might rise! **Today, we give thanks to God for the example of service set through Jesus!**

"THE WORD MADE FLESH"

Galatians 4:4,5 "But when the time had fully come, God sent His Son, born of a woman, born under the Law, to redeem those under the law, that we might receive our adoption as sons."

Time and eternity intersected with the coming of Jesus Christ. Through Jesus, God intervened in history to make it HIS-story. In order for Jesus to accomplish his purpose of dying for the sins of the whole world, Jesus had to be encased in a human body. God is amazing. Not only did He send Jesus, but as the scripture bears out, He sent Jesus in the right season and He sent Jesus through the body of Mary, who was the delivery mechanism. He was born of a woman, just like every other human being, but He was not created. Jesus is eternal, this just happened to how the plan of God was taking shape. The gifts to mankind from Jesus came in the form of our redemption and our adoption. Redemption means that we've been ransomed from sin. Adoption means that we are now ingrafted branches into the olive tree of Israel. **Today, thank God that in His infinite wisdom, He sent His Son to ransom us and to give us the right to be called children of God!**

_____

_____

_____

_____

_____

_____

_____

_____

_____

_____

_____

_____

_____

_____

_____

_____

_____

_____

_____

_____

DECEMBER 4TH

"A LITTLE CHILD SHALL LEAD THEM"

Isaiah 11:6 "And the wolf will dwell with the lamb, And the leopard will lie down with the young goat, And the calf and the young lion and the fatling together; And a little boy will lead them."

We all crave a time when the earth will be at peace. A time when the guns of war no longer shoot, the venom of hatred is neutralized by the anti-venom of love and humanity would value one another as being made in the image of God. This idyllic picture of the earth, while not impossible, is a distant desire that can only be accomplished by Jesus. Jesus will not only be a judge, but he will cause peace and unity to flourish in the place of malice. Isaiah's prophecy is partially fulfilled in the first coming of Jesus. At the second coming of Jesus, when the government will be upon His shoulders, then and only then will we have true peace. But the little child had to come first. This is why we celebrate during this season. There cannot truly be peace unless Christ is at the center. He can break down racial, socioeconomic, religious, cultural, political or spiritual barriers just through His presence! He can cause us to beat swords into plowshares and cause nations to no longer train for war. **Today, thank God that the little child came, and one day, we will all be at peace with one another because of it!**

DECEMBER 5TH

"IN THE SHADOW OF THE CROSS"

1 Peter 1:20 "He was known before the foundation of the world, but was revealed in the last times for your sake."

The pre-existence of Jesus is not debatable. The Bible is replete with examples of Christ being concealed in the Old Testament through typologies like the Angel of the Lord or the Rock in the wilderness. Peter tells us here that Jesus was known before the foundation of the world, another testament to His pre-existence. But what is also known is that He was also slain from the foundation of the world. While this may seem like a macabre way to discuss Christmas, this fact is a point of celebration for every believer. His slaying is our blessing! This is the beauty of Christmas: the manger sat in the shadow of the cross, but the cross sat in the shadow of the empty tomb! The purpose of Christ was pre-determined and the grace of God was poured out before any of us were created. What a gift given to us! **Today, let us thank God for His wisdom, His planning and His unlimited knowledge, without which, we would all be trapped in bondage to sin.**

"THE AMAZING GOD"

Matthew 1:11 "...and Josiah the father of Jeconiah and his brothers at the time of the exile to Babylon."

The situational engineering that it took for Jesus to get here to this planet is unfathomable. This meandering historical journey that began in eternity is a testament to how awesome God really is. The lineage of Jesus includes prostitutes, profligates, liars, cheaters and cursed kings and yet, not one iota of the Father's plan of salvation was interrupted by any of it! Mary and Joseph brought together two pieces of the puzzle. Joseph satisfied the legal requirement and Mary satisfied the biological requirement, both of which made Jesus the heir of David who was promised to sit on the throne in perpetuity! Joseph's presence made Jesus the legal heir to David's throne, Mary's DNA made her the biological vessel through which the Lord came. Add to that, death threats, traps, plots, a stint in Egypt and what you have is a miraculous example of God's ability to maneuver through and past sin and sinners to get His work done! Now, we can look at our own lives and know that what God maneuvered through then, He can maneuver through now. **Today, let us thank God for being the same God who overcame every obstacle in the life of Jesus and is also able to overcome every obstacle in our lives.**

DECEMBER 7TH

"JOSEPH, YOU ARE NOT THE FATHER"

Isaiah 9:6 "For a child will be born to us, a son will be given to us..."

The plan of God included He Himself coming in the flesh in the person of Jesus Christ. The casing of a human body was necessary for the Word to be made flesh. In Jesus, the fullness of deity dwelt in bodily form. But there was an issue with the parents of Jesus. The child was indeed born, but the son had to be given. Here is why: Joseph is a descendent of Jeconiah who is the son of Jehoiakim. Jehoiakim was cursed when he dismissed a prophecy from Jeremiah and burned the scroll on which the prophecy was inscribed. Because of his insubordination, God told him that a he would never have a descendant on the throne of David! This caused the entire lineage of Jehoiakim to be cursed, Joseph included. This precluded him from being the biological father of Jesus. So, Joseph, in the words of Maury Povich, you are not the father. But, Joseph's adoption made Jesus the LEGAL heir to the throne of David. Mary, who from Nathan's lineage, had no problem being the biological mother of Jesus. This also exempted Jesus from the curse! Keeping His word to David, God allowed Jesus to be born to Mary by her being overshadowed by the Holy Spirit and implanting the Messiah into her. In the same way, God so loved the world that He gave us His only begotten Son. **Today, let us give thanks for the birth of the child and the gift the Son!**

_____

_____

_____

_____

_____

_____

_____

_____

_____

_____

_____

_____

_____

_____

_____

_____

_____

_____

_____

_____

_____

_____

_____

DECEMBER 8TH

"UNWRAPPING THE GIFT"

Matthew 27:46 "About the ninth hour Jesus cried out with a loud voice, saying, "ELI, ELI, LAMA SABACHTHANI?" that is, "MY GOD, MY GOD, WHY HAVE YOU FORSAKEN ME?"

While the time of his birth is debated, the birth of Jesus had to occur. His existence is historically verifiable so we know that He had to be born. We must always keep the reason for the season at the forefront of our minds. A well informed theology causes us to glorify God rather than chase material fulfillment during the holiday season. So, we are here at the foot of the cross during Christmas because the cross was the end goal of the birth of Jesus! We are able to celebrate right now because of what happened at Calvary! We wrap boxes to surprise the recipients, but there was no surprise here! God sent us a gift that it took 33 years to unwrap. How do we know that He was a gift? Because when the world was in darkness, the Father sent the Son to be a LIGHT to the nations! The Father gift wrapped the Son. As a baby, He was wrapped in swaddling clothing! As a man, he was unwrapped and the soldiers took His clothes as they cast lots for them. The wrapping opened up when the nails pierced his skin, when the crown of thorns pierced his scalp, when the spear pierced his side! We were saved with the precious blood. **Today, let us thank God for the unwrapping, for the piercing, for the blood and for the resurrection!**

_____

_____

_____

_____

_____

_____

_____

_____

_____

_____

_____

_____

_____

_____

_____

_____

_____

_____

_____

"THE GOOD AND PERFECT GIFT"

1 John 4:9 "By this the love of God was manifested in us, that God has sent His only begotten Son into the world so that we might live through Him."

James says that every good and perfect gift comes down from God. There are some things that we know about God that will never change. We know that God is all wise in knowing exactly what we need. We know that God is omniscient in knowing what we need before we need it. We know that God sends perfect gifts. Jesus is a gift who was wrapped in eternity, unwrapped in time and revealed to us for such a time as this! The beauty of a gift sent by God is that the gift is tangible. John says by this the love of God was manifested. The word this is a demonstrative pronoun that points to something that we can tangibly know, the fact that the gift was manifested also indicates something tangible that we can actually see and discern. God's gifts are planned out. God planned the gift from eternity. The tense of sent indicates that the gift was given in a past time but still affects our present reality. God sends unique gifts. Jesus, the only begotten is the unique son of God. The word begotten is translated from the word monogenes which means there is no other like Jesus. God sends effective gifts! Jesus was sent into the whole world. And God sends life-giving gifts! He was sent into the world so that we might live through Him! **Today, let us give God praise for sending this gift!**

DECEMBER 10TH

"A KING'S GLORY FOR A SLAVE'S WAGE"

Philippians 2:7 "...but emptied Himself, taking the form of a servant, being made in human likeness."

The wise men showed up to Jerusalem looking for the One who was born King of Israel. I am sure that they were surprised to find Him in a stable. The king of Israel, resting in a place for animals. The king of Israel, born into a poor family of no reputation; the king of Israel born into this life to work as a carpenter with his "step" father. The king of Israel, born as a common man. The truth is, Jesus did this on purpose. He did it to fulfill what was written by the prophet Isaiah, "Like a root out of parched ground; He has no stately form or majesty that we should be attracted to Him." Jesus is the Christian standard of self-renunciation of rights and obedience to God. The king, Jesus, took the form of a bondservant. Bondservants were the lowest in the hierarchy of slave workers. They washed feet and did very undesirable chores. Jesus, the king, took off His kingly vestments and took the form of a slave. Jesus the king, allowed Himself to be made in human likeness. Jesus the king, voluntarily emptied Himself and came as a pauper. Make no mistake, just because His clothes and appearance changed, His status as God in the flesh did not. **Today, let us praise the King of kings for His sacrifice!**

DECEMBER 11TH

"BULLSEYE"

Micah 5:2 "But as for you, Bethlehem Ephrathah, Too little to be among the clans of Judah, From you One will go forth for Me to be ruler in Israel. His goings forth are from long ago, From the days of eternity."

A bullseye by definition is the center of a target. Archery, shooting and darts are some examples of sports where a target is used. It does not matter what circumstances come up, what obstacles stand in the way or who neglects their duties, God never misses His target. The bible is a book of targets that have been or will be hit. The prophets speak, in some cases, with pinpoint accuracy! Micah's accuracy is stunning. Micah pinpoints the exact city in which the Savior would be born. Historians have debated the location of Bethlehem but location is not the issue. Micah prophesies this hundreds of years before the birth of Jesus. The level of accuracy in the prophecy isn't uncanny. Prophets spoke directly from God and God knows everything, so He could tell these prophets things that the average mind could not fathom. We thank God that from Bethlehem, the ruler of Israel came forth and His eternality is cemented in the words of the Prophets. **Today, let us thank God for His accuracy and His ability to speak the end from the beginning.**

DECEMBER 12TH

"GOD CAN DO A LOT WITH A LITTLE"

Micah 5:2 "But as for you, Bethlehem Ephrathah, Too little to be among the clans of Judah..."

Nathaniel famously asked if anything good could come from Nazareth. He literally meant it with condescending intent. When Philip came to him and told him that they had found the Messiah, and said where the Messiah was from, Nathaniel became a little indignant. But, we know that God is able to bring something amazing from nothing. He did so when he created the universe ex nihilo. When we think of where Jesus was born, this place was called by the prophet as too little to be among the clans of Judah. Bethlehem was an obscure place. Joshua 15 lists 116 cities that are in the territory allotted to the tribe of Judah; also states that those cities had villages and yet NO MENTION of Bethlehem. Here is a testament to the power of God: that He can take a city that is unnamed and make it powerful and bless the whole world by who came from it. It was where Ruth and Boaz settled; it was David's hometown, he was anointed there by Samuel. Yet, it was an insignificant city. But God can take the foolish things to shame the wise. The humility of Jesus Christ is shown by the place where He chose to be born in human form. Here is the King of Kings choosing to come into the world in the most meager way possible! **Today, let us thank God for His work and His ways!**

DECEMBER 13TH

"A LONG TIME COMING"

Micah 5:2 "...One to be ruler over Israel, whose origins are of old, from the days of eternity."

The baby in Mary's womb was not a created being. The baby in Mary's womb was not the result of a sperm and an egg coming together. The baby in Mary's womb was a miraculous feat of spiritual engineering. That baby was the vehicle that God chose to come in human form. Free from the curse of Adam's sin, Mary's womb was a conduit by which the Savior would come into the world. The Most High overshadowed Mary, the Holy Spirit came upon Mary and the Lord Jesus was implanted into her womb. The same Lord Jesus who had glory with the Father from before time began! This is why Micah could say that the origins of the One who would be born in Bethlehem are from old, from days of eternity. The appearance of Jesus at the moment of His birth was the culmination of a journey that began in eternity and crossed over into time when Jesus was born in that stable in Bethlehem. He has ALWAYS EXISTED, and when the time was right, the plan was to come to the earth as a man, a human being, to Bethlehem! From eternity to Bethlehem; Bethlehem to Calvary; Calvary to His seat at the Father's right hand! **Today, let us thank say thank you Jesus for taking the journey from eternity for our sake!**

"BREAD FROM HEAVEN"

Micah 5:2 "But as for you, Bethlehem Ephrathah, Too little to be among the clans of Judah..."

Jesus called Himself the Bread of Life. It is amazing how many connections exist within the scriptures. Yes, there are 66 books and 40 authors of the biblical texts that are included in the Canon, but there are some very specific details that carry over between the Old and New Testaments. When Jesus called Himself the bread of life, He was making a reference to the manna that came down from heaven, which would spoil if more of it was collected than God allowed. He was telling the people who were following Him that He is the true bread; bread that does not spoil and bread that is able to nourish us to life. How fitting is it that this Bread of Life was born in Bethlehem. The word Bethlehem is translated as "house of bread". So, that the Bread of Life came forth from the house of bread! **Today, let us thank God for the Bread of Life, and that the Bread was broken for you and for me!**

DECEMBER 15TH

"THE LION OF JUDAH"

Micah 5:2 "But as for you, Bethlehem Ephrathah, Too little to be among the clans of Judah..."

During the days of Micah's prophesying, Babylon was an imminent threat to Judah. There was not anyone in Judah or Israel who could withstand the Babylonian military. But, there was one who would come from Bethlehem to whom Babylon and all other nations would have to bow. Micah spoke with pinpoint accuracy when he spoke of the coming King being brought forth from Bethlehem. Even more accurate is this: Bethlehem was a city within Judah! The consistency and the cohesiveness of scripture are evident in this passage. In the book of Revelation, John said that he was weeping because there was no one worthy to open the book that was sealed with the seven seals. One of the 24 elders spoke to John and said "Do not weep, the Lion of the tribe of Judah, the Root of David, He is worthy to open the seven scrolls." Bethlehem produced our King! He is worthy to open the book! He is worthy of all of our praises! He is God and besides him there is no other! **Today, we thank God for the Lion of Judah who will fight for His people!**

DECEMBER 16TH

"THE GOOD SHEPHERD"

Micah 5:4 "And He will arise and shepherd His flock In the strength of the LORD, In the majesty of the name of the LORD His God. And they will remain, because at that time He will be great to the ends of the earth."

Bethlehem graced us with so much. We now know that the city was prophesied as the birthplace of Jesus with remarkable accuracy, we know that the city had symbolic meaning as the "house of bread" which brought forth the Bread of Life and we know that God did a new thing by completely shifting from the Levitical priesthood to bring the Great High Priest from the tribe of Judah. What other treasures can we find in Bethlehem? Today's scripture says that the one who would come forth from Bethlehem would be our shepherd. Jesus is the Good Shepherd, guiding us to green pastures, leading us beside the still waters, doing so in the strength of the LORD, in the majesty of the LORD! The Good Shepherd, whose greatness will extend to the ends of the earth, is our Lord and Savior Jesus Christ! How is it that all of this magnificence came from such an obscure little town like Bethlehem? Because God is able! Do not despise small beginnings. Furthermore, the Bible says the Shepherd feels compassion for those who are like "sheep without a shepherd"! When He saw you and me wandering aimlessly like a sheep without a shepherd, He rescued us! **Today, give Him praise!**

DECEMBER 17TH

"PICKING UP THE PIECES"

Luke 2:14 "Glory to God in the highest, And on earth peace among men with whom He is pleased."

Imagine if you would, a very costly, very rare vase. This vase has the handprints of the Master Potter of the universe all over it. It was turned on the Potter's wheel, formed and shaped in His hand; in His image and likeness. It was fired and heated and finally, from the dust of the earth, it was created! When the Potter saw the work of His hands, He referred to it as "very good". This vase was created with the entirety of heaven watching. Some had a plan to destroy it. One in particular, took the form of a serpent, resolved to break the vase and caused the vase to be shattered! It lay strewn in millions of pieces. In the mind of the serpent, there was no hope of the vase being put back together. But in the mind of God, there was not only hope, there was a plan. Mankind is the vase, shattered into pieces from the effects of sin. Jesus Christ, the Prince of Peace, is the one who picked up the pieces that sin left scattered all over the earth. When translated, the word peace literally means a state of all things coming together. His birth signaled that God would repair the state of brokenness and close the chasm between God and man. **Today, we give thanks for His birth, His mission and His blood that unites us all!**

DECEMBER 18TH

"A PROMISE KEEPER"

Romans 15:13 "Now may the God of hope fill you with all joy and peace as you believe in Him, so that you may overflow with hope by the power of the Holy Spirit."

Hope is a powerful emotion. Hope carries with it expectation that what we are hoping for we will receive. The object of our hope it's just as important as the hope itself. When we hope in people, we are sometimes disappointed. But as believers, our hope is in Jesus Christ. During this time of year, we reflect on the hope that was given to us in the person of Jesus Christ. We reflect on the fact that God sent Jesus to us As a Savior. Hope in Christ is so powerful because we do not only hope for what we see but we also hope for what we have not seen yet. Scripture reminds us that eyes have not seen and ears have not heard, neither has it entered into the hearts of men the things that God has prepared for those who love Him. So, as Believers, our hope is not limited to this realm nor is it simply pie-in-the-sky. We literally expect God to keep his promises and we wait patiently for Him to do what He said. Sending Jesus Christ, and the hope that He represents was a promise that God kept. **Today, let us hold on to the hope that is within us, knowing that God is a promise keeper!**

"THE GIFT THAT KEEPS ON GIVING"

Romans 5:15 "But the gift is not like the trespass. For if the many died by the trespass of the one man, how much more did God's grace and the gift that came by the grace of the one man, Jesus Christ, abound to the many!"

Christmas time is a time for shopping bundles. Many of us are familiar with the phrase, "your free gift with the purchase of $200 dollars or more..." Many merchants use this as a ploy because they know we will do anything for something free! We will spend 500 dollars to get a 10 dollar umbrella from Lancôme! That is not a free gift, but rather, a gift that had stipulations. It was only available because we did something in advance to get it. This is why I love God. Most "gifts" require a purchase but God's gift was a purchase. We have been bought with a price. God redeemed us from the pit and gave us life when we deserved death. Unlike Adam's contribution to humanity, which brought death, the gift of Jesus Christ was given to us through the grace of God. God's gift to us, in the person of Jesus Christ did not require the purchase of a bottle of perfume or some other item. It is 100% free to us. Because the gift of Jesus is a consequence of the grace of God, it is not based on merit, but rather, the unmerited favor of God! It reversed the effects of Adam's trespass by bringing life where there was only death. **Today, let us reflect on the free, unmerited gift of Jesus Christ!**

_____

_____

_____

_____

_____

_____

_____

_____

_____

_____

_____

_____

_____

_____

_____

_____

_____

_____

_____

_____

_____

_____

"THE GLORY OF THE LORD"

Luke 2:9 "And an angel of the Lord suddenly stood before them, and the glory of the Lord shone around them; and they were terribly frightened."

The glory of the Lord is something of an enigma. Moses was in the presence of the Lord until his face shone. But when Moses asked God to see His glory, God answered Him and said that no one could see Him face to face and live. So, God offered to show Moses His hind parts as He hid Moses in the cleft of a rock. Needless to say, that the glory of the Lord is something magnificent. It brings to mind the heaviness of God, the power and the majesty of God. Daniel fell on his face, Ezekiel fell on his face, Moses fell on his face and Elijah fell on his face in the presence of God's glory. So, these shepherds in the field had every right to be terrified. They saw an angel and they saw a glimpse of the glory of the Lord. Men are no longer terrified of God because we cannot comprehend His greatness. But for those who have seen His glory and know that He is real, the fear of the Lord is a legitimate emotion. The beauty of the fear lies in what came next. **Today, we magnify and bless God in all of His glory!**

DECEMBER 21ST

"DON'T BE AFRAID"

Luke 2:10,11 "But the angel said to them, "Do not be afraid! For behold, I bring you good news of great joy that will be for all the people: Today in the City of David a Savior has been born to you. He is Christ the Lord!"

We don't know how it would feel to be engulfed by the glory of God. We know that the shepherds in the field were terrified. Terrifying moments happen in life every single day. What is God's remedy to the terror of being in His presence? Not like a bully who would relish that fear and use it as a tool against us, God tells us not to be afraid. Amazing, considering the circumstances. The angel, speaking on behalf of God, calms the fears of the shepherd and gives them the best news ever heard! The angel says I bring you good news of great joy! The Gospel is often called the good news but what is this news? The good news, that was for everyone, every sinner, was this: In Bethlehem, A Savior has been born! Why was this good news? It was not just another human being born, but a Savior. One who would save His people from their sins, who would make peace with God through His blood; One who is the Christ, the Son of the Living God! The Messiah was born and this is good news for all of us! Now, we do not have to be afraid in the presence of God. **Today, let us thank God for the confidence that Jesus gives to us that we may be in His presence and not fear death.**

DECEMBER 22ND

"SQUARE ONE"

Luke 2:11,12 "Today in the City of David a Savior has been born to you. He is Christ the Lord! And this will be a sign to you: You will find a baby wrapped in swaddling cloths and lying in a manger."

The City of David is also known as Bethlehem. How fitting is it that God would take everything back to square one? Remember where Abraham settled? He settled in Canaan. Remember where the Israelites were trying to get back to when they left Egypt? Canaan! Think about this, the Garden of Eden was secured after Adam's sin so that no one could enter. Flaming swords covered every entrance. But when we get to the Book of Revelation, there are elements of that same garden. There are two trees, separated by a crystal river, both have healing for the nations in their leaves and both bear fruit with no prohibition from God on whether or not the residents of heaven can touch it. God has a master plan. So, it made sense that God would cause the Son of David to be born in the city of David. After all, Jesus is the heir to the throne of David. This is another piece of evidence of the wisdom of God. He weaves the most intricate historical quilts and every thread matters. **Today, let us be reminded that if God took such pains to organize history, then He has done the same for our lives.**

"AIN'T NO MOUNTAIN HIGH ENOUGH"

Ruth 4:6 "The kinsman-redeemer replied, "I cannot redeem it myself, or I would jeopardize my own inheritance. Take my right of redemption, because I cannot redeem it."

It cannot be stressed enough how many mountains God moved to ensure that the birth of Jesus would take place when it was supposed to. Once God made the promise to Abraham that his Seed would bless the whole world, God began arranging pieces on the chess board of the universe. He overcame many obstacles just to keep His promises throughout the ages. One place in particular that is of great importance, is the relationship between Boaz and Ruth. In order for Boaz to marry Ruth, he had to redeem her. But there was someone who had the first right of redemption who could have redeemed Ruth. Boaz, ever the gentleman, went to the kinsman redeemer and gave him the option to redeem Ruth, but the man refused when he considered how his own inheritance would be jeopardized. Think of how He drove Ruth to Boaz. Ruth's husband died in Moab and she ended up having to come back to Bethlehem. The royal lineage that followed is a testament to God's incredible power. Boaz fathered Obed, Obed fathered Jesse, and Jesse fathered David. **Today, think across 42 generations, God fulfilled His greatest promise; a baby, the Son of David, was born in Bethlehem who would die for our sins!**

DECEMBER 24TH

"BLESSED AND HIGHLY FAVORED"

Luke 1:28 "And coming in, he said to her, "Greetings, favored one! The Lord is with you."

With the rampant materialism that we are saturated with during the holiday season, we can often be deluded into thinking that material wealth and possessions connote God's favor. Contrary to the popular use of the phrase, blessed and highly favored does not always mean materially blessed. There is another popular phrase, "favor isn't (ain't) fair". This is true because sometimes favor will turn your entire life upside down! Many of the most favored men and women of the Bible led lives of great suffering, but their lives brought immense glory to God! The favor that Mary experiences has nothing to do with houses, cars or money. While the amenities of life were nowhere to be found, God's will and plan for Mary were on full display! Rather than viewing favor as material prosperity, let us rethink what it means to be blessed and highly favored. We are blessed and highly favored whether we are in plenty or in lack! Blessed and highly favored means that God has His hands on us for His purposes! Mary, a young, unmarried virgin was chosen by God to give birth to the Savior of the world. Her soul would be pierced with a sword as she watched this same baby be hung from a cross as a man. **Today, give thanks in all circumstances knowing that we are blessed and highly favored by God.**

DECEMBER 25TH

"SILENT NIGHT"

Luke 2:7 "And she gave birth to her firstborn, a Son. She wrapped Him in swaddling cloths and laid Him in a manger, because there was no room for them in the inn."

There is a period of time where God is said to have gone silent. There was no prophetic word coming from heaven, no pillar of cloud to guide the people, no rock to get water from. Everything dried up. This period is known as the inter-testamental period or the time in between the last book of the Old Testament and the ushering in of the Messianic age. God was not speaking corporately to His people, but individuals like Mary, Joseph, Simeon, Anna, Zacharias all heard from God. Word of the birth of Jesus had even spread all the way to Persia. But not by mouth, the stars and planets were lining up to welcome the King! The Magi were Persian astrologers. They studied the stars. It is possible that they had been waiting for this day to come! Then, on a cold night in Bethlehem, before the shepherds showed up, before the magi showed up, the baby Jesus, Christ the Lord, took His first breath of earthly air in His human body, His lungs filled with oxygen for the first time, and when He cried out, as all newborns do, God's silence was broken. God was again ready to speak to His people. **Today, thank God that the silence was broken and communion was restored.**

_____

_____

_____

_____

_____

_____

_____

_____

_____

_____

_____

_____

_____

_____

_____

_____

_____

_____

_____

DECEMBER 26TH

"THE LONG JOURNEY"

Isaiah 53:1 "Who has believed our message? And to whom has the arm of the LORD been revealed?"

The picture of the suffering servant is an amazing picture of God's grace towards us. His mission was to save by the most humiliating means possible. He stepped out of glory into an unbelieving world of atheists, theists, polytheists, idolaters and sinners knowing that those 33 years spent here would be filled with the stench of moral and spiritual decay! His journey began before time. He came to us in the fullness of time in Bethlehem, in a stable. His journey was beset with ploys, potholes, and perfidy. Plots to have Jesus killed surfaced from the time of His birth, leading Him into Egypt as a refugee. His own people in Nazareth refused to accept Him. He was called "the carpenter's son", a devil, a possessed man, a blasphemer, a seditionist and accused of colluding with Beelzebub! What a long journey from Bethlehem! **Today, let us be grateful to God that no matter how treacherous the journey was, Jesus made it to the end!**

_____

_____

_____

_____

_____

_____

_____

_____

_____

_____

_____

_____

_____

_____

_____

_____

_____

_____

_____

_____

DECEMBER 27TH

"NO RESPECTER OF PERSON"

Hebrews 7:14 "For it is clear that our Lord descended from Judah, a tribe as to which Moses said nothing about priests."

In the lineage of Jesus there were prostitutes, liars, paupers, blasphemers and the like. From that wreckage of humanity, the Savior of the world emerged. God shows us immediately that our origins do not matter to Him. He can use anyone! God initially gave the priesthood to the Levites. They were responsible for all priestly duties. No one could be a priest unless they were a Levite. But the priesthood would become obsolete because One would come who would supersede all. The priesthood could never perfect anyone because the priesthood was based on the Law. One would come who would be a priest, not because of His pedigree or lineage, but by the power on an indestructible life. The Hebrew writer reminds us that, not only was Jesus not a Levite, He was from a totally different tribe. A tribe that never produced a priest. Top that off with his humble birth in a manger and we see something special. This is the nature of God. To do things His own way rather than doing them according to tradition. Tradition would have meant that we would still need feeble men to intercede for us. But Jesus, because He can never die, can be a priest forever, in the order of Melchizedek. **Today, let us give thanks to God for not being a respecter of pedigree!**

"DO WHAT GOD SAID PART I"

Matthew 1:19 "And Joseph her husband, being a righteous man and not wanting to disgrace her, planned to send her away secretly."

The story of Joseph is often overlooked in light of Mary's role in the birth of Jesus. Matthew even took pains to list Mary's name before Joseph's in the lineage of Jesus. This is uncommon, especially since Matthew's gospel has the most Jewish slant to it. Women were overlooked in the culture, but not this woman. Joseph, after learning that Mary was pregnant, was chagrined. But, because he was a good man, his plan was not to shame Mary. Joseph knew that she would be stoned to death because of being unwed and pregnant. He must have really loved her. God knows our emotions and knows when we need reassurance to carry out hard assignments. So, God did what God does, sent reassurance to empower Joseph's faith! An angel came to Joseph later in this story and told him to stay with Mary and even explained how Mary got pregnant. The angel also told Joseph what to name the baby, Jesus (Yeshua), which means "in Yahweh there is salvation". The greatest blessing comes when the angel tells Joseph that the baby would save His people from their sins! That is the good news of Christmas! God sent a savior. Needless to say, Joseph listened and the rest is history. **Today, let us be mindful of the need for obedience as we carry out God's work in the earth!**

DECEMBER 29TH

"DO WHAT GOD SAID PART II"

Matthew 2:13,14 "When they had gone, an angel of the Lord appeared to Joseph in a dream. "Get up!" he said. "Take the Child and His mother and flee to Egypt. Stay there until I tell you, for Herod is going to search for the Child to kill Him." So he got up, took the Child and His mother by night, and withdrew to Egypt..."

The reason that it is important to be obedient to God is because there are often multiple events connected to the one event that we are experiencing. Joseph was in a precarious predicament. His wife-to-be was pregnant, but the baby was not his. However, this was not the time for Joseph to be caught up in his emotions or trying to figure out how to do things his own way. The simple answer is this: Joseph had to do what God said. Had he not listened when the angel told Him to stay with Mary, the story would have immediately broken down. But Joseph's initial obedience led to the angel coming back to him and telling him to get the child and Mary out of Bethlehem and to go to Egypt. Can you imagine a pregnant teenager having to get to Egypt alone? That's 428 miles! There are other events and prophecies connected to the flight to Egypt, most notably, Hosea's prophetic words "out of Egypt, I called my Son" [Hosea 11:1]. Doing what God said cannot ever be the wrong thing to do because God is never wrong. **Today, let us pray to have the obedience of Joseph when a hard assignment is presented to us.**

"GREAT IS THY FAITHFULNESS"

Malachi 3:6 "For I, the LORD, do not change; therefore you, O sons of Jacob, are not consumed."

Resolutions are made to be broken. Towards the end of the holiday season, we usually start making checklists and resolutions, trying to figure out what we can do to reinvent ourselves in the upcoming year. Oddly, we wait until the end of the year to take inventory. In actuality, we should take multiple inventories. That would make our planning much better and give us smaller, more attainable goals to reach for. While we wait 365 days to make a resolution that we'll break in a week, the LORD is faithful to His Word every hour of every day of every year. Malachi says here that the Lord does not change. You cannot be any clearer than that. God is faithful, consistent and dependable. Thank you Jesus for being faithful even when we are faithless, for keeping Your word even when we renege on ours, for NEVER making promises You cannot keep and for the grace to cover our faults. **Today, let us be resolved to be more like Christ!**

"NOT A BABY ANYMORE"

Revelation 1:17,18 "... "Do not be afraid. I am the First and the Last, the Living One. I was dead, and behold, now I am alive forever and ever! And I hold the keys of Death and of Hades."

We often muse during the holiday season about the "baby" Jesus. We lose ourselves in the imagery of the nativity. Even the most anti-religious person is not offended by the baby Jesus. But there is MORE to Christmas than just the baby! There are some deep implications of the incarnation of Jesus as a babe in Bethlehem! The baby Jesus was hunted because His enemies knew what was at stake. The baby Jesus was the fulfillment of prophecy: Isaiah prophesied the virgin birth, Micah prophesied where he would be born, Jeremiah prophesied that He would occupy David's throne. The baby Jesus was the Lord donning flesh for the purpose of tasting death for everyone, saying to sin, I'm coming with the antidote! It was the LORD saying to the principalities, THIS is the plan that was hidden for all ages and is now revealed in My Son! **While we celebrate the first advent, we need to understand that the baby was just a temporary situation and that One day, that baby would grow to be a man, one day that man would die for the sins of the World, and one day, that man is coming back to judge the world, not as a baby or a lamb but a lion coming to put his enemies into final submission! Amen.**

ABOUT THE AUTHOR

Dr. Russell is currently the Pastor at Grace Community Church in Millbrook, AL. He is the father of two wonderful teens, Donovan and Genesis Russell. Dr. Russell is also the Department Chair of Chemistry at Tuskegee University where he has taught for the last 15 years. He is a graduate of Williamson High School in Mobile, AL where he was raised. He has a B.S. in Chemistry from Alabama State University and a Ph.D. in organic chemistry from The University of North Carolina at Chapel Hill. Dr. Russell has been dedicated to community service since moving to the River Region and has done community outreach through Grace Community Church as well as through Freewill Missionary Baptist Church under Pastor Edward Nettles. For more information on Dr. Russell, please visit the website: www.aer251books.com

Made in the USA
Middletown, DE
18 March 2021